THE
Essential
Andrew
MURRAY
Collection

The *Essential* Andrew MURRAY *Collection*

HUMILITY

ABIDING IN CHRIST

LIVING A PRAYERFUL LIFE

BETHANYHOUSE
a division of Baker Publishing Group
Minneapolis, Minnesota

Previously published in three separate volumes by Bethany House Publishers:
  Humility © 2001
  Abiding in Christ © 2003
  Living a Prayerful Life © 2002

Published by Bethany House Publishers
11400 Hampshire Avenue South
Bloomington, Minnesota 55438
www.bethanyhouse.com

Bethany House Publishers is a division of
Baker Publishing Group, Grand Rapids, Michigan

Bethany House 3-in-1 edition published 2021

Printed in the United States of America

Library of Congress Cataloging-in-Publication Data
Names: Murray, Andrew, 1828–1917, author. | Murray, Andrew, 1828–1917. Humility. | Murray, Andrew, 1828–1917. Abide in Christ. | Murray, Andrew, 1828–1917. Prayer life.
Title: The essential Andrew Murray collection : Humility, Abiding in Christ, Living a prayerful life / Andrew Murray.
Description: 3 in 1 edition. | Minneapolis, Minnesota : Bethany House, a division of Baker Publishing Group, 2021.
Identifiers: LCCN 2021005282 | ISBN 9780764238376 (paperback) | ISBN 9780764239120 (casebound)
Subjects: LCSH: Christian life—Reformed authors. | Spiritual life—Christianity.
Classification: LCC BV4501.3 .M8954 2021 | DDC 248.4/842—dc23
LC record available at https://lccn.loc.gov/2021005282

Cover design by Rob Williams, InsideOut Creative Arts, Inc.

21 22 23 24 25 26 27   7 6 5 4 3 2 1

Contents

◆

Humility

Abiding in Christ

Living a Prayerful Life

Humility

foreword

The words in this book changed my life forever. There is no other way to say it. Some ten years ago I stumbled upon an old version of this long-lost treasure, hidden under a pile of ninety-nine-cent books on a liquidation table. At the time, I had so many misconceptions about humility. For one thing, I confused it with self-loathing. Humility is not the same as beating yourself up or letting other people put you down. Humility is not the same as low self-esteem and it's not the opposite of confidence. In fact, the truly humble person walks with absolute confidence, knowing that we are simply empty vessels through whom God wants to accomplish His work. When we understand true humility, we understand that it's not about us at all. It's about God. That's a tremendously freeing realization.

No writer has had more impact on my understanding of what it takes to become a vessel God can use than Andrew

Murray. No writer has ever drawn me nearer to God than Andrew Murray. He writes with the gentle heart of the Father. The healing touch of Jesus flows from the tip of his pen. And the life-changing power of the Holy Spirit pulsates through every word.

It's my fervent hope that this book will become a constant companion to thousands of believers. That it will occupy a special place—on your nightstand, desk, or coffee table—right next to your Bible. I urge you to prayerfully undertake a careful reading of *Humility*. I believe it will open your eyes to a whole new way of living, as God, the Almighty Three-in-One, speaks to you very personally through the pages set before you now.

His Vessel,
Donna Partow
Author, *Becoming a Vessel
God Can Use*

preface

There are three great motivations to humility: it becomes us as creatures; it becomes us as sinners; and it becomes us as saints. Humility is first seen in the angels, in man before the Fall, and in Jesus as the Son of Man. In our fallen state, humility points us to the only way by which we can return to our rightful place as creatures. As Christians, the mystery of grace teaches us that as we lose ourselves in the overwhelming greatness of redeeming love, humility becomes to us the consummation of everlasting blessedness.

It is common in Christian teaching to find the second aspect taught almost exclusively. Some have gone so far as to say that we must keep on sinning in order to remain humble! Others have thought that the strength of self-condemnation is the secret of humility. As a result, the Christian life has suffered where believers have not been guided to see that even in our relationships as creatures, nothing is more natural and beautiful and blessed than to be nothing in order that God may be everything. It needs to be made clear that it is not sin that humbles but grace. It is the soul occupied with God in His wonderful glory as Creator and Redeemer that will truly take the lowest place before Him.

In these meditations I have, for more than one reason, almost exclusively directed our attention to the humility that becomes us as creatures. It is not only because the connection between humility and sin is so commonly taught but also because I believe that for the fullness of the Christian life it is indispensable that prominence be given to the other aspect. If Jesus is to be our example in His lowliness, we need to understand the principles in which this quality is rooted and where we find the common ground to stand with Him. If we are to be humble not only before God but toward men, and if humility is to be our joy, we must see that it is not only the mark of shame because of sin, but apart from sin, it is being clothed with the very beauty and blessedness of Jesus. We will see that just as Jesus found glory in taking the form of a servant, so when He said to us, "Whoever wants to become great among you must be your servant" (Matthew 20:26), He was teaching us the truth that there is nothing so divine as being the servant and helper of all. The faithful servant who recognizes his position finds real pleasure in supplying the wants of the master or his guests. When we realize that humility is something infinitely deeper than contrition, and accept it as our participation in the life of Jesus, we will begin to learn that it is our true nobility, and that to prove it in being servants of all is the highest fulfillment of our destiny as men created in the image of God.

When I look back upon my own Christian experience, or at the church of Christ as a whole, I am amazed at how little humility is seen as the distinguishing feature of discipleship. In our preaching and in our living, in our daily interaction in our families and in our social life, as well as fellowship with other Christians, how easy it is to see that humility is not esteemed the cardinal virtue, the root from which grace can grow and the one indispensable condition of true fellowship with Jesus. The fact that it is possible for anyone to say of those who claim to seek holiness that the profession has not been accompanied with increasing humility, is a loud call to all earnest Christians, whatever truth there be in the charge, to prove that meekness and lowliness of heart are the chief marks by which they who follow the Lamb of God are to be known.

chapter one

humility: the glory of the creature

"Humility is the proper estimate of oneself."

CHARLES SPURGEON

They lay their crowns before the throne and say: "You are worthy, our Lord and God, to receive glory and honor and power, for you created all things, and by your will they were created and have their being."

Revelation 4:10–11

When God created the universe, it was with the objective of making those he created partakers of His perfection and blessedness, thus showing forth the glory of His love and wisdom and power. God desired to reveal himself in and through His creatures by communicating to them as much of His own goodness and glory as they were capable of receiving. But this communication was not meant to give created beings something they could possess in themselves, having full charge and access apart from Him. Rather, God as the ever-living, ever-present, ever-acting One, who upholds all things by the word of His power, and in whom all things exist, meant that the relationship of His creatures to himself would be one of unceasing, absolute dependence. As truly as God by His power once created all things, so by that same power must God every moment maintain all things. We as His creatures have not only to look back to the origin and beginning of our existence and acknowledge that we owe everything to God—our chief care, highest virtue, and only happiness, now and throughout all eternity—but we must also present ourselves as empty vessels, in which God can dwell and manifest His power and goodness.

The life God bestows is imparted not once for all but each moment by the unceasing operation of His mighty power. Humility, the place of entire dependence upon God, is from the very nature of things the first duty and the highest virtue of His creatures.

And so pride—the loss of humility—is the root of every sin and evil. It was when the now-fallen angels began to look upon themselves with self-complacency that they were led to disobedience and were cast down from the light of heaven into outer darkness. Likewise, it was when the serpent breathed the poison of his pride—the desire to be as God— into the hearts of our first parents, that they too fell from their high estate into the wretchedness to which all humankind has sunk. In heaven and on earth, pride or self-exaltation is the very gateway to hell.[1]

And so it follows that nothing can save us but the restoration of our lost humility, the original and only true relationship of the creature to its God. And so Jesus came to bring humility back to earth, to make us partakers of it, and by it to save us. In heaven He humbled himself to become a man. The humility we see in Him possessed Him in heaven; it brought Him here. Here on earth "He humbled himself and became obedient to death"; His humility gave His death its value, and so became our redemption. And now the salvation He imparts is nothing less and nothing else than a communication of His own life and death, His own disposition and spirit, His own humility, as the ground and root of His relationship with God and His redeeming work. Jesus Christ took the place and ful-filled the destiny of man as a creature by His life of perfect humility. His humility became our salvation. His salvation is our humility.

The life of those who are saved, the saints, must bear this stamp of deliverance from sin and full restoration to their original state; their whole relationship to God and to man marked by an all-pervading humility. Without this there can be no true abiding in God's presence or experience of His favor and the power of His Spirit; without this no abiding faith or love or joy or strength. Humility is the only soil in which virtue takes root; a lack of humility is the explanation of every defect and failure. Humility is not so much a virtue along with the others, but is the root of all, because it alone takes the right attitude before God and allows Him, as God, to do all.

God has so constituted us as reasonable beings that the greater the insight into the true nature or the absolute need of a command, the quicker and more complete will be our obedience to it. The call to humility has been too little regarded in the church because its true nature and importance have been too little apprehended. It is not something that we bring to God, or that He bestows; it is simply the sense of entire nothingness that comes when we see how truly God is everything. When the creature realizes that this is a place of honor, and consents to be—with his will, his mind, and his affections—the vessel in which the life and glory of God are to work and manifest themselves, he sees that humility is simply acknowledging the truth of his position as creature and yielding to God His place.

In the life of earnest Christians who pursue and profess

holiness, humility ought to be the chief mark of their upright-ness. Often it is said that this is not the case. Perhaps one reason is that the teaching and example of the church has not placed the proper importance on humility. As strong as sin is a motive for it, there is one still wider and mightier influence: it is that which made the angels, Jesus himself, and the holiest saints humble. It is the first and chief mark of the relationship of the creature to God, of the Son to the Father—it is the secret of blessedness, the desire to be nothing, that allows God to be all in all.

I am sure there are many Christians who will confess that their experience has been very much like my own. I had long known the Lord without realizing that meekness and lowliness of heart are to be the distinguishing feature of the disciple, just as they were of the Master. And further, that this humility is not something that will come of itself, but that it must be made the object of special desire, prayer, faith, and practice. As we study the Word, we will see what very distinct and oft-repeated instructions Jesus gave His disciples on this point, and how slow they were to understand them.

Let us at the very outset of our meditations, then, admit that there is nothing so natural to man, nothing so insidious and hidden from our sight, nothing so difficult and dangerous as pride. And acknowledge that nothing but a very determined and persevering waiting on God will reveal how lacking we are in the grace of humility and how powerless we are to obtain what we seek. We must study the character of Christ until our souls are filled with the love and admiration of His lowliness.

We must believe that when we are broken under a sense of pride and our inability to cast it out, Jesus Christ himself will come to impart this grace as a part of His wonderful life within us.

chapter two

humility: the secret of redemption

"If you are looking for an example of humility,
look at the cross."

Thomas Aquinas

Your attitude should be the same as that of Christ Jesus:
Who, being in very nature God, did not consider equality
with God something to be grasped, but made himself
nothing, taking the very nature of a servant, being made in
human likeness. And being found in appearance as a man, he
humbled himself and became obedient to death—even death
on a cross! Therefore God exalted him to the highest place
and gave him the name that is above every name.

Philippians 2:5–9

No tree can grow except on the root from which it sprang. Through all its existence it can only live by the life that was in the seed that gave it being. The full apprehension of this truth in its application to the first and the Second Adam cannot but help us to understand both the need and the nature of the redemption that is in Jesus.

The Need

When the Old Serpent, who had been cast out of heaven for his pride, whose whole nature was pride, spoke temptation into Eve's ear, those words carried with them the very poison of hell. And when she listened, and yielded her desire and her will to the prospect of being like God, knowing good and evil, the poison entered into her soul, destroying forever that blessed humility and dependence upon God that would have been our everlasting inheritance and happiness. Her life and the life of the race that sprang from her became corrupted to its very root with that most terrible of all sins and curses—Satan's pride. All the wretchedness of which this world has been the scene, all its wars and bloodshed among the nations, all its selfishness and suffering, all its vain ambitions and jealousies, all its broken hearts and embittered lives, with all its daily unhappiness, have their origin in what this cursed pride—our own or that of others—has brought upon us. It is pride that made redemption necessary; it is from our pride that we need, above everything else, to be redeemed. And our insight into the need of redemption will largely depend upon our knowledge of the terrible nature of the power of pride that has entered our being.

As we have said, no tree can grow except on the root from which it sprang. The pride that Satan brought from hell and whispered into the life of humankind is working daily, hourly, and with mighty power throughout the world. Men and women suffer from it; they fear and fight and flee it; and yet they don't always know where it has come from or how it has gained such terrible supremacy. No wonder they don't know how to overcome it. Pride has its root and strength in a spiritual power, outside of us as well as within us; as needful as it is that we confess and deplore it, it is satanic in origin. If this leads us to utter despair of ever conquering or casting it out, it will lead us all the sooner to that supernatural power in which alone our deliverance is to be found—the redemption of the Lamb of God. The hopeless struggle against the workings of self and pride within us may indeed become still more hopeless as we think of the power of darkness behind it; the utter despair will fit us better for realizing and accepting a power and a life outside of ourselves, the humility of heaven brought down by the Lamb of God to cast out Satan and his pride.

Even as we need to look to the first Adam and his failure to know the power of sin within us, we need to know the Second Adam and His power to give us the life of humility as real and abiding and enabling as was the life of pride. We have our life from and in Christ even more certainly than from and in Adam. We are to walk "rooted in him, holding fast the head from whom the whole body increases with the increase of God." The life of God that entered human nature through the Incarnation, is the root in which we are to stand and grow; it is the same almighty power that worked there, at the Cross, and onward to the Resurrection, which works daily in us. It is of utmost importance that we study to know and trust the life that has been revealed in Christ as the life that is now ours, and waits for our consent to gain possession and mastery of our whole being.

In view of this, it is important that we know who Christ is, especially the chief characteristic that is the root and essence of His character as our Redeemer. There can be but one answer: it is His humility. What is the Incarnation but His heavenly humility, His emptying himself and becoming man? What is His life on earth but humility; His taking the form of a servant? And what is His atonement but humility? "He humbled himself and became obedient to death." And what is His ascension and His glory but humility exalted to the throne and crowned with glory? "He humbled himself . . . therefore God exalted Him to the highest place." In heaven, where He was one with the Father; in His birth, His life, and His death on earth; in His return to the right hand of the Father—it is all humility. Christ is the expression of the humility of God embodied in human nature; the Eternal Love humbling itself, clothing itself in the garb of meekness and gentleness, to win and serve and save us. As the love and condescension of God makes Him the benefactor and helper and servant of all, so Jesus of necessity was the Incarnate Humility. And so He is still, in the midst of the throne, the meek and lowly Lamb of God.

If this is the root of the tree, its nature must be seen in every branch and leaf and fruit. If humility is the first, the all-inclusive grace of the life of Jesus—if humility is the secret of His atonement—then the health and strength of our spiritual life will depend entirely upon our putting this grace first and making humility the chief quality we admire in Him, the chief attribute we ask of Him, the one thing for which we sacrifice all else.[1]

Is it any wonder that the Christian life is so often weak and fruitless, when the very root of the Christian life is neglected or unknown? Is it any wonder that the joy of salvation is so little felt, when that by which Christ brings it is so seldom sought? Until a humility that rests in nothing less than the end and death of self, and which gives up all the honor of men as Jesus did to seek the honor that comes from God alone (which absolutely makes and counts itself nothing) that God may be all, that the Lord alone may be exalted—until such a humility is what we seek in Christ above our chief joy, and welcome at any price, there is very little hope of a faith that will conquer the world.

I cannot too greatly impress upon my readers the need of realizing the lack there is today of humility within Christian circles. There is so little of the meek and lowly Lamb of God in those who are called by His name. Let us consider how our lack of love, indifference to the needs and feelings of others, even sharp comments and hasty judgments that are often excused as being honest and straightforward, are thwarting the effect of the influence of the Holy Spirit on others. Manifestations of temper and touchiness and irritation, feelings of bitterness and estrangement, have their root in nothing but pride. Pride creeps in almost everywhere, and the assemblies of the saints are not exceptions. Let's ask ourselves what would be the effect if all of us were guided by the humility of Jesus, that the cry of our whole heart, night and day, would be, "Oh, for the humility of Jesus in myself and all around me!" Let us honestly fix our heart on our lack of humility—that which has been revealed in the likeness of Christ's life, in the whole character of His redemption—and realize how little we know of Christ and His salvation.

Study the humility of Jesus. This is the secret, the hidden root of redemption. Believe with your whole heart that Christ, whom God has given you, will enter in to dwell and work within you and make you what the Father would have you to be.

humility in the life of Jesus

"The only hope of a decreasing self
is an increasing Christ."

F. B. MEYER

I am among you as one who serves.

Luke 22:27

In the gospel of John we have the inner life of our Lord laid open before us. Jesus spoke frequently of His relationship to the Father, of the motives by which He was guided, of His consciousness of the power and Spirit in which He acted. Though the word *humble* does not occur in Scripture, the humility of Christ is clearly revealed. We have already said that this virtue is nothing but the simple consent of the creature to let God be all, the surrender of itself to His working alone. In Jesus we see how both as the Son of God in heaven and the Son of Man on earth, He took the place of entire subordination and gave God the Father the honor and glory due Him. What He taught so often was true of himself: "He who humbles himself will be exalted" (Luke 18:14). As it is written, "He humbled himself. . . . Therefore God exalted him to the highest place" (Philippians 2:8–9).

Listen to the words our Lord speaks of His relationship to the Father and see how consistently He uses the words *not* and *nothing* of himself. The *not I* that Paul uses to express his relationship to Christ, is in the same spirit that Christ speaks of His relationship to the Father.

"The Son can do *nothing* by himself" (John 5:19).

"By myself I can do *nothing*; I judge only as I hear, and my judgment is just, for I seek *not* to please myself but him who sent me" (John 5:30).

"I do *not* accept praise from men" (John 5:41).

"For I have come down from heaven *not* to do my will" (John 6:38).

"My teaching is *not* my own" (John 7:16).

"I am *not* here on my own" (John 7:28).

"I do *nothing* on my own" (John 8:28).

"I have *not* come on my own; but he sent me" (John 8:42).

"I am *not* seeking glory for myself" (John 8:50).

"The words I say to you are *not* just my own" (John 14:10).

"These words you hear are *not* my own" (John 14:24).

These words of testimony, spoken by the Lord himself, reveal the deepest motivation of His life and work. They show how the Father was able to work His redemption through the Son. They show the state of heart that became Him as the Son of the Father. They teach us the essential nature and life of the redemption that Christ accomplished and now communicates to us. It is this: He was nothing that God might be all. He resigned himself to the Father's will and power that He might work through Him. Of His own power, His own will, His own glory, His whole mission with its works and teaching—of all this, He said, I am nothing. I have given myself to the Father to work; He is all.

This life of entire self-abnegation, of absolute submission and dependence upon the Father's will, Christ found to be the source of perfect peace and joy. He lost nothing by giving all to God. God honored His trust and did all for Him, and then exalted Him to His own right hand in glory. And because Christ humbled himself before God, and God was ever before Him, He found it possible to humble himself before men, too, and to be the Servant of all. His humility was simply the surrender of himself to God, to allow Him to do in Him what He pleased, regardless of what men might say of Him or do to Him.

It is in this state of mind, in this spirit and disposition, that the redemption of Christ has its virtue and efficacy. It is to bring us to this disposition that we are made partakers of Christ. This is the true self-denial to which our Savior calls us, the acknowledgment that self has nothing good in it, except as an empty vessel for God to fill. Its claim to be or do anything may not for a moment be allowed. It is in this, above and before everything, that the conformity to Jesus consists—the being and doing nothing of ourselves that God may be all in all.

Here we have the nature of true humility. It is because this is not understood or sought after, that our humility is so superficial and weak. We must learn of Jesus, how He is meek and lowly of heart. He teaches us where true humility begins and finds its strength—in the knowledge that it is God who works all in all, that our place is to yield to Him in perfect resignation and dependence, in full consent to be and to do nothing of ourselves. This is the life Christ came to reveal and to impart—a life to God that came through death to sin and self. If we feel that this life is too high for us and beyond our reach, it must all the more urge us to seek it in Him. It is the indwelling Christ who will live this life in us. If we long for it, let us above everything seek the secret of the knowledge of the nature of God, the secret of which every child of God is to be a witness: nothing but a vessel, a channel through which the living God can manifest the riches of His wisdom, power, and goodness. The root of all virtue and grace, of all faith and acceptable worship, is that we know that we have nothing but what we receive, and bow in deepest humility to wait upon God for it.

It was because this humility was not only a temporary sentiment awakened in Him when He thought of God but also was the spirit of His whole life, that Jesus was as humble in His relationship with men and women as He was with God. He felt himself to be the Servant of God for those whom God created and loved. As a natural consequence, He counted himself the Servant of men and women so that through Him God might do His work of love. He never for a moment sought His own honor or asserted His power to vindicate himself. His whole spirit was that of a life yielded to God. When we study the humility of Jesus as the very essence of His redemption, as the blessedness of the life of the Son of God, and as the virtue Jesus gives us if we are to have any part with Him, we will begin to comprehend how serious it is to lack humility in our lives.

Are you clothed with humility? Look at your daily life. Ask your friends about it. Begin to praise God that there is opened to you in Jesus a heavenly humility that you have hardly known and through which a heavenly blessedness you have never tasted can come.

chapter four

humility in the teaching of Jesus

"Humility must always be doing its work like a bee
making its honey in the hive: without humility
all will be lost."

TERESA OF AVILA

Learn from me, for I am gentle and humble in heart.

Matthew 11:29

Whoever wants to be first must be your slave—just as the Son of Man did not come to be served, but to serve.

Matthew 20:27–28

We see humility in the life of Christ demonstrated in how He laid open His heart to us. Through His teaching we hear Him speak of it—how He expects His disciples to be humble as He was. Let us carefully study the passages to see how often and how earnestly He taught it: it may help us to realize what He asks of us.

1. Look at the commencement of His ministry. In the Sermon on the Mount, He opens with the Beatitudes: "Blessed are the poor in spirit, for theirs is the kingdom of heaven. Blessed are the meek, for they will inherit the earth" (Matthew 5:3, 5). The very first words of His proclamation of the kingdom of heaven reveal the open gate through which we may enter. The kingdom comes to the poor, who have nothing in themselves. The earth is for the meek, who seek nothing for themselves. The blessings of heaven and earth are for the lowly. Humility is the secret of blessing for the heavenly and the earthly life.

2. "Learn from me, for I am gentle and humble in heart, and you will find rest for your souls" (Matthew 11:29). Jesus offers himself as Teacher. He tells us both what the Spirit is and what we can learn and receive from Him. Meekness and

41

lowliness are the qualities He offers us; in them we will find perfect rest. Humility is our salvation.

3. The disciples had been disputing among themselves who would be the greatest in the kingdom, and had agreed to ask the Master (Luke 9:46; Matthew 18:3). He placed a child in their midst, and said, "Whoever humbles himself like this child is the greatest in the kingdom of heaven" (Matthew 18:4). "Who is the greatest in the kingdom of heaven?" The question is far-reaching. What will be the chief distinction in the heavenly kingdom? The glory of heaven, the mind of heaven, is humility. "He who is least among you all—he is the greatest" (Luke 9:48).

4. The sons of Zebedee asked Jesus if they could sit on His right hand and on His left, the highest places in the kingdom. Jesus said it was not His to give but the Father's, who would give it to those for whom it was prepared. They must not seek it or ask for it. Their thoughts must be of the cup and the baptism of humiliation. And then He added, "Whoever wants to be first must be your slave—just as the Son of Man did not come to be served, but to serve" (Matthew 20:27–28). Humility, as it is the mark of Christ, will be the one standard of glory in heaven: the lowliest is the nearest to God.

5. Speaking to the multitude and the disciples, of the Pharisees and their love of the chief seats, Christ said once again, "The greatest among you will be your servant" (Matthew 23:11). Humiliation is the only ladder to honor in God's kingdom.

6. On another occasion, in the house of a Pharisee, He spoke the parable of the guest who would be invited to come

up higher, and added, "For everyone who exalts himself will be humbled, and he who humbles himself will be exalted" (Luke 14:1–11). The demand is inexorable; there is no other way. Self-abasement alone will be exalted.

7. After the parable of the Pharisee and the Publican, Christ spoke again, "For everyone who exalts himself will be humbled, and he who humbles himself will be exalted" (Luke 18:14). In the temple and presence and worship of God, everything is worthless that is not pervaded by deep, true humility toward God and humankind.

8. After washing the disciples' feet, Jesus said, "Now that I, your Lord and Teacher, have washed your feet, you also should wash one another's feet" (John 13:14). The authority of command and example, every thought, either of obedience or conformity, makes humility the first and most essential element of discipleship.

9. At the Lord's Supper table, the disciples still disputed who should be greatest. Jesus said, "The greatest among you should be like the youngest, and the one who rules like the one who serves. . . . I am among you as one who serves" (Luke 22:26–27). The path Jesus walked, which He opened up for us, the power through which He wrought our salvation and by which He saves us, is the humility that makes us the servant of all.

How little this is preached. How seldom it is practiced. How faintly the lack of it is felt or confessed. I cannot say how few attain to some recognizable measure of likeness to Jesus in His humility. But fewer ever think of making it a distinct object of continual desire or prayer. How little the world has seen it. How scarcely it is seen in the inner circle of the church.

"Whosoever will be chief among you, let him be your servant." Oh that God would convince us that Jesus means this! We all know what the character of a faithful servant or slave implies. Devotion to the master's interests, thoughtful study and care to please him, delight in his prosperity and honor and happiness. There are servants on earth in whom these dispositions have been seen, and to whom the name of servant has never been anything but glory. To how many of us has it been a new joy in the Christian life to know that we may yield ourselves as servants, as slaves to God, and to find that His service is our highest liberty—the freedom from sin and self? We need to learn another lesson—that Jesus calls us to be servants of one another, and that as we accept it heartily, this service will be a most blessed one, a new and fuller deliverance from sin and self. At first it may appear hard—this is because of the pride that still counts itself something. If once we learn that to be nothing before God is the glory of the creature, the spirit of Jesus, the joy of heaven, we shall welcome with our whole heart the discipline we may have in serving even those who try or annoy us. When our own heart is set upon this true sanctification, we will study each word of Jesus on self-abasement with new zeal, and no place will be too low, no stooping too far, and no service too mean or too long if we may but share and prove the fellowship with Him who said, "I am among you as one who serves" (Luke 22:27).

Here is the path to the higher life. It is the lowest path! This was what Jesus said to the disciples who were thinking of being great in the kingdom and of sitting on His right hand and His left. Ask not for exaltation. That is God's work. See that you humble yourselves, and take no place before God or man but that of a servant. That is your work; let that be your one purpose and prayer. God is faithful. Just as water seeks and fills the lowest place, so the moment God finds the creature empty, His glory and power flow in to exalt and to bless. He that humbles himself—that must be our one aim—shall be exalted; that is God's aim. By His mighty power and in His great love He will do it.

People sometimes speak of humility and meekness as something that would rob us of what is noble and bold. Oh, that all would realize that this is the nobility of the kingdom of heaven, that this is the royal spirit that the King of heaven displayed, that this is godlike, to humble oneself and to become the servant of all! This is the path to the gladness and the glory of Christ's presence in us, of His power resting upon us.

Jesus, the meek and lowly One, calls us to learn of Him the path to God. Let us study the words we have been reading until our heart is filled with the thought: *My one need is humility.* And let us believe that what He shows He gives, and what He is He imparts. As the meek and lowly One, He will come into and dwell within the longing heart.

chapter five

humility in the disciples of Jesus

"God created the world out of nothing, and as long as
we are nothing, He can make something out of us."

MARTIN LUTHER

The greatest among you should be like the youngest, and the one who rules like the one who serves.

Luke 22:26

W e have studied humility in the person and teaching of Jesus; now we will look for it in the circle of His chosen companions—the twelve apostles. If we see a lack of humility in the disciples, and a contrast between Christ and men is brought out more clearly, it will help us to appreciate the mighty change that Pentecost brought and prove how real our participation can be in the triumph of Christ's humility over the pride Satan breathed into humankind.

In the texts quoted from the teaching of Jesus, we have seen the occasions on which the disciples proved how much they lacked the grace of humility. Once they were disputing about who should be the greatest. Another time the sons of Zebedee, with their mother, had asked for the first places—the seats on the right hand and the left of Jesus in glory. And later on, at the Last Supper, there was a contention again about who should be counted the greatest. This is not to say that there were not moments when they did humble themselves before the Lord. Peter cried out, "Go away from me, Lord; I am a sinful man!" (Luke 5:8). On another occasion, the disciples fell down and worshiped Him when He stilled the storm. But such infrequent expressions of humility only emphasize the general habit of their minds, as shown in the natural and spontaneous revelations of the place and power of self. The study of the meaning of their behavior will teach us some important lessons.

First, is the fact that there may be the enthusiastic and active practice of Christianity while humility is still sadly lacking. The disciples had a fervent attachment to Jesus. They had forsaken all to follow Him. The Father had revealed to them that He was the Christ of God. They believed in Him, they loved Him, and they obeyed His commandments. When others fell away, they remained faithful to Him. They were ready to die with Him. But deeper than all of this devotion was the existence of an inner power of sin and selfishness. This power had to be dealt with before they could be witnesses of the power of Jesus to save. It is so with all of us. We may find professors and ministers, evangelists and Christian workers, missionaries and teachers, in whom the gifts of the Spirit are many and manifest, and who are the channels of blessing to multitudes, but of whom, when tested, or close interpersonal relationships reveal their true characters, it is only too evident that the grace of humility, as an abiding characteristic, is rarely to be seen. All of this tends to confirm the reality that humility is one of the chief and highest virtues, one of the most difficult to attain, and one to which our first and greatest efforts ought to be directed. Humility is a virtue that only comes in power when the fullness of the Spirit makes us partakers of the indwelling Christ and He lives within us.

Second, is the reality that external teaching and personal effort are powerless to conquer pride or create the meek and lowly heart in a person. For three years the disciples had been in the training school of Jesus. He had told them what the main lesson was that He wished to teach them: "Learn from me, for I am gentle and humble in heart" (Matthew 11:29). Time after time He had spoken to them, to the Pharisees, and to the multitudes, of humility as the only path to the glory of God. He had not only lived before them as the Lamb of God in His divine humility but He had also more than once unfolded to them the inmost secret of His life: "The Son of Man did not come to be served, but to serve" (Matthew 20:28); "I am among you as one who serves" (Luke 22:27). He had washed their feet and told them to follow His example. But all was to little avail. At the Last Supper there was still contention as to who should be greatest. They had doubtless tried to learn His lessons, and firmly resolved not to grieve Him again. But all was in vain. To teach them and us the lesson that no outward instruction, not even of Christ himself; no argument, however convincing; no sense of the beauty of humility, however deep; no personal resolve or effort, however sincere and earnest, can cast out pride. When Satan casts out Satan, it is only that he might enter afresh in a mightier, subtler power. Nothing works but this: that the new nature in its divine humility be revealed in power to take the place of the old—to become our true nature.

Third, is the revelation that it is only by the indwelling of Christ in His divine humility that we can become truly humble. We have our pride from Adam; we must have our humility from Christ. Pride rules in us with incredible power; it is ourselves, our very nature. Humility must become ours in the same way; it must be our true selves, our very nature. As natural and easy as it has been to be proud, it must become natural for us to be humble. The promise is "Where sin abounded, grace did abound more exceedingly." All Christ's teaching of His disciples, and all their vain efforts, were the needful preparation for His entering into them in divine power, to give and be in them what He had taught them to desire. In His death, He destroyed the power of the devil. He put away sin and produced an everlasting redemption. In His resurrection He received from the Father an entirely new life, the life of man in the power of God, capable of being communicated to men, and entering and renewing and filling their lives with His divine power. In His ascension He received the Spirit of the Father, through whom He might do what He could not do while upon earth—make himself one with those He loved, actually live their life for them, so that they could live before the Father in a humility like His own. On Pentecost He came and took possession of the church. The work of preparation and conviction, the awakening of desire and hope that His teaching brought about, was perfected by the mighty change of Pentecost. The lives and the epistles of James and Peter and John bear witness that all was changed, and that the spirit of the meek and suffering Jesus had taken possession of them.

Is this new information? There may be some readers who have never given particular thought to the subject, and therefore do not yet realize its immense importance as a question for the church. There are others who have felt condemned for their lack of humility, and have made great efforts, only to fail and to be discouraged. Still others may be able to give joyful testimony of spiritual blessing and power, yet there has never been conviction concerning the lack in those around them. Some may be able to witness to the Lord's deliverance and victory in this area, but realize how much they still need and may expect from the fullness of Jesus. To whatever class you belong, may I urge the pressing need to seek a deeper conviction of the unique place that humility holds in the life of every believer. Let us consider how far the disciples were advanced while this grace was still lacking, and let us pray that other gifts may not so satisfy us that we never grasp the fact that the absence of humility is no doubt the reason why the power of God cannot do its mighty work. It is only where we, like the Son, truly know and show that we can do nothing of ourselves that God will do everything.

It is when the truth of the indwelling Christ takes the place it deserves in the experience of believers that the church will put on her beautiful garment and humility will be seen in her teachers and members as the beauty of holiness.

chapter six

humility in daily life

"The more humble a man is in himself, the more obedient toward God, the wiser will he be in all things, and the more shall his soul be at peace."

THOMAS À KEMPIS

For anyone who does not love his brother, whom he has seen, cannot love God, whom he has not seen.

1 John 4:20

It is a solemn thought that our love for God is measured by our everyday relationships with others. Except as its validity is proven in standing the test of daily life with our fellowmen, our love for God may be found to be a delusion. It is easy to think that we humble ourselves before God, but our humility toward others is the only sufficient proof that our humility before God is real. To be genuine, humility must abide in us and become our very nature. True humility is to be made of no reputation—as did Christ. In God's presence, humility is not a posture we assume for a time—when we think of Him or pray to Him—but the very spirit of our life. It will manifest itself in all our bearing toward others. A lesson of deepest importance is that the only humility that is really ours is not the kind we try to show before God in prayer, but the kind we carry with us, and carry out, in our ordinary conduct. The seemingly insignificant acts of daily life are the tests of eternity, because they prove what spirit possesses us. It is in our most unguarded moments that we truly show who we are and what we are made of. To know a truly humble person, you must follow that one in the common course of daily life.

This is what Jesus taught. He gave them an example when

He washed their feet. He taught His lessons of humility by demonstration. Humility before God is nothing if it is not proven in humility before others.

It is so in the teaching of Paul. To the Romans he writes, "Honor one another *above yourselves*" (Romans 12:10); "Do not be proud, but be willing to associate with *people of low position*. Do not be conceited" (Romans 12:16). And to the Corinthians: "Love"—and there is no love without humility as its root—"does not boast, it is not proud. . . . It is not self-seeking, it is not easily angered" (1 Corinthians 13:4–5). To the Galatians: "Serve *one another* in love (Galatians 5:13). Let us not become conceited, provoking and envying *each other*" (Galatians 5:26). To the Ephesians, immediately after the three wonderful chapters on the heavenly life, he said, "Live a life . . . completely humble and gentle; be patient, bearing with *one another* in love" (Ephesians 4:1–2); "Always giving thanks. . . . Submit to *one another* out of reverence for Christ" (Ephesians 5:20–21). To the Philippians: "Do nothing out of selfish ambition or vain conceit, but in humility consider *others* better than yourselves" (Philippians 2:3). "Your attitude should be the same as that of Christ Jesus: "Who . . . made himself nothing, taking the very nature of a servant . . . he humbled himself" (Philippians 2:5–8). And to the Colossians: "Clothe yourselves with compassion, kindness, humility, gentleness and patience. Bear with *each other* and forgive whatever grievances you may have against *one another*. Forgive as the Lord forgave you" (Colossians 3:12). It is in our relationships with one another, in our treatment of each other, that true lowliness of mind and a heart of humility are seen. Our humility before God has no value except as it prepares us to reveal the humility of Jesus to our fellowmen. Let us study humility in daily life in light of these words.

The humble person seeks at all times to live up to the rule "Honor one another above yourselves; serve one another; consider others better than yourselves; submit to one another." The question is often asked how we can count others better than ourselves when we see that they are far below us in wisdom, in holiness, in natural gifts, or in grace received. The question proves at once how little we understand what real lowliness of mind is. True humility comes when before God we see ourselves as nothing, have put aside self, and let God be all. The soul that has done this, and can say, "I have lost myself in finding you," no longer compares itself with others. It has given up forever any thought of self in God's presence; it meets its fellowmen as one who is nothing and seeks nothing for itself; who is a servant of God and for His sake is a servant of all. A faithful servant may be wiser than his master and yet retain the true spirit and posture of a servant. The humble man looks upon every child of God, the most weak and unworthy, and honors him and prefers him as a son of the King. The spirit of Him who washed the disciples' feet makes it a joy to be the least, to be servants of one another.

The humble person feels no jealousy or envy. He can praise God when others are preferred and blessed before him. He can hear others praised and himself forgotten, because in God's presence he has learned to say with Paul, "I am nothing." He has received the spirit of Jesus, who pleased not himself and sought not His own honor as the spirit of his life.

Amid temptations to impatience and irritableness, to hard thoughts and sharp words that come in response to the failings and sins of fellow-Christians, the humble person carries the oft-repeated injunction in his heart and shows it in his life: "Forbearing one another, and forgiving one another, even as the Lord forgave you." He has learned that in putting on the Lord Jesus he puts on the heart of compassion, kindness, humility, meekness, and long-suffering. Jesus has taken the place of self, and it is not an impossibility to forgive as Jesus forgave. His humility does not consist merely in thoughts or words of self-depreciation, but, as Paul puts it, in "a heart of humility," the sweet and lowly gentleness recognized as the mark of the Lamb of God.

In striving after the higher experiences of the Christian life, the believer is often in danger of seeking the more visible virtues, such as joy, boldness, zeal, contempt of the world, self-sacrifice—even the old Stoics taught and practiced these—rather than the gentler graces, those which are more distinctly connected with Jesus' cross and death to self: poverty of spirit, meekness, humility, lowliness. Therefore, let us put on a heart of compassion, kindness, humility, meekness, long-suffering; and let us prove our Christlikeness not only in our zeal for saving the lost but also in our relationships with others—forbearing and forgiving one another, even as the Lord forgave us.

Let us study the Bible portrait of the most humble man that ever lived—the Lord Jesus. And let us ask our brethren, and the world, whether they recognize in us the likeness to the original. Let us be content with nothing less than taking each of these texts as the promise of what God will work in us, as the revelation of what the Spirit of Jesus will put within us. Allow each failure and shortcoming to only the more quickly turn us to the meek and lowly Lamb of God in the assurance that where He is enthroned in the heart, His humility and gentleness will be the streams of living water that flow from within us. George Foxe said, "I knew Jesus, and He was very precious to my soul, but I found something in me that would not keep sweet and patient and kind. I did what I could to keep it down, but it was there. I besought Jesus to do something for me, and when I gave Him my will, He came to my heart, and took out all that would not be sweet, all that would not be kind, all that would not be patient, and then He shut the door."

Once again, let me repeat what I have said before. I feel deeply that we have very little concept of what the church suffers as a result of its lack of humility—the self-abasement that makes room for God to prove His power. A Christian who was acquainted with mission stations of various societies, expressed his deep sorrow that in some cases the spirit of love and forbearance was sadly lacking. Men and women who could choose their own circle of friends, joined together in fellowship with those of contrary opinions, making it difficult to bear and to love and to keep the unity of the Spirit in the bond of peace. And those who should have been encouragers became a hindrance to the work. It appeared the lack of humility was the cause of much of the difficulty. Humility always seeks, like Jesus, to be the servant, the helper, and the comforter of others, even to the lowest and most unworthy.

Why is it that those who have joyfully given themselves up for Christ find it so hard to give themselves up for fellow Christians? It seems that the church has failed to teach its people the importance of humility—that it is the first of the virtues, the best of all the graces and powers of the Spirit. It has failed to show that a Christlike humility is what is needed and is also in the realm of possibility. But let us not be discouraged. Rather, let the discovery of the lack of this grace stir us up to greater expectation from God. Let us look upon everyone who tries us as God's means of grace, God's instrument for our purification, for our exercise of the humility of Jesus. May we have true faith in the sufficiency of God and admit to the inefficiency of self, that by God's power we will serve one another in love.

chapter seven

humility and holiness

"It is no great thing to be humble when you are
brought low; but to be humble when you are praised
is a great and rare achievement."

BERNARD OF CLAIRVAUX

All day long I have held out my hands to an obstinate people . . . who say, "Keep away; don't come near me, for I am too sacred for you!"

Isaiah 65:2, 5

We speak of the holiness movement in our times and praise God for it. We hear a great deal of seekers after holiness and professors of holiness, of holiness teaching and holiness meetings. The blessed truths of holiness in Christ and holiness by faith are being emphasized as never before. The great test of whether the holiness we profess to seek or to attain is truth and life will be whether it is manifest in the increasing humility it produces. In the individual, humility is the one thing needed to allow God's holiness to dwell in and shine through him or her. In Jesus—the Holy One of God, who makes us holy—divine humility was the secret of His life, His death, and His exaltation. The one infallible test of our holiness will be our humility before God and others. Humility is the bloom and the beauty of holiness.

The chief mark of counterfeit holiness is its lack of humility. Every seeker after holiness needs to be on his guard lest unconsciously what was begun in the spirit is perfected in the flesh, and pride creep in where its presence is least expected. Two men went into the temple to pray: the one a Pharisee, the other a tax collector. There was no place or position so sacred that the Pharisee could not enter there. Pride can lift its head in the very temple of God and make His worship the scene of its self-exaltation. Since the time Christ so exposed his pride, the Pharisee has put on the garb of the tax collector. The confessor of deep sinfulness and the professor of highest holiness must both be on watch. Just when we are most anxious to have our heart be the temple of God, we will find the two men coming to pray. And the tax collector will find that his danger is not from the Pharisee beside him, who despises him, but the Pharisee within, who commends and exalts himself. In God's temple, when we think we are in the holy place, in the presence of His holiness, let us beware of pride. "One day the angels came to present themselves before the Lord, and Satan also came with them" (Job 1:6).

"God, I thank you that I am not like other men, or even like this tax collector" (Luke 18:11). It is in the thanksgiving that we render to God or the confession that God has done it all, that self finds cause for complacency. Yes, even when the language of penitence and trust in God's mercy alone is heard, the Pharisee may take up the note of praise and in thanking God be congratulating himself. Pride can clothe itself in the garments of praise or of penitence. Even though the words "I am not as other men" are rejected and condemned, their spirit may too often be found in our feelings and language toward our fellow worshipers and fellowmen. If you wonder if this is so, listen to the way Christians speak of one another. How little of the meekness and gentleness of Jesus is seen. It is seldom remembered that deep humility must be the keynote of what we say of ourselves or of each other. There are countless assemblies of saints, mission conventions, societies, or committees, where the harmony has been disturbed and the work of God hindered because men who are counted saints are touchy and impatient, self-defensive and self-assertive to the point of sharp judgments and unkind words. They do not reckon others better than themselves, and their holiness has little meekness in it.

" 'Me' is a most exacting person, requiring the best seat and the highest place for itself, and feeling grievously wounded if its claim is not recognized. Most of the quarrels among Christian workers arise from the clamoring of this gigantic 'me.' How few of us understand the true secret of taking our seats in the lowest rooms."*

In their spiritual history, men may have had times of great humbling and brokenness, but what a different thing this is from being clothed with humility, from having a humble spirit, from having that lowliness of mind in which each counts himself the servant of others and so shows forth the mind that was in Jesus Christ.

Our text is a parody on holiness! Jesus the Holy One is the humble One: the holiest will always be the humblest. There is none holy but God: we have as much holiness as we have God. And according to what we have of God will be our real humility, because humility is nothing but the disappearance of self in the vision that God is all. The holiest will be the humblest. Though the barefaced boasting Jew of the days of Isaiah is not often to be found—our manners have taught us not to speak that way—how often his spirit is still seen, whether in

---

*Quoting Mrs. Smith in *Everyday Religion*, n.d.

the treatment of fellow Christians or of the children of the world. In the spirit in which opinions are given, work is undertaken, and faults are exposed, how often, though the garb be that of the tax collector, the voice is still that of the Pharisee: "God, I thank you that I am not like other men" (Luke 18:11).

Is there such humility still to be found that men count themselves "less than the least of all saints," the servants of all? "Love ... does not boast, it is not proud. ... It is not self-seeking" (1 Corinthians 13:4–5). Where the spirit of love is shed abroad in the heart, where the divine nature comes to full birth, and where Christ the meek and lowly Lamb of God is truly formed within, there comes the power of a perfect love that forgets itself and finds its blessedness in blessing others. Where this love enters, God enters. And where God has come in His power and revealed himself, the vessel becomes nothing. This is the condition in which true humility can be displayed toward others. The presence of God is not dependent upon times and seasons, but upon a soul ready to do His will and forget itself.

Let all teachers of holiness, whether in the pulpit or on the platform, and all seekers after holiness, whether in the closet or the convention, take warning: There is no pride so dangerous, so subtle and insidious, as the pride of holiness. It is not that a man ever says, or even thinks, "Stay away. I am too sacred for you!" The thought would be considered ludicrous. But unconsciously there can develop a private habit of soul that feels complacency in its attainments and cannot help but see how far it is ahead of others. It isn't always seen in self-assertion or self-praise, but in the absence of self-denial and modesty that reveals a lack of the mark of the soul that has seen the glory of God (Job 42:5–6; Isaiah 6:5). It is a tone, a way of speaking of oneself or others, in which those who have the gift of discernment cannot but recognize the power of self. Even the world with its keen eye notices it, and points to it as proof that the profession of a spiritual life does not always bear spiritual fruits. Beware, lest we make a profession of holiness, delighting in beautiful thoughts and feelings, in solemn acts of consecration and faith, while the mark of the presence of God—the disappearance of self—is obviously missing. Flee to Jesus and hide yourselves in Him until you are clothed with His humility. That alone is holiness.

chapter eight
humility and sin

"Nothing sets a person so much out of the devil's reach as humility."

JONATHAN EDWARDS

Christ Jesus came into the world to save sinners—of whom I am the worst.

1 Timothy 1:15

Humility is often identified with penitence and contrition. As a consequence, there appears to be no way of fostering humility but by keeping the soul occupied with its sin. But I think we have learned that humility is something else and something more than being consumed with our own sinfulness. We have seen in the teaching of our Lord Jesus and the Epistles how often the virtue is mentioned without any reference to sin. In the very nature of things, in the whole relationship of the creature to the Creator, in the life of Jesus as He lived it and imparts it to us, humility is the very essence of holiness. It is the displacement of self by the enthronement of God. Where God is all, self is nothing.

But though it is this aspect of the truth I have felt especially constrained to emphasize, I hardly need to say what new depth and intensity man's sin and God's grace give to the humility of the saints. We have only to look at a man like the apostle Paul to see how throughout his life as a ransomed and a holy man, the deep consciousness of having been a sinner lived in him inextinguishably. We all know the passages in which he refers to his life as a persecutor and blasphemer: "I am *the least of the apostles* and *do not even deserve to be called an apostle,* because I persecuted the church of God. But by the grace of God I am what I am, and his grace to me was not without effect. No, I worked harder than all of them—yet not I, but the grace of God that was with me" (1 Corinthians 15:9–10, emphasis added). "Although I am *less than the least of all God's people*, this grace was given me: to preach to the Gentiles" (Ephesians 3:8). "Even though I was once *a blasphemer and a persecutor and a violent man*, I was shown mercy because I acted in ignorance and unbelief. . . . Christ Jesus came into the world to save *sinners—of whom I am the worst*" (1 Timothy 1:13, 15).

God's grace had saved Paul; God remembered his sins no more; but never could Paul forget how terribly he had sinned. The more he rejoiced in God's salvation, and the more his experience of God's grace filled him with joy unspeakable, the clearer was his consciousness that he was a saved sinner and that salvation had no meaning or sweetness except that his being a sinner made it precious and real to him personally. Never for a moment could he forget that it was a sinner God had taken up in His arms and crowned with His love.

The texts we have quoted are often appealed to as Paul's confession of sinning daily. But one has only to read them carefully in their context to see that this is not the case. They have a far deeper significance. They refer to the power of God that endures throughout eternity to keep us in awe of the humility with which the ransomed bow before the throne as those who have been washed from their sins in the blood of the Lamb. Never, even in glory, can they be any other than ransomed sinners; never for a moment in this life can God's child live in the full light of His love without feeling that the sin out of which he has been saved is his one right to grace. The humility with which first he came as a sinner acquires a new meaning when he learns how it becomes him as a creature. And again, the humility in which he was born as a creature has its deepest, richest tones in the memory of what it is to be a monument of God's redeeming love.

The true importance of what these expressions of Paul teach us comes out all the more strongly when we notice the remarkable fact that through his whole Christian journey we never find from his pen anything like confession of sin. Nowhere is there any mention of shortcoming or defect, nowhere any suggestion to his readers that he has failed in duty or sinned against the law of perfect love. On the contrary, there are passages in which he vindicates himself in language that appeals to a faultless life before God and men. "You are witnesses, and so is God, of how holy, righteous and blameless we were among you who believed" (1 Thessalonians 2:10). "This is our boast: Our conscience testifies that we have conducted ourselves in the world, and especially in our relations with you, in the holiness and sincerity that are from God" (2 Corinthians 1:12). This is not an ideal or an aspiration; it is an admission of what his actual life had been. However we may account for this absence of confession of sin, all will admit that it must point to a life in the power of the Holy Spirit such as is seldom realized or expected in our day.

The point I wish to emphasize is this: the very fact of the absence of such confession of sin only gives more strength to the truth that it is not in daily sinning that the secret of humility is found, but rather in the position of dependence upon the grace of God. Our only place of blessing before God is among those whose highest joy is to confess that they are sinners saved by grace.

With Paul's fresh reminder of having sinned in the past, and his consciousness of being kept from sin daily, he was well aware of the power of sin that could overtake him without the daily presence and power of the indwelling Christ. "I know that nothing good lives in me" (Romans 7:18) describes the flesh as it is to the end. The glorious deliverance of Romans 8:2: "Through Christ Jesus the law of the Spirit of life set me free from the law of sin and death" is neither the annihilation nor the sanctification of the flesh, but a continuous victory given by the Spirit. As health expels disease, light swallows up darkness, and life conquers death, the indwelling Christ through the Spirit is the health, light, and life of the soul. But with this the conviction of helplessness tempers our faith with a sense of dependence that creates the proper humility in us and results in the greatest joy.

The passages above show that it was the wonderful grace bestowed upon Paul, of which he felt the need every moment, that humbled him so deeply. The grace of God that was with him and enabled him to labor more abundantly than they all, the grace to preach to the heathen the unsearchable riches of Christ, is what kept his sense of being liable to sin so alive. "But where sin increased, grace increased all the more" (Romans 5:20). This reveals how the very essence of grace deals with and takes away sin. The more abundant the experience of grace the more intense the consciousness of being a sinner. It is not sin, but God's grace showing a man and ever reminding him what a sinner he was that will keep him truly humble. It is not sin but grace that will make me know myself as a sinner.

I'm afraid that there are many who by strong expressions of self-condemnation and self-denunciation have sought to humble themselves, but who have to confess with sorrow that a humble spirit with its accompanying kindness and compassion, meekness and forbearance, is still as far off as ever. Being occupied with self, even having the deepest self-abhorrence, can never free us from self. It is the revelation of God not only by the law condemning sin but also by His grace delivering from it that will make us humble. The law may break the heart with fear; it is only grace that works that sweet humility that becomes joy to the soul as its second nature. It was the revelation of God in His holiness, drawing nigh to make himself known in His grace that made Abraham, Jacob, Job, and Isaiah bow so low. It is the soul that finds God to be everything that is so filled with His presence there is no place for self. So alone can the promise be fulfilled: "The pride of men brought low; the Lord alone will be exalted in that day" (Isaiah 2:11).

It is the sinner basking in the full light of God's holy, redeeming love, in the experience of that indwelling divine compassion of Christ, who cannot but be humble. Not to be occupied with your sin but to be fully occupied with God brings deliverance from self.

chapter nine
humility and faith

"Be not angry that you cannot make others as you
wish them to be, since you cannot make yourself
as you wish yourself to be."

THOMAS À KEMPIS

How can you believe if you accept praise from one another, yet make no effort to obtain the praise that comes from the only God?

John 5:44

In an address I heard recently, the speaker said that the blessings of the higher Christian life were often like the objects displayed in a shop window: one could see them clearly and yet could not reach them. If told to reach out and help himself, a man would answer, "I can't; there's a thick pane of plate glass between me and them." In the same way, Christians may see clearly the blessed promises of perfect peace and rest, overflowing love and joy, abiding communion and fruitfulness, and yet feel that there is something hindering their possession. What is it that hinders? The promises made to faith are free and sure; the invitation and encouragement strong; the mighty power of God close at hand and free. All that hinders the blessing being ours is pride or a lack of faith. In our text, Jesus reveals to us that it is indeed pride that makes faith impossible: "How can you believe if you accept praise from one another?" As we see how in their very nature pride and faith are irreconcilably at odds, we learn that faith and humility are at their root one, and that we can never have more of true faith than we have of true humility. It is possible to have strong intellectual convictions and assurance of the truth while pride is still in the heart, but it makes living faith, which has power with God, impossible.

We have only to think for a moment what faith is. Is it not a confession of helplessness, the surrender to God that waits to let Him work? Is it not in itself the most humbling thing there can be—the acceptance of our place as dependents who can claim, or get, or do nothing but what grace bestows? Humility is simply the disposition that prepares the soul for living in trust. Even the most secret breath of pride, in self-seeking, self-will, self-confidence, or self-exaltation, is only the strengthening of that self that cannot enter the kingdom or possess the things of the kingdom because it refuses to allow God to be who He is.

Faith is the means by which we perceive and apprehend the heavenly world and its blessings. Faith seeks the glory that comes when God is all. As long as we take glory from one another, as long as we seek and love and jealously guard the glory of this life, the honor and reputation that comes from men, we do not seek and cannot receive the glory that comes from God. Pride renders faith impossible. Salvation comes through the cross and the crucified Christ. Salvation is the fellowship with the crucified Christ in the Spirit of His cross. Salvation is union with and delight in, even participation in the humility of Jesus. Is it any wonder that our faith is weak when pride still reigns and we have hardly learned to long or pray for humility as the most necessary and blessed part of salvation?

Humility and faith are more nearly allied in Scripture than many realize. See it in the life of Christ. There are two cases in which He spoke of great faith. He marveled at the faith of the centurion, saying, "I have not found anyone in Israel with such great faith." The centurion had said, "Lord, I do not deserve to have you come under my roof" (Matthew 8:5–13). And the mother to whom He said, "It is not right to take the children's bread and toss it to their dogs," replied, "Yes, Lord, but even the dogs eat the crumbs." To her, he replied, "Woman, you have great faith! Your request is granted" (Matthew 15:22–28). It is humility that brings a soul to be nothing before God and that also removes every hindrance to faith and makes it only fear lest it dishonor Him by not trusting Him completely.

If there is failure in the pursuit of holiness, it most surely has pride and self at its root. We have no idea to what extent pride and self secretly work within us, or how God alone by His indwelling power can cast them out. Nothing but the new and divine nature taking the place of the old self can make us truly humble. Absolute, unceasing humility must be the core disposition of every prayer and approach to God as well as every relationship with our fellowmen.

We go to such lengths to believe, while the old self in its pride seeks to avail itself of God's blessing and riches. No wonder we can't believe. We need to change our course. We need to humble ourselves under the mighty hand of God: He will exalt us. The cross, death, and the grave, into which Jesus humbled himself, were His path to the glory of God. And they are our path too. Let humility be our one desire and our fervent prayer. Let us gladly accept whatever humbles us before God or men—this alone is the path to the glory of God.

I have spoken of some who have blessed experiences or are the means of bringing blessing to others and yet are lacking in humility. You may ask whether these do not prove that they have true, even strong faith, though they show all too clearly that they still seek the honor that comes from men. There is more than one answer to this. But the principal answer in our present connection is this: they have a measure of faith in proportion to the blessing they bring to others. But the real work of their faith is hindered through their lack of humility. The blessing is often superficial or transitory because they by their failure to be "nothing" block the way for God to be all. A deeper humility would bring a deeper and fuller blessing. The Holy Spirit, working in them not only as a Spirit of power but also dwelling in them in the fullness of His grace, and especially that of humility, would through them communicate himself to others a life of power and holiness and steadfastness as yet unseen.

"How can you believe if you accept praise from one another?" Nothing can cure you of the desire to receive glory from men or of the sensitiveness and pain and anger that come when it is not given, but seeking alone the glory that comes from God. Let the glory of the all-glorious God be everything to you. You will be freed from the glory of men and of self and be content and glad to be nothing. Out of this nothingness you will grow strong in faith, giving glory to God, and you will find that the deeper you sink in humility before Him, the nearer He is to fulfill every desire of your faith.

humility and death to self

"Humility is the most difficult of all virtues to achieve; nothing dies harder than the desire to think well of oneself."

T. S. ELIOT

He humbled himself and became obedient to death.

Philippians 2:8

Humility is the path to death, because in death it gives the highest proof of its perfection. Humility is the blossom of which death to self is the perfect fruit. Jesus humbled himself unto death and opened the path in which we too must walk. As there was no way for Him to prove His surrender to God to the uttermost or to give up and rise out of our human nature to the glory of the Father but through death, so it is with us. Humility must lead us to die to self: so we prove how wholly we have given ourselves up to it and to God; so alone we are freed from our fallen nature and find the path that leads to life in God, to that full birth of the new nature, of which humility is the breath and the joy.

We have spoken of what Jesus did for His disciples when He communicated His resurrection life to them, when in the descent of the Holy Spirit, glorified and enthroned meekness, He actually came from heaven himself to dwell in them. He won the power to do this through death: in its inmost nature, the life He imparted was a life out of death, a life that had been surrendered to death and been won through death. He who came to dwell in them was himself one who had been dead and lives forevermore. His life, His person, His presence, bears the marks of death, a life begotten out of death. That life in His disciples ever bears the marks of death too; it is only as the Spirit of the dying One dwells and works in the soul that the power of His life can be known. The first mark of the dying of the Lord Jesus—the mark that shows the true follower of Jesus—is humility. For these two reasons: only humility leads to perfect death; only death perfects humility. Humility and death are in their very nature one: humility is the bud; in death the fruit is ripened to perfection.

Humility leads to perfect death. Humility means giving up self, taking the place of perfect nothingness before God. Jesus humbled himself and became obedient unto death. In death He gave the highest and perfect proof of having given up His will to the will of God. In death He gave up self with its natural reluctance to drink the cup; He gave up the life He had in union with our human nature; He died to self and the sin that tempted Him; so, as man, He entered into the perfect life of God. If it had not been for His boundless humility, counting himself as nothing except as a servant to do and suffer the will of God, He never would have died.

This gives us the answer to the question so often asked and seldom clearly understood: How can I die to self? Death to self is not your work; it is God's work. In Christ *you are dead* to sin; your life has gone through the process of death and resurrection. But the full manifestation of the power of this death in your disposition and conduct depends upon the measure in which the Holy Spirit imparts the power of the death of Christ. And here it is that the teaching is needed: If you would enter into full fellowship with Christ in His death, and know the full deliverance from self, humble yourself. This is your duty. Place yourself before God in your helplessness; consent to the fact that you are powerless to slay yourself; give yourself in patient and trustful surrender to God. Accept every humiliation; look upon every person who tries or troubles you as a means of grace to humble you. God will see such acceptance as proof that your whole heart desires it. It is the path of humility that leads to the full and perfect experience of our death with Christ.

Beware of the mistake so many make. They have so many qualifications and limitations, so many thoughts and questions as to what true humility is to be and to do that they never unreservedly yield themselves to it. Humble yourself unto death. It is in the death to self that humility is perfected. At the root of all real experience of grace and true advance in consecration is conformity to the likeness of Jesus, which affects our dispositions and our habits. The reason I mention disposition and habit is that it is possible to speak of walking in the Spirit while there is still evidence of self. True humility will manifest itself in daily life. The one who has it will take the form of a servant. It is possible to speak of fellowship with a despised and rejected Jesus and of bearing His cross, while the meek and lowly Lamb of God is not seen and rarely sought. The Lamb of God means two things: meekness and death. Let us seek to receive Him in both forms.

What a hopeless task if we had to do the work ourselves! Nature never can overcome nature, not even with the help of grace. Self can never cast out self, even in the regenerate man. Praise God! The work has been done, finished, and perfected forever. The death of Jesus, once and for all, is our death to self. And the ascension of Jesus, His entering once and forever into the Holy of Holies, has given us the Holy Spirit to communicate to us with power. As the soul in the pursuit and practice of humility follows in the steps of Jesus, its consciousness of the need of something more is awakened, its desire and hope is quickened, its faith strengthened, and it learns to look up and claim that true fullness of the Spirit of Jesus that can daily maintain His death to self and sin in its full power and make humility the all-pervading spirit of our life.[1]

"Or don't you know that all of us who were baptized into Christ Jesus were *baptized into his death?* . . . Count yourselves *dead to sin* but alive to God in Christ Jesus. . . . Offer yourselves to God, as those who have been *brought from death to life*" (Romans 6:3, 11, 13). The whole self-awareness of the Christian is to be imbued by the spirit of the sacrifice of Christ. He must present himself to God as one who has died with Christ and in Christ is alive again. His life will bear the twofold mark: its roots in the humility of Jesus, death to sin and self; its head lifted up in resurrection power.

Claim in faith the death and the life of Jesus as your own. Enter into rest from self and its work—the rest of God. With Christ, who committed His spirit into the Father's hands, humble yourself and acknowledge each day your helpless dependence upon God. God will raise you up and exalt you. Every morning remind yourself afresh of your emptiness so that the life of Jesus may be manifested in you. Let a willing, loving, restful humility be the mark that you have claimed your birthright—the baptism into the death of Christ. "By one sacrifice he has made perfect forever those who are being made holy" (Hebrews 10:14). The souls that enter into *His* humiliation will find *in Him* the power to see and count self as dead and, as those who have learned and received of Him, to walk with all lowliness and meekness, forbearing one another in love.

chapter eleven

humility and happiness

"Should you ask me: What is the first thing in religion? I should reply: the first, second, and third thing therein is humility."

AUGUSTINE

Therefore I will boast all the more gladly about my weaknesses, so that Christ's power may rest on me. That is why, for Christ's sake, I delight in weaknesses. . . . For when I am weak, then I am strong.

2 Corinthians 12:9–10

It seems that Paul's thorn in the flesh was sent to humble him so that he might not exalt himself as a result of the great revelations given to him. Paul's first desire was to have the thorn removed, and he asked the Lord three times that it might be taken away. The answer came to him that the trial was a blessing—that through the weakness and humiliation it brought, the grace and strength of the Lord could better be manifested. Paul at once entered upon a new stage in his relationship to the trial: instead of simply enduring it, *he gladly gloried* in it; instead of asking for deliverance, *he took pleasure* in it. He had learned that the place of humiliation is the place of blessing, of power, and of joy.

Many Christians fear and flee and seek deliverance from all that would humble them. At times they may pray for humility, but in their heart of hearts they pray even more to be kept from the things that would bring them to that place. They have not reached the level of seeing humility as a manifestation of the beauty of the Lamb of God. There is still a sense of burden connected with humility in their minds; to humble themselves has not become the spontaneous expression of their lives.

Can we hope to reach the stage in which this will be the case? Certainly. By the same way that Paul reached it: a new revelation of the Lord Jesus. Nothing but the presence of God can reveal and expel self. A clearer insight was to be given to Paul into the deep truth that the presence of Jesus banishes every desire to seek anything in ourselves. It will make us delight in every humiliation that prepares us for His fuller manifestation.

We may know advanced believers, eminent teachers, and men of great spiritual experience who have not yet learned to embrace humility. We see this danger in Paul's situation. The inevitability of exalting himself was close at hand. He didn't yet know what it was to be nothing; to die, that Christ alone might live in him; to take pleasure in all that brought him low. It appears that this was the greatest lesson that he had to learn.

Every Christian who seeks to advance in holiness should remember this: there may be intense consecration and fervent zeal, and if the Lord himself does not step in, there may be unconscious self-exaltation. Let us learn the lesson that the greatest holiness comes in the deepest humility.

Let us look at our lives in the light of this experience and see whether we gladly glory in weakness, and whether we take pleasure, as Paul did, in injuries, in necessities, in distresses. Yes, let us ask whether we have learned to regard a reproof, just or unjust, a reproach from a friend or an enemy, an injury, or trouble, or difficulty as an opportunity for proving that Jesus is all to us. It is indeed the deepest happiness of heaven to be so free from self that whatever is said of us or done to us is swallowed up in the thought that Jesus is all and we are nothing.

Let us trust Him who took care of Paul to take care of us too. Paul needed special discipline, and with it special instruction to learn what was more precious than even the unutterable things he had heard from heaven: what it is to glory in weakness and lowliness. We need it too. The school in which Jesus taught Paul is our school as well. He watches over us with a jealous, loving care, lest we exalt ourselves. When we do this, He seeks to show to us the evil of it and to deliver us from it. Through trials and failures and troubles, He seeks to bring us to the place where His grace is everything. His strength is made perfect in our weakness; His presence fills and satisfies our emptiness; and becomes the secret of humility. Paul could say, "I am not in the least inferior to the 'super-apostles,' even though I am nothing" (2 Corinthians 12:11).

"I will boast all the more gladly about my weaknesses, so that Christ's power may rest on me" (2 Corinthians 12:9). The humble man has learned the secret of abiding joy. The weaker he feels, the lower he sinks, the greater his humiliations, the more the power and presence of Christ is his portion. When he says, "I am nothing," the word of his Lord comes: "My grace is sufficient for you" (2 Corinthians 12:9).

The danger of pride is greater and nearer than we think, and especially at the time of our greatest experiences. The preacher of spiritual truth with an admiring congregation hanging on his every word, the gifted speaker of a holiness convention expounding the secrets of the heavenly life, the Christian giving testimony to a blessed experience—no man knows the hidden, unconscious danger to which these are exposed. Paul was in danger without knowing it: what Jesus did for him is written for our admonition, that we may know our danger and know our only safety. If ever it has been said of a teacher or professor of holiness: he is so full of self; or he does not practice what he preaches; or his blessing has not made him humbler or gentler—let it be said no more. Jesus, in whom we trust, can make us humble.

The grace for humility is also greater and nearer than we think. The humility of Jesus is our salvation: Jesus himself is our humility. His grace is sufficient for us to meet the temptation of pride. His strength will be perfected in our weakness. Let us choose to be weak, to be low, to be nothing. Let humility be to us joy and gladness. Let us gladly glory and take pleasure in weakness, in all that will humble us and keep us low; the power of Christ will rest upon us. Christ humbled himself, therefore God exalted Him. Christ will humble us and keep us humble; let us heartily consent, let us trustfully and joyfully accept all that humbles; the power of Christ will rest upon us. We shall find that the deepest humility is the secret of the truest happiness, of a joy that nothing can destroy.

chapter twelve

humility and exaltation

"I used to think that God's gifts were on shelves—one above another—and the taller we grow, the easier we can reach them. Now I find that God's gifts are on shelves—and the lower we stoop, the more we get."

F. B. MEYER

He who humbles himself will be exalted.

Luke 14:11; 18:14

God . . . gives grace to the humble. . . . Humble yourselves
before the Lord, and he will lift you up.

James 4:6, 10

Humble yourselves, therefore, under God's mighty hand, that
he may lift you up in due time.

1 Peter 5:6

Recently I was asked the question, "How can I overcome my pride?" The answer is simple. Two things are needed. Do what God says to do: humble yourself. Trust Him to do what He says He will do: He will exalt you.

The command is clear. But to humble yourself does not mean that you must conquer and cast out the pride of your nature and then form within yourself the lowliness of Jesus. No, this is God's work. He lifts you up into the true likeness of His beloved Son. What the command does mean is this: take every opportunity to humble yourself before God and man. In the faith of the grace that is already working in you; in the assurance of the grace for the victory that is yet to be; stand persistently under the unchanging command: humble yourself. Accept with gratitude everything that God allows from within or without, from friend or enemy, in nature or in grace, to remind you of your need for humbling and to help you in it. Reckon humility to be the mother-virtue, your very first duty before God, the one perpetual safeguard of the soul, and set your heart upon it as the source of all blessing. The promise is divine and sure: He that humbles himself shall be exalted. See that you do the one thing that God asks, and He will see that He does the one thing He has promised. He will give more grace; He will exalt you in due time.

All God's dealings with man are characterized by two stages. There is the time of preparation, when command and promise, with the mingled experience of effort and impotence, of failure and partial success, with the holy expectancy of something better, that these waken, train, and discipline men for a higher stage. Then comes the time of fulfillment, when faith inherits the promise and enjoys what it had so often struggled for in vain. This law holds good in every part of the Christian life and in the pursuit of every separate virtue. And that is because it is grounded in the very nature of things. In all that concerns our redemption, God must take the initiative. When that has been done, it is man's turn. In the effort after obedience and attainment, he must learn to know his powerlessness, in self-despair to die to himself, and so be fitted voluntarily and intelligently to receive from God the end, the completion of that which he had accepted in the beginning in ignorance. So God who had been the Beginning before man rightly knew Him or fully understood what His purpose was, is longed for and welcomed as the End, as the All in All.

It is so, too, in the pursuit of humility. To every Christian the command comes from the throne of God himself: humble yourself. The earnest attempt to listen and obey will be rewarded with the painful discovery of two things: the depth of our pride, and the powerlessness of all our efforts to destroy it. Blessed is the man who has learned to put his hope in God. We know the law of human nature: acts produce habits, habits breed dispositions, dispositions form the will, and the rightly formed will becomes the character. It is no different in the work of grace. As acts, persistently repeated, beget habits and dispositions, and these strengthen the will, He who works both to will and to do in us comes with His mighty power and Spirit; and the humbling of the proud heart with which the penitent saint so often casts himself before God is rewarded with the "more grace" of the humble heart.

Humble yourselves in the sight of the Lord, and He will exalt you. It cannot be repeated too often. The highest glory of the creature is in being a vessel, to receive and enjoy and show forth the glory of God. It can do this only as it is willing to be nothing in itself, that God may be everything. Water always fills first the lowest places. The lower, the emptier a man lies before God, the speedier and the fuller will be the inflow of the divine glory. The exaltation God promises is not, cannot be, any external thing apart from himself: all that He has to give or can give is only more of himself, in order that He might take the more complete possession. The exaltation is not, like an earthly prize, something arbitrary, in no connection with the conduct to be rewarded. It is in its very nature the effect and result of the humbling of ourselves. It is nothing but the gift of such a divine indwelling humility, such a conformity to and possession of the humility of the Lamb of God, as fits us for receiving fully the indwelling of God.

He that humbles himself shall be exalted. Of the truth of these words Jesus himself is the proof; of the certainty of their fulfillment to us He is the pledge. Let us take His yoke upon us and learn of Him, for He is meek and lowly of heart. If we are but willing to stoop to Him, as He has stooped to us, He will yet stoop to each one of us again, and we shall find ourselves not unequally yoked with Him. As we enter deeper into the fellowship of His humiliation—and either humble ourselves or bear the humbling of men—we can count upon the fact that the Spirit of His exaltation, "the Spirit of God and of glory," will rest upon us. The presence and the power of the glorified Christ will come to them that are of a humble spirit. When God can again have His rightful place in us, He will lift us up. Make His glory your motivation to humble yourself; He will make your glory His motivation to perfect your humility. As the all-pervading life of God possesses you, there will be nothing so natural or sweet as to be nothing, with no thought or wish for self, because all is occupied with Him. "I will boast all the more gladly about my weaknesses, so that Christ's power may rest on me" (2 Corinthians 12:9).

Have we not here the reason that our consecration and our faith have availed so little in the pursuit of holiness? It was by self and its strength that the work was done under the name of faith; it was for self and its happiness that God was called in; it was, unconsciously, but still truly, in self and its holiness that the soul rejoiced. We never knew that humility—absolute, abiding, Christ-like humility—and self-effacement, pervading and marking our whole life with God and man, was the most essential element of the life of holiness for which we sought.

It is only in the possession of God that I lose myself. As it is in the height and breadth and glory of the sunshine that the smallest speck dancing in its beams is seen, even so humility is taking our place in God's presence to be nothing but a speck dancing in the sunlight of His love.

How great is God! How small we are! Lost, swallowed up, in love's immensity!

May God teach us to believe that to be humble, to be nothing in His presence, is the highest attainment and the fullest blessing of the Christian life. He speaks to us: "I live in a high and holy place, but also with him who is contrite and lowly in spirit" (Isaiah 57:15).

> Oh, to be emptier, lowlier,
> Mean, unnoticed, and unknown,
> And to God a vessel holier,
> Filled with Christ, and Christ alone!

a prayer for humility

The secret of secrets: humility is the soul of true prayer. Until the spirit of the heart is renewed, until it is emptied of all earthly desires and stands in a habitual hunger and thirst after God, which is the true spirit of prayer; until then, all our prayer will be more or less like lessons given to students. We will mostly say them only because we dare not neglect them. But be not discouraged; take the following advice, and then you may go to church without any danger of mere lip-service or hypocrisy, although there may be a hymn or a prayer whose language is higher than that of your heart. Go to the church as the tax collector went to the temple; stand inwardly, in the spirit of your mind, in that form that he outwardly expressed when he cast down his eyes and could only say, "God be merciful to me, a sinner." Stand unchangeably, at least in your desire, in this form or state of heart; it will sanctify every petition that comes out of your mouth; and when anything is read or sung or prayed that is more exalted than your heart is, if you make this an occasion of further identifying with the spirit of the tax collector, you will then be helped and highly blessed by those prayers and praises that seem to belong to a heart better than yours.

This, my friend, is the secret of secrets. It will help you to reap where you have not sown and will be a continual source of grace in your soul; for everything that inwardly stirs you or outwardly happens to you becomes good to you if it finds you in this humble state of mind. For nothing is in vain or without profit to *the humble soul*; it stands always in a state of divine growth, and everything that falls upon it is like dew from heaven. Close yourself, therefore, in this form of humility; all good is enclosed in it; it is a fresh spring from heaven that turns the fire of the fallen soul into the meekness of the divine life, and creates that oil out of which the love to God and man gets its flame. Be always clothed in it; let it be as a garment wherewith you are always covered and a shield with which you are girded; breathe nothing but in and from its spirit; see nothing but with its eyes; hear nothing but with its ears. And then, whether you are in the church or out of the church, hearing the praises of God or receiving wrongs from men and the world, all will be edification, and everything will help promote your growth in the life of God.

I will here give you an infallible touchstone that will test all to the truth: retire from the world and all conversation for one month. Neither write, nor read, nor debate anything with yourself; stop all the former workings of your heart and mind, and with all the strength of your heart stand as continually as you can in the following form of prayer to God. Offer it frequently on your knees; but whether sitting, walking, or standing, be always inwardly longing and earnestly praying this one prayer to God: that of His great goodness He would make known to you, and take from your heart every kind and form and degree of pride, whether it be from evil spirits or your own corrupt nature; and that He would awaken in you the deepest depth and truth of that humility which can make you capable of His light and Holy Spirit. Reject every thought but that of waiting and praying in this manner from the bottom of your heart—with such truth and earnestness as people in agony pray and be delivered from their torment. In this spirit of prayer, I will venture to affirm that if you had twice as many evil spirits in you as Mary Magdalene had, they would all be cast out of you, and you would be forced with her to weep tears of love at the feet of the holy Jesus. (Adapted from *The Spirit of Prayer*, part 2, 121, 124, n.d.)

notes

Chapter One

1. "All this to make it known through the region of eternity
   that *pride* can degrade the highest angels into devils, and
   humility can raise fallen flesh and blood to the thrones of
   angels. This is the great end of God: raising a new creation
   out of a fallen kingdom of angels; for this end it stands in
   its state of war between the fire and pride of fallen angels
   and the humility of the Lamb of God—that the last trum-
   pet may sound the great truth through the depths of eternity that evil can have no beginning but from pride and no
   end but from humility.

   "The truth is this: Pride must die in you or nothing of
   heaven can live in you. Under the banner of the truth, give
   yourself up to the meek and humble spirit of the holy Jesus.

Humility must sow the seed or there can be no reaping in heaven. Look not at pride only as an unbecoming temper, nor at humility only as a decent virtue: for the one is death and the other is life; the one is hell and the other is heaven. So much as you have of pride within you, you have of the fallen angel alive in you; so much as you have of true humility, so much you have of the Lamb of God within you.

"If you could see what every stirring of pride does to your soul, you would beg of everyone you meet to tear the viper from you, though with the loss of a hand or an eye. If you could see what a sweet, divine, transforming power there is in humility, how it expels the poison of your nature, and makes room for the Spirit of God to live in you, you would rather wish to be the footstool of all the world than want the smallest degree of it." Taken from *The Spirit of Prayer*, edition of Moreton, Canterbury, 1893, part 2, 73.

Chapter Two

1. "We need to know two things: (1) Our salvation consists wholly in being saved from *ourselves*, or that which we are by nature; (2) In the whole nature of things, nothing could be salvation or savior to us but the humility of God beyond all expression. Hence the first unalterable term of 'Savior' of fallen man: 'Except a man deny himself he cannot be my disciple.' Self is the whole evil of the fallen nature. Self-denial is our capacity for being saved. Humility is our savior. . . . Self is the root, the branches, the tree, of all the evil of our fallen state. All the evil of fallen angels and of men

112

has its birth in the pride of self. On the other hand, all the virtues of the heavenly life stem from humility. It is humility alone that makes the impassable gulf between heaven and hell. What is then, or in what lies, the great struggle for eternal life? It all lies in the strife between pride and humility. Pride and humility are the two master powers, the two kingdoms at war for the eternal possession of man. There never was or ever will be but one humility, and that is the humility of Christ. Pride and self have the "all" of man, until man has his all in Christ. He only fights the good fight whose desire is that the self-idolatrous nature that he has from Adam may be put to death by the supernatural humility of Christ brought to life in him." Adapted from William Law, *Address to the Clergy*, n.d., 52.

Chapter Ten

1. "To die to self, or come from under its power, is not, cannot, be done by any active resistance we can make to it by the powers of nature. The one true way of dying to self is the way of patience, meekness, humility, and resignation to God. If I ask you what the Lamb of God means, would you not tell me that it means the perfection of patience, meekness, humility, and resignation to God? Would you say that a desire for these virtues is a desire to give yourself up to Him? Because this inclination of your heart is to seek patience, meekness, humility, and resignation to God, giving up all that you are and all that you have is your highest act of faith in Him. Christ is nowhere but in these virtues;

when they are there, He is in His own kingdom. Let this be the Christ you follow.

"The Spirit of divine love can have no birth in any fallen creature till it wills and chooses to be dead to all self, in patient, humble resignation to the power and mercy of God.

"I seek for all my salvation through the merits and mediation of the meek, humble, patient, suffering Lamb of God, who alone hath power to bring forth the blessed birth of these heavenly virtues in my soul. There is no possibility of salvation but in and by the birth of the meek, humble, patient, resigned Lamb of God in our souls. When the Lamb of God has brought forth a real birth of His own meekness, humility, and full resignation to God in our souls, then it is the birthday of the Spirit of love in our souls, which, whenever we attain it, will feast our soul with such peace and joy in God as will blot out the remembrance of everything that we called peace or joy before.

"This way to God is infallible. This infallibility is grounded in the twofold character of our Savior: (1) As He is the Lamb of God, it is a principle of meekness and humility in the soul; (2) As He is the Light of heaven, and blesses eternal nature and turns it into a kingdom of heaven when we are willing to get rest for our soul in meek, humble resignation to God, then it is that He, as the Light of God and heaven, joyfully breaks in upon us, turns our darkness into light, and begins that kingdom of God and of love within us that will never have an end." Taken from William Law, *Dying to Self: A Golden Dialogue*, n.d.

ABIDING
IN CHRIST

◆

Preface

During Jesus' life on earth, the phrase He used most often when speaking of the relationship of the disciples to himself was "Follow Me." When about to leave for heaven, He gave them a new phrase, which better described their more intimate and spiritual union with himself in glory: "Abide in Me."

Unfortunately there are many earnest followers of Jesus who fail to grasp the full meaning of these words. While trusting Him for pardon and help, and seeking to some extent to obey Him, they have not realized the closeness of union, the intimacy of fellowship, or the wondrous oneness of life and interest He invites them to when He says, "Abide in Me." This is not only an unspeakable loss to them personally but also a great loss to the church and the world around them.

If we ask why those who have accepted the Savior, and have experienced the renewing of the Holy Spirit, come short of the full salvation prepared for them, I am sure the answer will in many cases be ignorance, which leads to unbelief. If the reality of abiding in Christ, the living union with Him, the experience of His daily and hourly presence and keeping, were preached in our orthodox churches with the same distinctness and urgency as is His Atonement and our pardon through His blood, no doubt many would accept with gladness the invitation to such a life. And its influence would shine forth in the believers as they experience the purity and power, the love and joy, the fruit-bearing, and all the other blessings associated with abiding in Christ.

My desire to help those who have not yet fully understood what it means to abide in Him, or who have feared that it is a life beyond their reach, is why these meditations are now published. It is only by frequent repetition that a child learns its lessons. Only by continuously fixing the mind for a time on one of the lessons of faith is the believer gradually helped to take and thoroughly assimilate its benefits. I hope that to some, especially young believers, it will be a help to consider carefully the precious words, "Abide in Me," with the lessons connected with them in the parable of the Vine. Step by step we will see how truly this promise–precept is meant for us, how surely grace is provided to enable us to obey it, how indispensable the experience of its blessing is to a healthy Christian life, and how awesome are the blessings that flow from it. As we listen, meditate, and pray, the Holy Spirit will make the words to be spirit and life to us. This word of Jesus will become to us the power of God unto salvation, and through it will come the faith that grasps the long-desired blessing.

I pray earnestly that our gracious Lord may be pleased to bless this book, to help those who seek to know Him fully, as He has already blessed it in its original issue in the Dutch language. I pray that He would, by whatever means, make the multitudes of His dear children who are still living divided lives, to see how He claims them wholly for himself, and how wholehearted surrender to abide in Him alone brings a joy that is "unspeakable and full of glory" (1 Peter 1:8). May all of us who have begun to taste the sweetness of this life yield ourselves to be witnesses of the grace and power of our Lord to keep us united with Him. And may we seek by word and walk to win others to follow Him fully. It is only in such fruit-bearing that our own abiding can be maintained.

In conclusion, I would give one word of advice to my readers: It *takes time* to grow into Jesus the Vine; do not expect to abide in Him unless you will give Him that time. It is not enough to read God's Word, or meditations as found in this book; and when we think we understand the concepts and have asked God for His blessing, to go out in the hope that the blessing will remain. No, abiding requires day-by-day time with Jesus and the Father. We all know that we must take time for our meals each day. Every workman sets aside his time for dinner because it is important in his daily routine. In the same way, if we are to live through Jesus, we must feed on Him (John 6:57); we must thoroughly take in and assimilate the heavenly food the Father has given us in His life. Therefore, anyone who wants to learn to abide in Jesus must take time each day, before reading, while reading, and after reading, to put himself into contact with the living Jesus. He must yield himself distinctly and consciously to His blessed influence—giving Him the opportunity to take hold of him so that He may draw him up and keep him safe in His almighty life.

And now, to all God's children whom He allows me the privilege of pointing to the Heavenly Vine, I offer my fraternal love and greetings, with the prayer that to each one of them may be given the rich and full experience of abiding in Christ. And may the grace of Jesus, the love of God, and the fellowship of the Holy Spirit be their daily portion. Amen.

John 15:1-12

I am the true vine, and My Father is the vinedresser. Every branch in Me that does not bear fruit He takes away; and every branch that bears fruit He prunes, that it may bear more fruit. You are already clean because of the word which I have spoken to you. Abide in Me, and I in you. As the branch cannot bear fruit of itself, unless it abides in the vine, neither can you, unless you abide in Me. I am the vine, you are the branches. He who abides in Me, and I in him, bears much fruit; for without Me you can do nothing. If anyone does not abide in Me, he is cast out as a branch and is withered; and they gather them and throw them into the fire, and they are burned. If you abide in Me, and My words abide in you, you shall ask what you desire, and it shall be done for you. By this My Father is glorified, that you bear much fruit; so you will be My disciples. As the Father loved Me, I also have loved you; continue in My love. If you keep My commandments, you will abide in My love, just as I have kept My Father's commandments and abide in His love. These things I have spoken to you that My joy may remain in you, and that your joy may be full. This is My commandment, that you love one another as I have loved you.

All You Who Have Come to Him

Come to Me.

Matthew 11:28

Abide in Me.

John 15:4

It is to you who have heard and responded to the call, *"Come to Me,"* that this new invitation comes, *"Abide in Me."* The message comes from the same loving Savior. No doubt you have never regretted responding to His call and coming to Him. You experienced that His word was truth; all His promises He fulfilled; He made you a partaker of the blessings and the joy of His love. His welcome was heartfelt, His pardon full and free, His love most sweet and precious, was it not? You more than once, at your first coming to Him, had reason to say, "The half was not told me."

And yet you have had some disappointment. As time went on, your expectations were not always realized. The blessings you once enjoyed were lost; the love and joy of your first meeting with your Savior, instead of deepening, have become faint and weak. And you have often wondered why, with such a mighty and loving Savior, your experience of salvation was not a fuller one.

The answer is very simple. You wandered from Him. The blessings He bestows are all connected with His "Come to Me," and are only to be enjoyed in close fellowship with Him. You either did not fully understand, or did not rightly remember, that the call meant "Come to Me and remain with Me." This was His object and purpose when He first called you to himself. It was not to refresh you for a few short hours after your conversion with the joy of His love and deliverance, and then to send you forth to wander in sadness and sin. He destined you to something better than a short-lived blessing, to be enjoyed only in times of special earnestness and prayer, and then to pass away as you had to return to the more mundane duties of life.

No, indeed, He has prepared for you an abiding dwelling with himself, where your whole life and every moment of it might be spent and where the work of your daily life might be done as you enjoy unbroken communion with Him. This is what He meant when to that first word, "*Come* to Me," He added "*Abide* in Me." Just as earnest and faithful, as loving and tender, as the compassion contained in the invitation to "Come" was the grace that added a further invitation to "Abide." As mighty as the attraction with which that first word drew you were the bonds with which this second—had you but listened to it—would have kept you. And as great as were the blessings associated with coming, so much greater were the treasures to which abiding would have given you access.

Notice that He did not say, "Come to me and abide with

Me," but, "Abide *in* Me." The relationship was not only to be unbroken, but also intimate and complete. He opened His arms, to press you to himself; He opened His heart, to welcome you there; He opened up all His divine fullness of life and love, and offered to take you up into its fellowship, to make you wholly one with Him. There was a depth of meaning you have not yet realized in His words "Abide in Me."

Just as earnestly as He cried, "Come to Me," did He plead—had you but noticed it—"Abide in Me." Was it the fear of sin and its curse that first drew you to Him? The pardon you received on first coming could, with all the blessings flowing from it, only be confirmed and fully enjoyed by abiding in Him. Was it the longing to know and enjoy Infinite Love that was calling you? The first coming gave but single drops to taste; it is only the abiding that can really satisfy the thirsty soul and enable you to drink of the rivers of pleasure that are at His right hand (Psalm 16:11; 36:8). Was it the weary longing to be set free from the bondage of sin, to become pure and holy, and so find rest, the rest of God for the soul that drew you to Him? This too can only be realized as you abide in Him; only abiding in Jesus gives rest in Him. Or if it was the hope of an inheritance in glory, and an everlasting home in the presence of the Infinite One, the true preparation for this, as well as a taste of its glory in this life, is granted only to those who abide in Him.

The truth is, there is nothing that moved you to come that does not plead with even greater force: *Abide in Him.* You did well to come; you do better to abide. Who would be content, after seeking the King's palace, to stand in the door, when he is invited in to dwell in the King's presence, and share with Him in all the glory of His royal life? Let us enter in and abide, and enjoy fully all the rich supply His wondrous love has prepared for us!

I fear that there are many who have indeed come to Jesus, and who yet mournfully confess that they know little of this blessed abiding in Him. With some the reason is that they never fully understood that this was the meaning of the Savior's call. With others, though they heard the word, they did not know that such a life of abiding fellowship was possible and within their reach. Others will say that, though they did believe that such a life was possible, and seek after it, they have not yet discovered the secret of its attainment. And others, alas, will confess that it is their own unfaithfulness that has kept them from the enjoyment of the blessing. When the Savior would have kept them, they were not found ready to stay; they were not prepared to give up everything and to always, only, completely identify with Jesus.

To all such I come now in the name of Jesus, their Redeemer and mine, with the blessed message: "Abide in Me." In His name I invite them to come, and for a season meditate with me daily on its meaning, its lessons, its claims, and its promises. I know how many, and, to the young believer, how difficult, the questions are which suggest themselves in connection with the idea of abiding. There is especially the question to the possibility, in the midst of tiring work and continual distraction, of keeping up, or rather being kept in, abiding communion. I do not attempt to remove all difficulties; this Jesus Christ himself must do by His Holy Spirit.

What I will do, by the grace of God, is to repeat day by day the Master's blessed command, "Abide in Me," until it enters our hearts and finds a place there. In the light of Holy Scripture we should meditate on its meaning until the understanding, that gate to the heart, opens to grasp something of what it offers and expects. In this way we will discover the means of its attainment and learn what keeps us from it and what can help us to it. So we will feel its claims and be compelled to acknowledge that there can be no true allegiance to our King without simply and heartily accepting this important command.

Come, fellow believers, and let us day by day place ourselves at His feet, and meditate on this word of His with an eye fixed on Him alone. Let us set ourselves in quiet trust before Him, waiting to hear His holy voice—the still, small voice that is mightier than the storm that breaks the rocks—breathing its life-giving spirit within us as He speaks: "Abide in Me." The soul that hears *Jesus himself speak the word* receives with the word the power to accept and to hold the blessing He offers.

And may it please you, blessed Savior, to speak to us; let each of us truly hear your blessed voice. May the feeling of our deep need, and the faith of your wondrous love, combined with the sight of the wonderfully blessed life you are waiting to bestow upon us, compel us to listen and to obey as often as you speak: "Abide in Me." Let the answer from our heart day by day be ever clearer and fuller: "Blessed Savior, I do abide in you."

You Will Find Rest for Your Souls

*Come to Me, all you who labor and are heavy laden, and I will
give you rest. Take My yoke upon you and learn from Me, for I
am gentle and lowly in heart, and you
will find rest for your souls.*

Matthew 11:28–29

Rest for the soul: Such was the first promise extended by the
Savior to win the burdened sinner. Simple though it appears,
the promise is as large and comprehensive as can be found. Rest
for the soul—does it not imply deliverance from every fear, the
supply of every want, the fulfillment of every desire? And now
this is the prize with which the Savior woos back the wandering
one, the one who is mourning that his rest has not been so
abiding or so full as he had hoped, to return and abide in Him.
This was the reason that rest either has not been found, or, if
found, has been disturbed or lost again: you did not abide in
Him.

Have you ever noticed how, in the original invitation of the

129

Savior to come to Him (Matthew 11:28–29), the promise of rest was repeated twice, with such a variation in the conditions as might suggest that abiding rest can only be found in abiding nearness. First the Savior says, "Come to Me, and I will give you rest"; the very moment you come, and believe, I will give you rest, the rest of pardon and acceptance found in my love. But we know that all that God bestows needs time to become fully our own. It must be embraced, appropriated, and assimilated into our soul; without this not even Christ's giving can make it our own in terms of full experience and enjoyment.

And so the Savior repeats His promise, in words that clearly speak not so much of the initial rest with which He welcomes the weary one who comes, but of the deeper and personally appropriated rest of the soul that abides in Him. Now He not only says "Come to Me" but also "Take My yoke upon you and learn from Me"; become My scholars, yield yourselves to My training, submit in all things to My will, let your whole life be one with mine—in other words, abide in Me. And then He adds not only "I will give" but also "you will find rest for your souls." The *rest* that He gave at your first coming will become something you have really found and made your very own— the deeper, abiding rest which comes from longer acquaintance, closer fellowship, and entire surrender. "Take My yoke, and learn from Me," "Abide in Me"—this is the path to abiding rest.

These words of the Savior uncover what you have perhaps often wondered: How is it that the rest you at times enjoy is so often lost? This must have been the reason: You did not understand how *entire surrender to Jesus is the secret of perfect rest.* Giving up one's whole life to Him to rule and order, taking up His yoke, and allowing ourselves to be led and taught of Him, abiding in Him, to be and do only what He wills—these are the conditions of discipleship without which there can be no thought of maintaining the rest that was bestowed on first coming to Christ. This rest is in Christ, not something He gives apart from himself, and so it is only in having Him that the rest can really be kept and enjoyed.

It is because so many young believers fail to grasp this truth that their rest so quickly evaporates. With some it is that they really did not know; they were never taught how Jesus claims undivided allegiance of the whole heart and life. They were unaware that there is not a spot in the whole of life over which He does not wish to reign. They did not know how entire the consecration was that Jesus claimed. With others, who had some idea of what a very holy life a Christian ought to lead, the mistake was a different one: They could not believe such a life could be attained. Taking, bearing, and never for a moment laying aside the yoke of Jesus appeared to them to require such a strain of effort, and such an enormous amount of goodness that they assumed it was beyond their reach. The very idea of always, all the day, abiding in Jesus was too high—something they might attain to after a life of holiness and growth, but certainly not what an immature beginner was to start with.

They did not know how, when Jesus said, "My yoke is easy," He spoke the truth; how it is actually *the yoke* which gives the rest, because the moment the soul yields itself to obey, the Lord himself gives the strength and joy to do it. They did not notice how when He said, "Learn from Me," He added, "for I am gentle and lowly in heart," to assure them that His gentleness would meet their every need and sustain them as a mother upholds her weakest child. They did not know that when He said, "Abide in Me," He only asked that His followers surrender to Him; His almighty love would keep and bless them. And so, as some fell short of full consecration, they failed because they did not fully trust. These two, consecration and faith, are the essential elements of the Christian life—the giving up of all to Jesus, the receiving of all from Jesus. They are implied in each other; they are united in one word: *surrender*. A full surrender is to obey as well as to trust, to trust as well as to obey.

With such misunderstanding at the outset, it is no wonder that the disciple's life is often not filled with as much joy or strength as had been hoped. In some things you were led into sin without knowing it, because you had not learned how wholly Jesus wanted to rule you and how you could not remain righteous for a moment unless you had Him very near you. In other things you knew what sin was, but did not have the power to conquer, because you did not know or believe how entirely Jesus would keep and help you. Either way, it was not long before the bright joy of your first love was lost, and your path, instead of being like the "path of the righteous . . . shining ever brighter till the full light of day" (Proverbs 4:18 NIV), became like Israel's wandering in the desert, ever on the way, never very far, and yet always coming short of the promised rest. Weary soul, come and learn this day the lesson that there is a spot where safety and victory, peace and rest, are always sure. That place, which is the heart of Jesus, is always open to you.

But, sadly, I hear someone say it is just this abiding in Jesus, always bearing His yoke to learn from Him, that is so difficult, and the very effort to attain to this often disturbs my rest even more than sin or the world. What a mistake it is to speak like this, yet how often the words are heard! We must ask ourselves, does it make the traveler even wearier to rest in the house or on the bed where he seeks relief from his fatigue? Or is it work to a little child to rest in his mother's arms? Is it not the house that keeps the traveler within its shelter? Do not the arms of the mother sustain and keep the little one? And so it is with Jesus.

The soul has only to yield itself to Him, to be still and to rest in the confidence that His love has undertaken, and that His faithfulness will perform, the work of keeping it safe. It is because the blessing is so great that our frail hearts cannot rise to grasp it; it is as if we cannot believe that Christ, the Almighty One, will actually teach and keep us all day. And yet this is just what He has promised, for without this He cannot really give us rest. It is His own work to keep us abiding when we yield ourselves to Him. We must risk casting ourselves into the arms of His love, and so abandon ourselves to His blessed keeping. It is not the yoke, but resistance to the yoke, that makes the difficulty; wholehearted surrender to Jesus, our Master and our Keeper, is what finds and secures our rest.

Come, my fellow believers, and let us this very day begin to accept the word of Jesus in all its simplicity. It is a distinct command to "Take My yoke . . . and learn from Me"; "Abide in Me." A command has to be obeyed. The obedient scholar asks no questions about possibilities or results; he accepts every order in the confidence that his teacher has provided for all that is needed. The power and the perseverance to abide in His rest, and the blessing in abiding, belongs to the Savior: 'tis mine to obey, 'tis His to provide. Let us this day in immediate obedience accept the command, and answer boldly, "Savior, I abide in you. At your bidding I take your yoke upon me; I undertake the duty without delay; I abide in you." May each time we fail only give new urgency to the command, and teach us to listen more earnestly than ever until the Spirit gives us the voice of Jesus saying with love and authority the words that inspire both hope and obedience: "Child, abide in Me." That word, heard as coming from Jesus himself, will be an end to all doubting—a divine promise of what will surely be granted. And with ever-increasing simplicity its meaning will be interpreted. Abiding in Jesus is nothing but the giving up of oneself to be ruled, taught, and led, enabling the disciple to rest in the arms of Everlasting Love.

What a blessed rest it is! The fruit, the foretaste, and the fellowship of God's own rest are found by them who have come to Jesus to abide in Him. It is the peace of God, the great calm of the eternal world, that passes all understanding and that keeps the heart and mind. With this grace secured, we have strength for every duty, courage for every struggle, a blessing in every cross, and the joy of life eternal in death itself.

O my Savior, if ever my heart should doubt or fear again, as if the blessing were too great to expect, or too high to attain, let me hear your voice, which alone can create faith and obedience in me: "Abide in Me"; "Take My yoke upon you and learn from Me; you will find rest for your souls."

Trusting Him to Keep You

I press on to take hold of that for which
Christ Jesus took hold of me.

Philippians 3:12 NIV

More than one admits that it is a sacred duty and a blessed privilege to abide in Christ but shrinks back continually before the question: Is it possible, a life of unbroken fellowship with the Savior? Eminent Christians, to whom special opportunities of cultivating this grace have been granted, may attain to it; but for the large majority of disciples whose lives are so fully occupied with the everyday concerns of this life, it cannot be expected. The more they hear of this life, the deeper their sense of its glory and blessing, and there is nothing they would not sacrifice to be made partakers of it. But they feel they are too weak, too unfaithful; they are sure they can never attain it.

How little such dear souls know about this life. They don't realize that abiding in Christ is meant for the weak and is beautifully suited to their frailty. It is not the doing of some great thing and does not demand that we first lead a very holy and devoted life. No, it is simply weakness entrusting itself to a Mighty One to be kept, the unfaithful one casting itself on One who is altogether trustworthy and true. Abiding in Him is not a work that we have to do as the condition for enjoying His salvation, but rather a consenting to let Him do all for us, in us, and through us. It is a work He does for us as the fruit and the power of His redeeming love. Our part is simply to yield, to trust, and to wait for what He has promised to perform.

It is this quiet expectation and confidence, resting on the word of Christ that *in Him* there is an abiding place prepared, which is so sadly lacking among Christians. For when He says, "Abide in Me," He offers himself, the Keeper of Israel that neither slumbers nor sleeps (Psalm 121:4), with all His power and love, as *the living home of the soul*, where the mighty influences of His grace will be stronger to keep than all of the disciples' tendencies to be led astray. The idea so many Christians have of grace is this: that their conversion and pardon are God's work, but now, in gratitude to God, it is their work to live as Christians and follow Jesus. There is always the thought of a work that has to be done, and even though they pray for help, still the work is theirs. They fail continually and become hopeless; and their despondency only increases their feelings of helplessness.

No, wandering one; as it was Jesus who drew you when He said, "Come," so it is Jesus who keeps you when He says, "Abide." The grace to come and the grace to abide are both from Him alone. That word *come*—heard, meditated on, accepted—was the cord of love that drew you close; the word *abide* is the band with which He holds you fast and binds you to himself. Let the soul take time to listen to the voice of Jesus. *"In Me,"* He says, "is your place—in my almighty arms. It is I, the One who loves you so, who now speaks 'Abide in Me'; surely you can trust Me." The voice of Jesus entering and dwelling in the soul draws us to respond: "Yes, Savior, *in you* I can, I will abide."

"Abide in Me": These words are no law of Moses, demanding from the sinful what they cannot perform. They are the command of love, which is only a promise in a different shape. Think of this until all feeling of burden, fear, and despair pass away, and the first thought that comes as you hear of abiding in Jesus is one of bright and joyous hope: It is for me; I know I will enjoy it. You are not under the law, with its demanding *Do*, but under grace, with its blessed *Believe* what Christ will do for you. And if the question is asked, "But surely there is something for us to do," the answer is, "Our doing and working are but the fruit of Christ's work in us." It is when the soul becomes utterly passive, looking and resting on what Christ is to do, that its energies are stirred to their highest activity, and we work most effectively because we know that He works in us. It is as we see in the words "in Me" the mighty energies of love reaching out after us to have us and to hold us, that all the strength of our will is awakened to abide in Him.

This connection between Christ's work and our work is beautifully expressed in the words of Paul: "I press on, to *take hold of* that for which Christ Jesus *took hold* of me." It was because he knew that the mighty and the faithful One had grasped him with the glorious purpose of making him one with Christ that he did his utmost to grasp the glorious prize. The faith, the experience, the full assurance, "Christ Jesus took hold of me," gave him the courage and the strength to press on and take hold of that for which he was taken. Each new insight of the great end for which Christ had taken him spurred him on to aim for nothing less.

Paul's expression, and its application to the Christian life, can be best understood if we think of a father helping his child to climb the side of some steep precipice. The father stands above and has taken the son by the hand to help him on. He points him to the spot on which he will help him to plant his feet as he leaps upward. The leap would be too high and dangerous for the child alone, but the father's hand is his trust and he leaps to get hold of the point for which his father has taken hold of him. It is the father's strength that secures him and lifts him up, and so urges him to use his utmost strength.

Such is the relationship between Christ and you, O weak and trembling believer! Fix your eyes first on the *that* for which He has taken hold of you. It is nothing less than a life of abiding, unbroken fellowship with himself to which He is seeking to lift you up. All that you have already received—pardon and peace, the Spirit and His grace—are but preliminary to this. And all that you see promised to you in the future—holiness and fruitfulness and glory everlasting—are but its natural outcome. *Union with himself*, and so with the Father, is His highest object. Fix your eye on this, and gaze until it stands out before you clear and unmistakable: Christ's aim is to have me abiding in Him.

Then let the second thought enter your heart: *For this Christ Jesus took hold of me.* His almighty power has taken hold of me and offers now to lift me up to where He would have me. Fix your eyes on Christ. Gaze on the love that shines in those eyes and that asks whether you can trust Him, who sought, found, and brought you near, now to keep you. Gaze on that arm of power, and say whether you have reason enough to be assured that He is indeed able to keep you abiding in Him.

And as you think of the spot He points to—the blessed *that* for which He laid hold of you—and keep your gaze fixed on Him holding you and waiting to lift you up, begin at once to say, "O my Jesus, if you bid me, and if you will indeed lift me up and keep me there, I will venture. Trembling, but trusting, I will say, 'Jesus, I do abide in you.' "

My beloved fellow believers, go, and take time alone with Jesus, and say this to Him. I do not speak to you about abiding in Him for the mere sake of calling forth a pleasing religious sentiment. God's truth must be acted on at once. Yield yourself this very day to the blessed Savior by surrendering the one thing He asks of you: Give up yourself to abide in Him. He himself will work it in you. You can trust Him to keep you trusting and abiding.

And if ever doubts arise, or the bitter experience of failure tempts you to despair, just remember where Paul found His strength: "Christ Jesus took hold of me." In that assurance you have a fountain of strength. From that you can look up to where He has set His heart and set yours there too. From that truth you can gather confidence that the good work He began in you He will carry on to completion (Philippians 1:6). And in that confidence you will gather courage day by day to say, "I press on, to take hold of that for which Christ Jesus took hold of me." It is because Jesus has taken hold of me, and because Jesus keeps me, that I dare to say: "Savior, I abide in you."

As the Branch in
the Vine

I am the vine, you are the branches.

John 15:5

It was in connection with the parable of the Vine that our Lord first used the expression "Abide in Me." That parable, so simple and yet so rich in its teaching, gives us the best and most complete illustration of the meaning of our Lord's command and the union to which He invites us.

The parable teaches us *the nature* of that union. The connection between the vine and the branch is a living one. No external, temporary union is described here, and no work of man can make it happen. The branch, whether an original or an engrafted one, is the Creator's own work; the life, the sap, the fatness, and the fruitfulness of the branch are only possible because of its attachment to the vine. And so it is with the believer too. His union with his Lord is no work of human wisdom or human will, but an act of God, by which the closest and most complete life-union possible is forged between the

Son of God and the sinner. "God has sent forth the Spirit of His Son into your hearts" (Galatians 4:6). The same Spirit that dwelt and still dwells in the Son becomes the life of the believer; in the unity of that one Spirit, and the fellowship of the same life that is in Christ, he is one with Him. As between the vine and branch, it is a life-union that makes them one.

The parable teaches us the *completeness* of the union. So close is the union between the vine and the branch, that each is nothing without the other, each is wholly and only for the other.

Without the vine the branch can do nothing. To the vine it owes its right of place in the vineyard, its life and its fruitfulness. And so the Lord says, "Without Me you can do nothing." The believer can each day be pleasing to God only in that which he does through the power of Christ dwelling in him. The daily filling of the life-sap of the Holy Spirit is his only power to bring forth fruit. He lives in Him alone and is for each moment dependent on Him alone.

Without the branch the vine can also do nothing. A vine without branches can bear no fruit. No less indispensable than the vine to the branch is the branch to the vine. Such is the wonderful condescension of the grace of Jesus; just as His people are dependent on Him, He has made himself dependent on them. Without His disciples He cannot dispense His blessing to the world. I know it seems incredible, but it is true! This is God's own doing, giving such high honor to those He has called His redeemed ones, designing it so that as indispensable as He is to them in acquiring fruit and winning heaven, so indispensable are they to Him on earth, that through them His fruit may be found. Believers, meditate on this until your soul bows to worship in the presence of the mystery of the perfect union between Christ and the believer.

There is more: As neither vine nor branch is anything *without* the other, so is neither anything except *for* the other. *All the vine possesses belongs to the branches.* The vine does not gather from the soil its fatness and its sweetness for itself; all it has is at the disposal of the branches. As it is the parent, so it is the servant of the branches. How completely Jesus, to whom we owe our life, gives himself for us and to us: "The glory which You gave Me I have given them" (John 17:22); "He who believes in Me, the works that I do he will do also; and greater works than these he will do, because I go to My Father" (John 14:12). All His fullness and all His riches are for you, as His believer; for the vine does not live for itself, or keep anything for itself, but exists only for the branches. All that Jesus is in heaven, He is for us. He has no interest there separate from ours; as our representative He stands before the Father on our behalf.

And all the branch possesses belongs to the vine. The branch does not exist for itself, but to bear fruit that can proclaim the excellence of the vine; it has no reason to exist except to be of service to the vine. What a glorious image this is of the calling of the believer; the entirety of his consecration is only for service to his Lord. As Jesus gives himself so completely over to him, he feels himself urged to be wholly his Lord's. Every power of his being, every moment of his life, every thought and feeling belong to Jesus, that from Him and for Him he may bring forth fruit. As he realizes what the vine is to the branch, and what the branch is meant to be to the vine, he feels that he has but one thing to think of and to live for: the will, the glory, the work, the kingdom of his blessed Lord—the bringing forth of fruit to the glory of His name.

The parable also teaches us *the object* of the union. The branches are for *fruit* and *fruit alone.* "Every branch in Me that does not bear fruit He takes away." The branch needs leaves for the maintenance of its own life and the perfection of its fruit; the fruit it bears is to be given away to those around it. As the believer enters into his calling as a branch, he sees that he has to forget himself and to live entirely for others. To love them, to seek for them, and to save them, this is why Jesus came. For this purpose every branch on the Vine—as well as the Vine—must live. *It is for fruit, much fruit,* that the Father has made us one with Jesus.

Wondrous parable of the Vine—unveiling the mysteries of divine love, of the heavenly life, of the world of the Spirit—how little have I understood you! Jesus the living Vine in heaven, and I the living branch on earth—how profound are the implications of this revelation. I have scarcely grasped how great my need is, but also how perfect is my claim to all His fullness! How little have I understood how great His need is, but also how perfect is His claim to my emptiness! Let me, in its beautiful light, study the wondrous union between Jesus and His people until it becomes to me the guide into full communion with my beloved Lord. Let me listen and believe, until my whole being cries out, "Jesus is indeed to me the True Vine, bearing me, nourishing me, supplying me, using me, and filling me to the full to make me bring forth fruit abundantly." Then I will not be afraid to say, "I am indeed a branch of Jesus, the True Vine, abiding in Him, resting on Him, waiting for Him, serving Him, and living so that through me, too, He may exhibit the riches of His grace, and give His fruit to a dying world."

It is when we try to understand the meaning of the parable that the blessed command spoken in connection with it will come home to us in its true power. The thought of what the vine is to the branch, and Jesus to the believer, will give new power to the words "Abide in Me!" It will be as if He says, "Think, believer, how completely I belong to you. I have joined myself inseparably to you; all the fullness and fatness of the Vine are yours. It is My desire and My honor to make you a fruitful branch; only *Abide in Me*. You are weak, but I am strong; you are poor, but I am rich. Only abide in Me; yield yourself wholly to My teaching and rule; simply trust My love, My grace, and My promises. Only believe; I am wholly yours; I am the Vine, you are the branch. Abide in Me."

What is my response to such a revelation? Should I continue to hesitate, or withhold consent? Or should I—instead of only thinking about how hard and how difficult it is to live like a branch of the True Vine, because I thought of it as something I had to accomplish—now begin to look upon it as the most blessed and joyful thing under heaven? Should I not believe that, now that I am in Him, He himself will keep me and enable me to abide? On my part, abiding is nothing but the acceptance of my position, the consent to be kept there, the surrender of faith to the strong Vine to hold the frail branch. Yes, I will, I do abide in you, blessed Lord Jesus.

O Savior, how unspeakable is your love! "Such knowledge is too wonderful for me, too lofty for me to attain" (Psalm 139:6 NIV). I can only yield myself to your love with the prayer that, day by day, you would reveal to me the precious mysteries of such knowledge and so encourage and strengthen me to do what my heart longs to do indeed—ever, only, wholly to abide in you.

It Is As You Came to Him, by Faith

As you have therefore received Christ Jesus the Lord, so walk in Him, rooted and built up in Him and established in the faith, as you have been taught, abounding in it with thanksgiving.

Colossians 2:6–7

In these words the apostle teaches us an important lesson, that it is not only by faith that we first come to Christ and are united to Him but also by faith that we are to be rooted and established in our union with Christ. Faith is essential not only for the commencement, but also for the progress of the spiritual life. Abiding in Jesus can only be by faith.

There are sincere Christians who do not understand this; or, if they admit it in theory, they fail to realize its application in practice. They are very zealous for a free gospel in which our first acceptance of Christ and justification is by faith alone. But after this they think everything depends on our diligence and faithfulness. While most firmly grasp the truth "The sinner is justified by faith" (Galatians 2:16), they rarely find a place for

147

the larger truth, "The just shall *live* by faith" (Romans 1:17). They have not understood what a perfect Savior Jesus is, and how He will each day do for the sinner just as much as He did the first day he came to Him. They do not know that the life of grace is always and only a life of faith, and that in the relationship to Jesus the one daily and unceasing duty of the disciple is *to believe*, because believing is the one channel through which divine grace and strength flow out into the heart of His people.

The old nature of the believer remains evil and sinful to the last; it is only as he daily comes, empty and helpless, to his Savior to receive His life and strength, that he can bring forth fruits of righteousness to the glory of God. Therefore it is: "*As you have therefore received Christ Jesus the Lord, so walk in Him*, rooted and built up *in Him* and established *in the faith*, as you have been taught, abounding in it with thanksgiving." As you came to Jesus, so abide in Him, by faith.

And if you would know how faith is to be exercised in this abiding, how you can be rooted more deeply and firmly in Him, you will need to look back to the time when you first received Him. You remember well the obstacles that appeared to be in the way of your believing. There was first your corruption and guilt; it appeared impossible that the promise of pardon and love could be for a sinner like you. Then there was the sense of weakness and death: You did not feel the power necessary for the surrender and the trust to which you were called. And then there was the future: You did not dare to imagine you could be a disciple of Jesus while you felt so unable to stand. You were sure you would quickly revert to unfaithfulness and fall. These difficulties were like mountains in your way. And how were they removed? Simply by the word of God. That word compelled you to believe that despite guilt in the past, weakness in the present, and unfaithfulness in the future, the promise was sure that Jesus would accept you and save you. On that word you ventured to come, and were not deceived: You found that Jesus did indeed accept and save you.

Now apply this, your experience in coming to Jesus, to abiding in Him. Now, as then, the temptations to keep you from believing are many. When you think of your sins since you became a disciple, your heart is cast down with shame, and it looks as if it were too much to expect that Jesus would indeed receive you into perfect intimacy and the full enjoyment of His holy love. When you think how utterly, in times past, you have failed to keep the most sacred vows, the consciousness of present weakness makes you tremble at the very idea of answering the Savior's command with the promise "Lord, from now on I will abide in you." And when you set before yourself the life of love and joy, of holiness and fruitfulness, which in the future are to flow from abiding in Him, it is as if it only serves to make you still more hopeless; you are sure you can never attain to it. You know yourself too well. There is no use expecting it, only to be disappointed; a life fully and wholly abiding in Jesus is not for you.

Oh, that you would learn a lesson from the time of your first coming to the Savior! Remember, dear one, how you were then led—contrary to all that your experience, your feelings, and even your sober judgment said—to take Jesus at His word, and how you were not disappointed. He did receive you, and pardon you; He did love you, and save you. And if He did this for you when you were an enemy and a stranger, now that you are His own, will He not much more fulfill His promise? (See

Romans 5:10.) Oh, that you would come and begin simply to listen to His word, and to ask only one question: Does He really mean that I can abide in Him? The answer His word gives is so simple and so sure: By His almighty grace you are now *in Him*; that same almighty grace will indeed enable you to abide in Him. By faith you became a partaker of the initial grace; by that same faith you can enjoy the continuous grace of abiding in Him.

And if you ask what exactly it is that you now have to believe that you may abide in Him, the answer is not difficult. Believe first of all what He says: "I am the Vine." The safety and the fruitfulness of the branch depend upon the strength of the vine. Do not think so much of yourself as a branch, nor of the abiding as your duty, until you have first had your soul filled with faith in what Christ as the Vine is. *He really will be to you all that a vine can be*—holding you fast, nourishing you, and making himself responsible every moment for your growth and your fruit. Take time to know, set yourself to believe heartily: My Vine, on whom I can depend for all I need, is Christ. A large, strong vine bears a weak branch and holds it more than the branch holds the vine. Ask the Father by the Holy Spirit to reveal to you what a glorious, loving, mighty Christ this is, in whom you have your place and your life; it is *faith in what Christ is*, more than anything else, that will keep you abiding in Him. A soul filled with large thoughts of the Vine will be a strong branch and will abide confidently in Him. Turn your attention to Jesus and exercise your faith in Him as the True Vine.

And then, when Faith can confidently say, "He is my Vine," let it further say, "I am His branch, I am in Him." I speak to those who say they are Christ's disciples, and on them I cannot too earnestly press the importance of exercising their faith in saying, "I am in Him." It makes abiding so simple. If I realize clearly as I meditate: Now I am in Him, I see at once that there is nothing lacking but my consent to be what He has made me, to remain where He has placed me. *I am in Christ*: This simple thought, carefully, prayerfully, believingly uttered, removes the fear that there is yet some great attainment to be reached. No, *I am in Christ*, my blessed Savior. His love has prepared a home for me with himself. When He says, "Abide in My love," His power has undertaken to open the door and to keep me in this home He has prepared for me, if I will but consent. *I am in Christ*: now all I need to say is, "Savior, I thank you for this wondrous grace. I consent; I yield myself to your gracious keeping; I do abide in you."

It is astonishing how such faith will work out all that is further implied in abiding in Christ. There is in the Christian life a great need for watchfulness and prayer, of self-denial, obedience, and diligence. But "all things are possible to him who believes" (Mark 9:23). "This is the victory that has overcome the world—our faith"(1 John 5:4). It is faith that continually closes its eyes to the weakness of the creature, and finds its joy in the sufficiency of an almighty Savior, that makes the soul strong and glad. It gives itself up to be led by the Holy Spirit into an ever-deeper appreciation of that wonderful Savior given to us by God. This faith follows the leading of the Spirit from page to page of the blessed Word with the one desire to take each revelation of what Jesus is and what He promises as its nourishment and its life. In accordance with the promise "If what you have heard from the beginning abides in you, you also will abide in the Son and in the Father" (1 John 2:24), you will live "by every word that proceeds out of the mouth of God" (Matthew 4:4). And so the Word makes us strong with the strength of God, to enable us to abide in Christ.

Believer, if you would abide in Christ: only believe. Believe always; believe now. Bow even now before your Lord, and say to Him in childlike faith that, because He is your Vine and you are His branch, you will this day abide in Him.

Note: It is perhaps necessary to say, for the sake of young or doubting Christians, that there is something more necessary than the effort to exercise faith in each separate promise that is brought to our attention. What is of even greater importance is the cultivation of a trustful disposition toward God, the habit of always thinking of Him, of His ways and His works, with confidence and hope. In such soil alone can individual promises take root and grow.

God Has United You to Himself

*Of Him [God] you are in Christ Jesus, who became for us
wisdom from God—and righteousness and
sanctification and redemption.*

1 Corinthians 1:30

My Father is the vinedresser.

John 15:1

"You are in Christ Jesus." The believers at Corinth were still
weak and carnal, only babes in Christ. And yet Paul wanted
them, at the outset of his teaching, to know distinctly that they
were in Christ Jesus. The whole Christian life depends on the
clear consciousness of our position in Christ. Most essential to
abiding in Christ is the daily renewal of our faith's assurance, "I
am in Christ Jesus." All fruitful preaching to believers must
begin with: "You are in Christ Jesus."

But the apostle has an additional thought, of almost greater
importance: "Of God are you in Christ Jesus." He would have

us not only remember our union to Christ but also, more particularly, that it is not our own doing, but the work of God himself. As the Holy Spirit teaches us to realize this, we will see what a source of assurance and strength it is to us. If it is of God alone that I am in Christ, then God himself, the Infinite One, becomes my security for all I need or desire in seeking to abide in Christ.

Let me try to explain what it means, this wonderful truth "Of God in Christ." In becoming one with Christ, there is a work God does and a work we have to do. God does His work by moving us to do our work. The work of God is hidden and silent; what we do is something distinct and tangible. Conversion and faith along with prayer and obedience are conscious acts of which we can give a clear account, while the spiritual awakening and strengthening that come from above are secret and beyond the reach of human sight. So often when the believer tries to say, "I am in Christ Jesus," he looks more to the work *he* has done than to that wondrous secret work of God, which united him to Christ. This is to be expected at the beginning of the Christian course. "I know that I have believed," is a valid testimony. But it is important that the mind be led to see that at the back of our turning, believing, and accepting of Christ, God's almighty power was doing its work of inspiring our will, taking possession of us, and carrying out its own purpose of love in planting us into Christ Jesus. As the believer understands the divine side of the work of salvation, he will learn to praise and to worship with new enthusiasm and to rejoice more than ever in his salvation. At each step he reviews, the song will come, "This is the Lord's doing"— Divine Omnipotence working out what Eternal Love devised. "Of God I am in Christ Jesus."

The words will lead him even further and higher, and to the very depths of eternity. "And *those* he predestined, he also called" (Romans 8:30 NIV). The calling in time is the manifestation of God's purpose in eternity. For before the world came into existence, God had His eyes of sovereign love fixed on you in the election of grace and had chosen you in Christ. That you know you are in Christ is the key to understanding the full meaning of this word: "Of God I am in Christ Jesus." With the prophet, your language will be, "The Lord has appeared to us in the past, saying: 'I have loved you with an everlasting love, I have drawn you with loving-kindness'" (Jeremiah 31:3 NIV). And you will see your own salvation as a part of that "mystery of his will according to his good pleasure, which he purposed in Christ" (Ephesians 1:9 NIV) and join with the whole church as they say, "In him we were also chosen, having been predestined according to the plan of him who works out everything in conformity with the purpose of his will" (Ephesians 1:11 NIV). Nothing will exalt free grace more, and make man bow very low before it, than this knowledge of the mystery of His will: "Of God in Christ."

It is easy to see what a great influence this truth will exert on the believer who seeks to abide in Christ. What a sure standing-ground it gives him, as he rests his right to Christ and all His fullness on nothing less than the Father's own purpose and work! We have thought of Christ as the Vine, and the believer as the branch; let us not forget that other precious word, "My Father is the vinedresser." The Savior said, "Every plant which My heavenly Father has not planted will be uprooted" (Matthew 15:13); but every branch grafted by Him into the True Vine will never be plucked out of His hand (John 10:28). As it was the Father to whom Christ owed all He was, and in whom He had all His strength and His life as the Vine, so to the Father the believer owes his place and his security in Christ. It is with the same love and delight with which the Father watched over the beloved Son that God the Father now watches over every member of His body, every one who is in Christ Jesus.

What confident trust this faith inspires—not only in being kept in safety to the end, but also in being able to fulfill in every point the object for which I have been united to Christ. The branch is as much in the keeping of the vinedresser as is the vine. God's honor is as much at stake in the well-being and growth of the branch as it is in that of the vine. The God who chose Christ to be the Vine made Him thoroughly fit for the work He had to perform. The God who has chosen me and planted me in Christ as a branch has ensured (if I will let Him, by yielding myself to Him) that I will in every way be worthy of Jesus Christ. Oh, to fully realize this truth! What confidence and urgency it would give to my prayer to the God and Father of Jesus Christ! How it would deepen my sense of dependence and enable me to see that continual praying is the one need of my life—an unceasing waiting, moment by moment, on the God who has united me to Christ, to perfect His own divine work in me.

And what a motive this would be for the highest activity in the maintenance of a fruitful branch-life! Motives are mighty powers; it is of infinite importance that we keep them high and clear. Here surely is the highest motive of all: "We are His (God's) workmanship, created in Christ Jesus for good works" (Ephesians 2:10). We have been grafted by Him into Christ, to bring forth much fruit. Whatever God creates is exquisitely suited to its end. He created the sun to give light, and how perfectly it does its work! He created the eye to see, and how beautifully it fulfills its object! And He created the new man to do good works; can we affirm that our new nature is also perfectly formed for its purpose?

Of God I am in Christ: created anew, made a branch of the Vine, and made for bearing fruit. Oh, that believers would stop looking at their old nature so much, and complaining of their weakness, as if God called them for what they were unsuited! How much better for them to believingly and joyfully accept the wondrous revelation of how God, in uniting them to Christ, has made himself responsible for their spiritual growth and fruitfulness! Then all hesitancy and laziness would disappear, and under the influence of this mighty motive—faith in the faithfulness of Him of whom they are in Christ—their whole nature would arise to accept and fulfill their glorious destiny!

It is the same God of whom Christ is made all that He is for us, of whom we also are in Christ and will be made what we must be to Him. Take time to meditate and to worship, until the light that comes from the throne of God has shone into you, and you have seen your union to Christ as the work of His almighty Father. Take time, day after day, in your whole Christian walk, with all its claims, duties, needs, and desires, and let God be everything. See Jesus, as He speaks to you, "Abide in Me," pointing upward and saying, "My Father is the vinedresser. *Of Him* you are in Me, *through Him* you abide in Me, and *to Him* and to His glory shall be the fruit you bear." And let your answer be, Amen, Lord! So be it. From eternity Christ and I were ordained for each other; inseparably we belong to each other. It is God's will for me to abide in Christ. It is of God I am in Christ Jesus.

He Is Your Wisdom

*Of Him (God) you are in Christ Jesus, who became for us
WISDOM from God—and righteousness and
sanctification and redemption.*

1 Corinthians 1:30

Jesus Christ is not only Priest to purchase, and King to secure,
but also Prophet to reveal to us the salvation that God prepared
for them who love Him. Just as at creation the light was first
called into existence, that in it all God's other works might have
their life and beauty, so in our text wisdom is mentioned first
as the treasury in which are found the three precious gifts that
follow. The life is the light of man (John 1:4); in revealing this
to us, and enabling us to see the glory of God in His own face,
Christ makes us partakers of eternal life. It was by the Tree of
Knowledge that sin came; it is through the knowledge that
Christ gives that salvation comes. He is made of God wisdom
for us. *In Him* are hidden all the treasures of wisdom and
knowledge (Colossians 2:3).

And of God you are *in Him*, and only have to abide in Him
to be made partaker of these treasures of wisdom. *In Him* you

are, and *in Him* the wisdom is; dwelling in Him, you dwell in the very fountain of all light; abiding in Him, you have Christ, the wisdom of God, leading your whole spiritual life. He is ready to communicate, in the form of knowledge, just as much as is needful for you to know. Christ is made to us wisdom: You are in Christ.

It is this connection between what Christ has been made for us, and how we have it only as we are in Him, that we need to understand better. The blessings prepared for us in Christ cannot be obtained as special gifts in answer to prayer *apart from abiding in Him.* The answer to each prayer must come in a closer union and deeper abiding in Him; in Him—the unspeakable gift—all other gifts are treasured up, including the gifts of wisdom and knowledge.

How often have you longed for wisdom and spiritual understanding that you might *know God* better, whom to know is life eternal? Abide in Jesus: Your life in Him will lead you to that fellowship with God in which the only true knowledge of God can be found. You may not be able to grasp it with understanding, or to express it in words; but the knowledge that is deeper than thoughts or words will be given—the knowing of God that comes from being known of Him. "We preach Christ crucified . . . to those who are called . . . Christ the power of God and the wisdom of God" (1 Corinthians 1:23–24).

Would you count all things but loss for the excellency of the *knowledge of Jesus Christ* your Lord (Philippians 3:8)? Then abide in Jesus, and be found in Him. You will know Him in the power of His resurrection and the fellowship of His sufferings (Philippians 3:10). Following Him, you will not walk in darkness, but will have the light of life (John 8:12). It is only when

God shines into the heart, and Christ Jesus dwells there, that the light of the knowledge of God in the face of Christ can be seen.

Would you understand His blessed *work*, as He brings it to pass on earth or works it from heaven by His Spirit? Would you know how Christ has become our righteousness, our sanctification, and our redemption? It is by bringing, revealing, and communicating these that He is made to us wisdom from God. There are a thousand questions that at times come up, and the attempt to answer them sometimes becomes a burden. It is because you have forgotten you are in Christ, whom God has made to be your wisdom. Let it be your first aim to abide in Him in focused, fervent devotion of heart; when the heart and the life are right, rooted in Christ, knowledge will come in the measure we need. Without such abiding in Christ, knowledge does not really profit, but can actually be hurtful.

The soul may satisfy itself with thoughts that are but the forms and images of truth, without receiving the truth itself in its power. God's way is to first give us, even though it is but as a seed, the thing itself, the life and the power, and then comes the knowledge. Man seeks the knowledge first and often never gets beyond it. God gives us Christ, and in Him are *hidden* the treasures of wisdom and knowledge. Let us be content to possess Christ, to dwell in Him, to make Him our life. Only in a deeper searching into Him will we find the knowledge we desire. Such knowledge is life indeed.

Therefore, believer, abide in Jesus as your wisdom, and confidently expect from Him whatever teaching you may need for living your life to the glory of the Father. In all that concerns your *spiritual life*, abide in Jesus as your wisdom. The life you have in Christ is a thing of infinite sacredness, far too high and holy for you to naturally know how to act it out. He alone can guide you, as by a secret spiritual instinct, to know what will help and what will hinder your inner life, and enable you to abide in Him.

Do not think of it as a mystery or a difficulty you must solve. In whatever questions come up about abiding perfectly in Him at all times, and of obtaining all the blessing that comes from abiding, always remember: He knows, all is perfectly clear to Him, and He is your wisdom. Just as much as you need to know, and are capable of understanding, will be communicated, *if you only trust Him.* Never think of the riches of wisdom and knowledge hidden in Jesus as treasures without a key, or of your way as a path without a light. Jesus your wisdom is guiding you in the right way, even when you do not see it.

In all your meditations with the *blessed Word,* remember the same truth: Abide in Jesus, your wisdom. Study as much as you can to know the written Word; but study even more to know the living Word, in whom you are of God. Jesus, the wisdom of God, is only known by a life of implicit confidence and obedience. The words He speaks are spirit and life to those *who live in Him.* Therefore, each time you read, or hear, or meditate upon the Word, be careful to assume your true position. Realize first your oneness with Him who is the wisdom of God; know yourself to be under His direct and special training; go to the Word abiding in Him, the very fountain of divine light. *In His light* you can and will see light.

In all *your daily life,* its ways and its work, abide in Jesus as your wisdom. Your body and your daily life share in the great salvation: In Christ, the wisdom of God, provision has been made for their guidance too. Your body is His temple, your daily life the sphere for glorifying Him. It is a matter of deep interest to Him that all your earthly concerns be guided rightly. Trust His sympathy, believe His love, and wait for His guidance—it will be given. Abiding in Him, the mind will be calm and free from distraction, judgment will be clear as the light of heaven shines on earthly things, and your prayer for wisdom, like Solomon's, will be fulfilled "exceedingly abundantly above all that (you) ask or think" (Ephesians 3:20).

And so, especially in any *work* you do for God, abide in Jesus as your wisdom. Remember, we are "created in Christ Jesus for good works, which God has prepared beforehand that we should walk in them" (Ephesians 2:10). Put away any fears or doubts that you will not know exactly what these works are. In Christ we are created for them; He will show us what they are and how to do them. Cultivate the habit of rejoicing in the assurance that the God of divine wisdom is guiding you, even where you do not yet see the way.

All that you can wish to know is perfectly clear to Him. As Man, our Mediator, He has access to the counsels of Deity, to the secrets of Providence, in your interest and on your behalf. If you will but trust Him fully, and abide in Him entirely, you can be confident of having unerring guidance.

Yes, abide in Jesus as your wisdom. Seek to maintain the spirit of waiting and dependence, the spirit that always seeks to learn and moves only as the heavenly light leads on. Withdraw yourself from all needless distraction, close your ears to the voices of the world, and be as a docile learner, always listening for the heavenly wisdom the Master has to teach. Surrender all your own wisdom; seek a deep conviction of the utter blindness of the natural understanding in the things of God; and wait for Jesus to teach and to guide in all you believe and do. Remember that His teaching and guidance do not come outside you: It is by *His life in us* that Divine Wisdom does His work.

Retire frequently with Him into the inner chamber of the heart, where the gentle voice of the Spirit is only heard if all is still. Hang on with unshaken confidence, even in the midst of darkness and apparent desertion, to His own assurance that He is the light and the leader of His own. And live, above all, day by day in the blessed truth that, as He himself, the living Christ Jesus, is your wisdom, your first and last care must be this alone—to abide in Him. Abiding in Him, His wisdom will come to you as the spontaneous outflow of a life rooted in Him. I am, I abide, in Christ, who was *made to us* wisdom from God; wisdom will be given to me.

He Is Your Righteousness

Of Him (God) you are in Christ Jesus, who became for us wisdom from God—and RIGHTEOUSNESS and sanctification and redemption.

1 Corinthians 1:30

The first of the great blessings that Christ our wisdom reveals to us as prepared in himself, is *righteousness*. It is not difficult to see why this must be first.

There can be no real prosperity or progress in a nation, a home, or a soul without peace. As not even a machine can do its work unless it is at rest, secured on a good foundation, so quietness and assurance are indispensable to our moral and spiritual well-being. Sin disturbed all our relationships; we were out of harmony with ourselves, with others, and with God. The first requirement of a salvation that would bring blessing to us is peace. And peace can only come with righteousness. Peace can reign only where everything is as God would have it, in God's order and in harmony with His will. Jesus Christ came to restore peace on earth, and peace in the soul, by restoring righteousness. Because He is Melchizedek, King of righteousness, He reigns as King of Salem, King of peace (Hebrews 7:2). In this, He fulfills the promise the prophets held out: "A king will reign in righteousness ... the fruit of righteousness will be peace; the effect of righteousness will be quietness and confidence forever" (Isaiah 32:1, 17 NIV). God has made Christ to be righteousness for us; because of God we are in Him as our righteousness. In fact, we are made the righteousness of God in Him (2 Corinthians 5:21). Let us try to understand what this means.

When the sinner is first led to trust in Christ for salvation, he, as a rule, looks more to Christ's work than His person.

As he looks at the Cross, with Christ suffering there, the Righteous One *for* the unrighteous, he sees in that atoning death the only sufficient foundation for his faith in God's pardoning mercy. In becoming our substitute, bearing our curse and dying in our place, Christ atones for our sin and so gives us peace. As a believer understands how Christ's righteousness becomes his very own, and how, in the strength of that, he is counted righteous before God, he feels that he has what he needs to restore him to God's favor: "Having been justified by faith, we have peace with God" (Romans 5:1). The new Christian seeks to wear this robe of righteousness by ever-renewed faith in the glorious gift of righteousness that has been given to him.

But as time goes on, and he seeks to grow in the Christian life, new needs arise. He wants to understand more fully how it is that God can justify the ungodly on the strength of the righteousness of another. He finds the answer in the wonderful teaching of Scripture about true union of the believer with Christ as the Second Adam (Romans 5:12–21). He sees that it is possible because Christ made himself one with His people, and they were one with Him. In perfect accordance with all law in the kingdom of nature and of heaven, each member of the body has full benefit from the deeds and the suffering experienced by the Head. And so he is led to understand that it is only as he fully realizes his personal union with Christ as the Head that he can truly experience the power of His righteousness, which brings his soul into full fellowship with the Holy One. The work of Christ does not become less precious with this understanding, but the person of Christ becomes more so; the work leads up into the very heart, the love and the life of the God-man.

And this experience sheds its light again upon Scripture. It leads him to notice what he had overlooked before: how distinctly the righteousness of God, as it becomes ours, is connected with the person of the Redeemer. "This is His name whereby He shall be called, the Lord our righteousness" (Jeremiah 23:6). "Surely in the Lord have I righteousness and strength" (Isaiah 45:24). "That we might become the righteousness of God in Him" (2 Corinthians 5:21). "That I may gain Christ and be found *in Him*, not having my own righteousness which is from the law, but that which is through faith in Christ, the righteousness which is from God by faith" (Philippians 3: 8–9). The believer finally sees how inseparable righteousness and life in Christ are from each other: ". . . by one Man's righteous act the free gift came to all men, resulting in *justification of life*" (Romans 5:18). "Those who receive abundance of grace and of the gift of righteousness will *reign in life* through the

One, Jesus Christ" (Romans 5:17). And he understands what deep meaning there is in the key word of Paul's letter to the Romans: "The righteous will *live* by faith" (Romans 1:17 NIV). Now he is not content with only thinking of his robe of imputed righteousness that was given to him through the Atonement. He sees beyond this to the possibility of putting on Jesus Christ, and being wrapped up in and clothed with *Jesus himself and His life*; he knows how completely the righteousness of God is his because the Lord our righteousness is his. Before he understood this, he felt too often that it was difficult to wear his white robe all day; it was as if he had to put it on deliberately when he came into God's presence to confess his sins and seek new grace. But now the living Christ himself is his righteousness—that Christ who watches over, keeps, and loves us as His own; so it is no longer an impossibility to walk all day in the robe of his loving presence.

Such an experience leads still further. Christ's life and righteousness are inseparably linked, and the believer becomes more conscious than before of a righteous nature planted within him. The new man created in Christ Jesus, is "created according to God, in righteousness and true holiness" (Ephesians 4:24). "He who practices righteousness is righteous, just as He is righteous" (1 John 3:7). The union to Jesus has changed not only our relationship to God but also our personal state before God. And as this intimate fellowship is maintained, the growing renewal of the whole being makes righteousness our very nature.

To a Christian who begins to see the deep meaning of the truth that He was made to us righteousness, it is hardly necessary to say, "Abide in Him." As long as he only thought of the righteousness of the substitute, and our being counted judicially righteous for His sake, the absolute necessity of *abiding in Him* was not apparent. But as the glory of "the Lord our righteousness" unfolds to the view, he sees that abiding in Him personally is the only way to stand, at all times, complete and accepted before God, because it is the only way to realize how the new and righteous nature can be strengthened from Jesus our Head. To the repentant sinner the chief thought was *the righteousness* that comes through Jesus' dying for sin; to the intelligent and growing believer, *Jesus*, the Living One, through whom the righteousness comes, is everything, because in having Him, he has His righteousness too.

Believer, abide in Christ as your righteousness. You still have within you a nature altogether corrupt, which is always trying to rise up and discourage your sense of acceptance and access to unbroken fellowship with the Father. Nothing can enable you to dwell and walk in the light of God, without even the shadow of a cloud between, but habitual abiding in Christ as your righteousness. To this you are called. Seek to walk worthy of that calling. Yield yourself to the Holy Spirit to reveal to you the wonderful grace that permits you to draw near to God, clothed in a divine righteousness. Take time to realize that the King's own robe has been put on you, and in it you need not fear entering His presence. It is the token that you are the man or woman the King delights to honor. Take time to remember that as much as you need this robe of righteousness in the palace, you require it even more when He sends you forth into the world, where you are the King's messenger and representative.

Live your daily life in full consciousness of being righteous in God's sight, an object of delight and pleasure in Christ.

Connect every view you have of Christ in His other graces with this first one: Christ Jesus—our righteousness from God. This will keep you in perfect peace. You will enter into, and dwell in, the rest of God. And your inmost being will be transformed into being righteous and doing righteousness. In your heart and life it will become obvious where you dwell; abiding in Jesus Christ, the Righteous One, you will share His position, His character, and His blessedness. It is said of Him: "You have loved righteousness and hated wickedness; therefore God, your God, has set you above your companions by anointing you with the oil of joy" (Hebrews 1:9 NIV). This joy and gladness will be your portion too as you abide in Him.

He Is Your Sanctification

*Of Him (God) you are in Christ Jesus, who became for us
wisdom from God—and righteousness and
SANCTIFICATION and redemption.*

1 Corinthians 1:30

"Paul ... to the church of God which is at Corinth, to those
who are *sanctified* in Christ Jesus, called to be *saints*"—this is
how the chapter opens in which we are taught that Christ is our
sanctification, our holiness. In the Old Testament, believers
were called the righteous; in the New Testament they are called
saints, holy ones sanctified in Christ Jesus. Holy is higher than
righteous. Holiness in reference to God relates to His inmost
being; righteousness has to do with God's dealings with His
creatures. In man, righteousness is but a stepping-stone to holiness. It is in holiness that man can approach the nature of God
(Matthew 5:48; 1 Peter 1:16). In the Old Testament it was righteousness that was found, while holiness was only typified. In
Jesus Christ, the Holy One, and in His people, His saints or
holy ones, it is first realized.

As in Scripture, and in our text, so also in personal

experience: Righteousness comes before holiness. When the believer first finds Christ as his righteousness, he has such joy in being righteous that he hardly considers the idea of holiness. But as he grows, the desire for holiness makes itself felt, and he wants to know what provision his God has made for supplying that need. A superficial acquaintance with God's plan leads to the view that while justification is God's work, by faith in Christ, sanctification is our work, to be performed under the influence of the gratitude we feel for the deliverance we have experienced, and by the aid of the Holy Spirit. But the sincere Christian soon finds how little gratitude can supply the power. When he thinks that more prayer will bring it, he finds that, indispensable as prayer is, it is not enough. Often the believer struggles hopelessly for years, until he listens to the teaching of the Spirit, as He glorifies Christ again, and reveals Christ, our sanctification, to be appropriated by faith alone.

Christ is made sanctification to us by God. Holiness is the very nature of God, and *that alone is holy which God takes possession of and fills with himself.* God's answer to the question "How could sinful man become holy?" is "Christ, the Holy One of God." In Him, the One sanctified by the Father and sent into the world, God's holiness was revealed in the flesh, incarnated and brought within reach of man. Jesus declares, "For their sakes I sanctify Myself, that they also may be sanctified by the truth" (John 17:19). There is no other way for us to become holy but by becoming partakers of the holiness of Christ. And there is no other way of this taking place than by our personal spiritual union with Him, so that through His Holy Spirit His holy life flows into us. "Of Him you are in Christ Jesus, who was made to us sanctification." Abiding by faith in Christ our sanctification is the simple secret of a holy life. The measure of sanctification will depend on the measure of abiding in Him. As the soul learns to wholly abide in Christ, the promise is increasingly fulfilled: "May the God of peace Himself sanctify you completely" (1 Thessalonians 5:23).

To illustrate this relationship between the measure of the abiding and the measure of sanctification experienced, let us consider the grafting of a tree, that instructive symbol of our union to Jesus. The illustration is suggested by the Savior's words, "Make a tree good and its fruit will be good" (Matthew 12:33 NIV). Now I can graft a tree so that only a single branch bears good fruit, while many of the natural branches remain and bear their old fruit—a type of believer in whom a small part of the life is sanctified, but in whom, from ignorance or other reasons, the carnal life in many respects still has full reign.

I also can graft a tree so that every branch is cut off, and the whole tree becomes renewed to bear good fruit. Yet unless I watch over the tendency of the stems to give sprouts, they may again rise and grow strong, and, robbing the new graft of the strength it needs, make it weak. Such are Christians who, apparently powerfully converted, forsake all to follow Christ, and yet after a time, through carelessness, allow old habits to regain their power. As a result, their Christian life and fruit are weakened. But if I want a tree to be completely good, I take it when it is young, and, cutting the stem off right to the ground, I graft it just where it emerges from the soil. I watch over every bud that might arise from the old nature until the flow of sap from the old roots into the new stem is so complete that the old life has, as it were, been entirely conquered and covered by the new. Here I have a tree entirely renewed, an emblem of the

Christian who has learned by entire consecration to surrender everything for Christ, and in wholehearted faith to abide in Him.

If, in this last case, the old tree were a reasonable being that could cooperate with the gardener, what would the gardener say to it? Something like this, probably: "Now yield yourself entirely to this new nature I have given you; repress every tendency of the old nature to give buds or sprouts. Let all your sap and all your life-powers rise up into this graft taken from the beautiful tree over there, which I have put on you; in this way, you will bring forth much fruit that is sweet to the taste." And the reply of the tree to the gardener would be: "When you graft me, do not spare a single branch; let everything of the old self, even the smallest bud, be destroyed, that I may no longer live in my own, but in that other life that was cut off and brought and put upon me. That way I will be completely new and good."

Could you later ask the renewed tree, as it was bearing abundant fruit, what it could say of itself, its answer would be this: "In me, that is, in my roots, there dwells no good thing. I am always inclined toward evil; the sap I collect from the soil is corrupt in nature, and ready to show itself in bearing evil fruit. But just when the sap rises into the sunshine to ripen into fruit, the wise gardener covers me with a new life, through which my sap is purified, and all my powers are renewed to bear good fruit. All I have to do is abide in what I have received. He cares for the immediate repression and removal of every bud which the old nature would still like to put forth."

Christian, do not be afraid to claim God's promises to make you holy. Don't listen to the suggestion that the corruption of your old nature renders holiness an impossibility. In your flesh dwells no good thing, that is true, and that flesh, though crucified with Christ, is not yet dead, but it continually seeks to rise up and lead you to evil. But the Father is your Vinedresser. He has grafted the life of Christ onto your life. That holy life is stronger than your evil life; under the watchful care of the Vinedresser, that new life can keep down the workings of the evil life within you. The evil nature is there, with its unchanged tendency to rise up and show itself. But the new nature is there too; the living Christ, your sanctification, is there, and through Him all your powers can be sanctified as they rise into life. And you will be able to bear fruit to the glory of the Father.

Now, if you would live a holy life, abide in Christ your sanctification. Look upon Him as the Holy One of God, made man that He might communicate to us the holiness of God. Listen when Scripture teaches that there is within you a new nature, a new man, created in Christ Jesus in righteousness *and true holiness*. Remember that this holy nature that is in you is especially made for living a holy life and performing all holy duties, as much as the old nature is suited for doing evil. Understand that this holy nature within you has its root and life in Christ in heaven, and can only grow and become strong as the interaction between it and its source is uninterrupted.

Above all, believe most confidently that Jesus Christ himself delights in maintaining that new nature within you, and giving to it His own strength and wisdom for its work. Let faith in this reality lead you daily to surrender all self-confidence, and confess the utter corruption of all there is in you by nature. Let it fill you with a quiet and assured confidence that you are well able to do what the Father expects of you as His child, under the covenant of His grace, because you have Christ strengthening you. Let it teach you to lay yourself and your services on the altar as spiritual sacrifices, holy and acceptable in His sight, a sweet-smelling fragrance. Do not look upon a life of holiness as a strain and an effort, but as the natural outgrowth of the life of Christ within you. Let a quiet, hopeful, gladsome faith assure you that all you need for a holy life will be given you out of the holiness of Jesus. Then you will understand and prove what it is to abide in Christ our sanctification.

He Is Your Redemption

Of Him (God) you are in Christ Jesus, who became for us
wisdom from God—and righteousness and
sanctification and REDEMPTION.

1 Corinthians 1:30

Here we reach the top of the ladder as it ascends into heaven—
the blessed end to which Christ and life in Him is to lead. The
word *redemption,* though sometimes applied to our deliverance
from the guilt of sin, here refers to our complete and final
deliverance from all the consequences of sin, when the
Redeemer's work will be fully displayed, even to the redemption
of the body itself (Romans 8:21–23; Ephesians 1:14; 4:30). The
expression points us to the highest glory to be hoped for in the
future, and therefore also to the highest blessing to be enjoyed
in the present in Christ. We have seen how, as a Prophet, Christ
is our wisdom, revealing to us God and His love, along with the
nature and conditions of the salvation that love has prepared.
As a Priest, He is our righteousness, restoring us to right relationship to God and securing for us His favor and friendship.
As a King, He is our sanctification, forming and guiding us into

177

obedience to the Father's holy will. As these three offices work out God's one purpose, the grand consummation will be reached: complete deliverance from sin and all its effects, and ransomed humanity regaining all that was lost in the Fall.

Christ is made *redemption* to us by God. The word invites us to look upon Jesus, not only as He lived on earth—teaching us by word and by example as He died to reconcile us with God, as He lives again, a victorious King, rising to receive His crown—but also as, sitting at the right hand of God, He takes again the glory which He had with the Father before the world began and holds it there for us. There His human nature, His human body, free from all the consequences of sin to which He once was exposed, is now in heaven sharing the divine glory. As Son of Man, He dwells on the throne and in the presence of the Father; the deliverance from what He had to suffer for sin is complete and eternal. Complete redemption is fulfilled and revealed in His own Person; what He as man is and has in heaven is the complete redemption. He is made of God to us redemption.

We are in Him as such. And to the extent that we can receive this truth as we abide in Him as our redemption, the more we will experience, even here, "the powers of the coming age" (Hebrews 6:5 NIV). As our communion with Him becomes more intimate and intense and we let the Holy Spirit reveal Him to us in His heavenly glory, the more we realize how the life in us is the life of One who sits upon the throne of heaven. We feel the power of an endless life working in us. We taste eternal life; we have a foretaste of the eternal glory.

The blessings flowing from abiding in Christ as our redemption are great. The soul is delivered from all fear of death. There was a time when even the Savior feared death. But no longer. He has triumphed over death; even His body has entered into God's glory. The believer who abides in Christ as his full redemption realizes even now his spiritual victory over death. It becomes to him the servant that removes the last rags of the old carnal robe before he is clothed with the new body of glory. Death carries the body to the grave, to lie there as the seed from which the new body will arise as a worthy companion of the glorified spirit. The resurrection of the body is no longer an empty doctrine, but a living expectation, because the Spirit of Him who raised Jesus from the dead dwells in the body as the pledge that even our mortal bodies will be made alive (Romans 8:11–23). Faith in this expectation exercises its sanctifying influence by making us willing to surrender the sinful members of our bodies to Him—to be put to death and then subjected to the reign of the Spirit, as preparation for the time when our frail bodies will be changed to be fashioned like His glorious body (Philippians 3:21).

This full redemption of Christ as extending to the body has a depth of meaning not easily expressed. It was of man as a whole, soul and body, that it was said that he was made in the image and likeness of God. In the angels, God created spirits without material bodies; in the creation of the world, there was matter without spirit. Man was to be the highest specimen of divine art: the combination in one being of matter and spirit in perfect harmony, as a type of the most perfect union between God and His own creation. Sin entered in and appeared to block the divine plan. By sin the material obtained a dreaded supremacy over the spiritual. But God's plan was still in place.

The Word was *made flesh*, the divine fullness received an

embodiment in the humanity of Christ so that redemption might be complete and perfect; the whole creation, which now groans and labors in pain together, will be delivered from the bondage of corruption into the liberty of the glory of the children of God (Romans 8:21–22). God's purpose will not be accomplished, and Christ's glory will not be fully exhibited, until the body, which includes the whole of nature, has been transformed by the power of the spiritual life. It will then become the transparent garment that will shine forth with radiance as it reflects the glory of the Infinite Spirit. Only then will we understand the depth of meaning in these words: "Christ Jesus was made to us (complete) redemption."

In the meantime we know that: "Of Him (God) you are in Christ Jesus," as your redemption. This is not meant to be merely a future revelation; we must seek to enter into and apply it in our present abiding in Christ so that we may reach full development in the Christian life. We do this as we learn to triumph over our fear of death. We learn to look upon Christ as the Lord of our body, claiming its entire consecration on this side of heaven and victory over the terrible dominion sin has enjoyed in the body. Another way we do this is learning to look on all nature as part of the kingdom of Christ, destined, even though it might be through a baptism of fire, to take part in His redemption. We do it as we allow the powers of the coming age to possess us and to lift us up into a life in the heavenly places, to enlarge our hearts and our views, to anticipate, even here, the things which have never entered into the heart of man to imagine (1 Corinthians 2:9).

Believer, abide in Christ as your redemption. Let this be the crown of your Christian life. It is faithfulness in the previous steps of your Christian life that will best fit you for this spiritual reality. Abide in Him as your wisdom, the perfect revelation of all that God is and has for you. Follow, in the daily ordering of your inner and outer life, His teaching with humility, and you will be counted worthy to have secrets revealed to you, secrets that to most disciples are a sealed book. Such wisdom will lead you into the mysteries of our complete redemption.

Abide in Him as your righteousness, and dwell clothed with Him in that inner sanctuary of the Father's favor and presence to which His righteousness gives you access. As you rejoice in your reconciliation, you will understand how it includes all things, even full redemption; "For it pleased the Father that in Him all fullness should dwell, and by Him to reconcile all things to Himself, by Him, whether things on earth or things in heaven" (Colossians 1:19–20). And abide in Him as your sanctification; the experience of His power to make you holy in spirit, soul, and body will make your faith alive in a holiness that will not stop working until the bells of the horses and every pot in Jerusalem shall be holiness to the Lord (Zechariah 14:20–21).

Abide in Him as your redemption, and live, even here, as the heir of future glory. As you seek to experience on earth the full power of His saving grace, your heart will be enlarged to realize the position mankind has been destined to occupy in the universe, with all things made subject to Him. For your part, you can be assured that you will be readied by the Spirit of God to live worthy of that high and heavenly calling.

The Crucified One

I have been crucified with Christ: it is no longer I who live,
but Christ lives in me.

Galatians 2:20

We have been united together in the likeness of His death.

Romans 6:5

"I have been crucified with Christ": Here the apostle expresses his assurance of his fellowship with Christ in His sufferings and death, and his full participation in all the power and the blessing of that death. The apostle Paul was so convinced of this and the fact that he was now indeed dead that he adds: "It is *no longer I who live,* but Christ lives in me." How blessed must be the experience of such a union with the Lord Jesus—to be able to look upon His death as mine, just as really as it was His, to look upon His perfect obedience to God, His victory over sin, and complete deliverance from its power as mine, and to realize that the power of that death works by faith daily with a divine energy to put to death the flesh, to renew the whole life into perfect conformity to the resurrection life of Jesus! Abiding in

Jesus, the Crucified One, is the secret to the growth of that new life, which comes from the death of our old life.

Let us try to understand this. The suggestive expression "*united together* in the likeness of His death," will teach us what abiding in the Crucified One means. When a graft is united with the stock on which it is to grow, we know that it must be kept fixed; it must abide in the place where the stock has been cut and wounded to make an opening to receive the graft. No graft is possible without wounding, laying bare and opening up the inner life of the tree to receive the foreign branch. It is only through such wounding that access can be obtained to the fellowship of the sap and the growth and life of the stronger stem.

This reality holds true for the relationship between Jesus and the sinner. Only when we are united together in the likeness of His death will we also be in the likeness of His resurrection, partakers of the life and the power that are in Him. In the death of the Cross Christ was wounded, and in His opened wounds a place was prepared where we might be grafted in. And just as one might say to a graft as it is fixed in its place, "Abide here in the wound of the stem, it will now bear you"; so to the believing soul the message comes, "Abide in the wounds of Jesus; there is the place of union, life, and growth. There you will see how His heart was opened to receive you; His flesh was torn so that the way might be opened for your being made one with Him, and having access to all the blessings flowing from His divine nature."

You have also noticed how the graft has to be torn away from the tree where it naturally grew and cut into conformity to the place prepared for it in the wounded stem. Even so the believer has to be made conformable to Christ's death—to be crucified and to die with Him. The wounded stem and the wounded graft are cut to fit into each other, into each other's likeness. There is a fellowship between Christ's sufferings and your sufferings. His experiences must become yours. The disposition He showed in choosing and bearing the Cross must be yours. Like Him, you will have to give full assent to the righteous judgment and curse of a holy God against sin. Like Him, you have to consent to yield your life, the old nature full of sin and its curse, to death, and through it to pass to the new life. Like Him, you will experience that it is only through the self-sacrifice of Gethsemane and Calvary that the path to the joy and fruit-bearing of the resurrection life can be found. The more clear the resemblance between the wounded stem and the wounded graft, the more exactly their wounds fit into each other, and the more complete will be the union and the growth.

It is in Jesus, the Crucified One, I must abide. I must learn to look upon the Cross as not only atonement to God but also a victory over the devil; it is not only deliverance from the guilt but also from the power of sin. I must gaze on Him on the Cross, seeing Him as the One who offered himself in order to receive me into the closest possible union and fellowship. Through Him I can partake of the full power of His death to sin and the new life of victory to which it is but the gateway. My part is simply to yield myself to Him in undivided surrender, with much prayer and strong desire, asking to be admitted into the ever-closer fellowship and conformity of His death by the power of the Spirit in which He died that death.

Let me try to understand why the Cross is thus the place of union. *On the Cross* the Son of God enters into the greatest union with man—enters into the experience of what it means to become a son of man, a member of a race under the curse. It is in death that the Prince of life conquers the power of death; it is in death alone that He can enable me to partake of that victory. The life He imparts is a life from the dead; each new experience of the power of that life depends upon the fellowship of the death. The death and the life are inseparable. All of the grace that Jesus the Saving One gives is given only in the path of fellowship with Jesus the Crucified One.

Christ came and took my place; I must put myself in His place, and abide there. And there is but one place that is both His and mine—that place is the Cross: His place because of His free choice; my place because of the curse of sin. He came there to seek me; there alone can I find Him. When He found me there, it was the place of cursing; this He experienced, for "Cursed is everyone who hangs on a tree" (Galatians 3:13). But He made it a place of blessing; this I experienced because Christ delivered us from the curse, being made a curse for us. When Christ comes in my place, He remains what He was, the beloved of the Father; but in fellowship with me He shares my curse and dies my death.

When I stand in His place, which is still always mine, I am still what I was by nature, the cursed one, who deserves to die; but since I am united to Him, I share His blessing and receive His life. When He came to be one with me He could not avoid the Cross, for the curse always points to the Cross as its end and fruit. And when I seek to be one with Him, I cannot avoid the Cross, either; for life and deliverance are to be found only in the Cross. As inevitably as my curse pointed Him to the Cross as the only place where He could be fully united to me, His blessing points me to the Cross too as the only place where

186

I can be united to Him. He took my cross for His own; I must take His Cross as my own; I must be crucified with Him. It is as I abide daily, deeply in Jesus the Crucified One that I will taste the sweetness of His love, the power of His life, and the completeness of His salvation.

It is a deep mystery, this Cross of Christ. I am afraid there are many Christians who are content to look upon the Cross, with Christ on it dying for their sins, who have little heart for fellowship with the Crucified One. They hardly know that He invites them to it. Or they are content to consider the ordinary afflictions of life, of which the world's children often have as many as they do, as their share of Christ's Cross. They have no understanding of what it means to be crucified with Christ, not knowing that bearing the Cross means likeness to Christ in the principles that propelled Him in His path of obedience. The entire surrender of all self-will, the complete denial to the flesh of its every desire and pleasure, the perfect separation from the world in all its ways of thinking and acting, the losing and hating of one's life, the giving up of self and its interests for the sake of others—this is the disposition that marks him who has taken up Christ's Cross, who seeks to say, "I am crucified with Christ; I abide in Christ, the Crucified One."

Would you please your Lord and live in as close fellowship with Him as His grace could maintain in you? Then pray that His Spirit will lead you into this blessed truth, this secret of the Lord for those who fear Him. We know how Peter knew and confessed Christ as the Son of the living God while the Cross was still an offense to him (Matthew 16:16–17, 21, 23). The faith that believes in the blood that pardons, and the life that renews, can only reach its perfect growth as it abides beneath the Cross and in living fellowship with Him seeks for perfect conformity with Jesus the Crucified.

Jesus, our crucified Redeemer, teach us not only to believe on you but also to abide in you. Help us to take your Cross not only as the ground of our pardon but also as the law of our life. May we learn to love it not only because on it you bore our curse but also because on it we enter into intimate fellowship with you and are crucified with you. As we yield ourselves fully to be filled with the Spirit in which you bore the Cross, teach us how to be made partakers of the power and the blessing found only in the Cross.

God Himself Will Establish You in Him

*He who establishes us with you in Christ and
has anointed us is God.*

2 Corinthians 1:21

These words of Paul teach us a much-needed and most blessed truth—that just as our first being united with Christ was the work of divine omnipotence, so we may also look to the Father for being kept and being established more firmly in Him. "The Lord will perfect that which concerns me" (Psalm 138:8)—this expression of confidence should always accompany the prayer "Do not forsake the works of Your hands" (Psalm 138:8). In all his longings and prayers to reach a deeper and more perfect abiding in Christ, the believer must have this confidence: "He who began a good work in you will carry it on to completion until the day of Christ Jesus" (Philippians 1:6 NIV). There is nothing that will so help to root and ground him in Christ as faith in these words: "He who establishes us in Christ is God."

How many there are who can witness to the fact that this

faith is just what they need! They continually mourn over the ups and downs of their spiritual life. Sometimes there are hours and days of great continuity and even a profound experience of the grace of God. But how little is needed to mar their peace, to bring a cloud over the soul! And then, how the faith is shaken. All efforts to regain their standing appear utterly fruitless; and neither solemn vows, nor watching and prayer, help to restore to them the peace they had for a while tasted. What they need to understand is how their own efforts are the cause of their failure, because it is God alone who can establish us in Christ Jesus.

Just as in justification they had to cease from their own working, and to accept in faith the promise that God would give them life in Christ, so now, in the matter of their sanctification, their first need is *to cease from striving themselves to establish the connection with Christ more firmly, and to allow God to do it.* "God is faithful, by whom you were called into the fellowship of His Son, Jesus Christ our Lord" (1 Corinthians 1:9). What they need is simple faith in the fact that establishing us in Christ, day by day, is God's work—a work that He delights to do, in spite of all our weakness and unfaithfulness, if we will but trust Him for it.

Many can testify to the blessedness of such a faith and the experience it brings. What peace and rest to know that there is a Vinedresser who cares for the branch, to see that it grows stronger, and that its union with the Vine becomes more perfect, who watches over every hindrance and danger and supplies every need! What peace and rest to fully and finally give up our abiding into the care of God, and to never have a wish or thought, never offer a prayer or engage in an exercise connected with it, without first gladly remembering that what we do is only the manifestation of what God is doing in us! The establishing in Christ is His work: He accomplishes it by stirring us to watch, wait, and work. But this He can do with power only as we stop interrupting Him by our self-working, as we accept in faith the dependent posture that honors Him and opens the heart to let Him work. How such a faith frees the soul from care and responsibility! In the midst of the rush and bustle of the world's busy life, the subtle and ceaseless temptations to sin, and all the daily cares and trials that so easily distract and lead to failure, how wonderful to be an established Christian who is always abiding in Christ! How blessed even to have the faith that such a position can be attained and is within our reach!

Dear believer, the blessing is indeed within your reach. He who establishes you with us in Christ *is God*. What I want you to take in is this: Believing this promise will not only give you comfort but will also be the means of obtaining your desire. You know how Scripture teaches us that in all God's leadings with His people faith has everywhere been the one condition for seeing His power manifested. Faith is the ceasing from all our natural efforts and all other dependence; faith is confessed helplessness casting itself upon God's promise and claiming its fulfillment; faith is putting ourselves quietly into God's hands for Him to do His work. What you and I need now is to take time, until this truth stands out before us in all its spiritual brightness: It is God Almighty, God the Faithful and Gracious One, who has undertaken to establish me in Christ Jesus.

Listen to what the Word teaches you: "The Lord *will establish* you as a holy people to Himself" (Deuteronomy 28:9); "Your

God has loved Israel, to *establish* them forever" (2 Chronicles 9:8); "Now to Him who is able *to establish you,* be glory through Jesus Christ forever" (Romans 16:25, 27); "So that He *may establish your hearts blameless in holiness*" (1 Thessalonians 3:13); "The Lord is faithful, who will establish you and guard you from the evil one" (2 Thessalonians 3:3); "The God of all grace, who has called us to His eternal glory by Christ Jesus, after you have suffered a while, perfect, *establish,* strengthen, and settle you" (1 Peter 5:10). Can you take these words to mean anything less than that you too—however spasmodic your spiritual life has been up to now, however unfavorable your natural character or your circumstances may appear—can be established in Christ Jesus? If we take the time to listen, in simple childlike humility, to these words as the truth of God, the confidence will come: As surely as I am in Christ, I will also, day by day, be established in Him.

The lesson appears so simple; and yet most of us take so long to learn it. The main reason is that the grace the promise offers is so large, so Godlike, so beyond all our thoughts, that we do not take it to mean what it says. The believer who has finally come to see and accept what it brings can testify to the wonderful change that comes over the spiritual life. Before he had taken control of his own welfare; now he has God to take charge of it. He now knows himself to be in the school of God, with a Teacher who plans the whole course of study for each of His pupils with infinite wisdom, and delights to have them come daily for the lessons He has to give. All he asks is to feel himself constantly in God's hands and to follow His guidance, neither lagging behind nor getting ahead of Him. Remembering that it is God who works both to will and to do, he sees his only safety in yielding himself to God's working. He lays aside all anxiety about his inner life and its growth, because the Father is the Vinedresser. Under His wise and watchful care each plant is well secured. He knows that there is the prospect of a most blessed life of strength and fruitfulness to every one who will take God wholly as his only hope.

Believer, you must admit that such a life of trust is most blessed. You say, perhaps, that there are times when you do, with your whole heart, consent to this way of living and wholly abandon the care of your inner life to your Father. But somehow it does not last. You forget again; and instead of beginning each morning with the joyous transference of all the needs and cares of your spiritual life to the Father's charge, you again feel anxious, burdened, and helpless.

Could it be that you have not committed to the Father's care this matter, daily remembering to renew your entire surrender? Memory is one of the highest powers in our nature. By it day is linked to day, the unity of life through all our years is kept up, and we know that we are still ourselves. In the spiritual life, recollection is of infinite value. For the sanctifying of our memory, in the service of our spiritual life, God has provided most beautifully. The Holy Spirit is the Spirit of recollection. Jesus said, "He will bring to your remembrance all things that I said to you" (John 14:26). "He who *establishes* us with you in Christ is God, who also has *sealed* us and *given us the Spirit in our hearts* as a deposit" (2 Corinthians 1:21–22). It is for the purpose of establishing us that the Holy Spirit has been given. God's blessed promises, and your unceasing acts of faith and surrender that accept them—He will enable you to remember these each day. The Holy Spirit is—praise be to God—the memory of the new man.

Apply this to the promise of the text: "He who establishes us in Christ is God." As you now, at this moment, abandon all anxiety about your growth and progress to the God who has undertaken to establish you in the Vine, and feel what a joy it is to know that God alone has charge, ask and trust Him by the Holy Spirit to always remind you of your blessed relationship with Him. He will do it; and with each new morning your faith may grow stronger and brighter: The Father will see that each day I become more firmly united to Christ.

And now, beloved fellow-believer, "the God of all grace, who called us to His eternal glory by Christ Jesus, *perfect, establish, strengthen, and settle you*" (1 Peter 5:10). What more can you desire? Expect it confidently, ask for it fervently. Count on God to do His work. And learn in faith to sing the song, the notes of which each new experience will make deeper and sweeter: "Now to Him who is able to *establish* you, be glory through Jesus Christ forever. Amen" (Romans 16:25, 27). Yes, glory to God, who has undertaken to establish us in Christ!

Every Moment

*In that day sing to her, "A vineyard of red wine! I, the Lord,
keep it, I water it every moment; Lest any hurt it,
I keep it night and day."*

Isaiah 27:2–3

The vineyard was the symbol of the people of Israel, in whose
midst the True Vine was to stand. The branch is the symbol of
the individual believer, who stands in the Vine. The song of the
vineyard is also the song of the Vine and its every branch. The
command still goes out to the watchers of the vineyard—if only
they would obey it, and sing till every fainthearted believer
learned and joined the joyful strain—"Sing to her: I, the Lord,
keep it; I water it *every moment*; Lest any hurt it, I *keep* it night
and day."

What an answer from the mouth of God himself to the
question so often asked: Is it possible for the believer to always
abide in Jesus? Is a life of unbroken fellowship with the Son of
God possible here in this earthly life? If abiding is our work, to
be done in our strength, then the answer must be no. But
thankfully the things that are impossible with men are possible

195

with God. If the Lord himself will keep the soul night and day, and watch it and water it every moment, then surely uninterrupted communion with Jesus does become a blessed possibility to those who can trust God to mean and to do what He says.

In one sense, it is true, all believers are always abiding in Jesus; without this there could not be true spiritual life. "If anyone does not abide in Me, he is cast out" (John 15:6). But when the Savior gives the command "Abide in Me" with the promise "He who abides in Me bears much fruit" (John 15:4–5), He speaks of that willing, intelligent, and wholehearted surrender by which we accept His offer and consent to abiding in Him as the only life we choose or seek. The objections that are raised against our right to expect that we will be able to, voluntarily and consciously, abide always in Jesus are mainly two.

One is derived from the nature of man. It is said that our limited powers prevent us from being occupied with two things at the same moment. God's providence places many Christians in business, where for hours at a time close attention to the work they have to do is required. How can such a man, it is asked, with his whole mind on the work he has to do, be at the same time occupied with Christ and keep up fellowship with Him? The consciousness of abiding in Jesus is seen as requiring such a strain, and such a direct occupation of the mind with heavenly thoughts, that to enjoy the blessing would imply a withdrawing of oneself from all the ordinary activities of life. This is the same error that drove the first monks into the wilderness.

Praise be to God, there is no necessity for such a going out of the world. Abiding in Jesus is not a work that needs our minds to be engaged each moment, or our attention to be directly and actively occupied with it. It is an entrusting of ourselves to the keeping of Eternal Love, in the faith that it will abide near us and with its holy presence watch over us and ward off evil, even when we have to be intently occupied with other things. In this way the heart has rest, peace, and joy in the consciousness of being kept when it cannot keep itself.

In ordinary life, we have many illustrations of the influence of a supreme love reigning in and guarding the soul while the mind concentrates itself on work that requires its whole attention. Think of the father of a family, separated for a time from his home so that he may secure for his loved ones what they need. He loves his wife and children and longs to return to them. There may be hours of intense occupation when he does not have a moment to think of them, and yet his love is as deep and real as when he can recall their images. All the while his love and the hope of making them happy urge him on and fill him with a secret joy in his work. Think of a king: In the midst of work, pleasure, and trial, he all the while acts under the secret influence of the consciousness of royalty, even while he is unaware of it. A loving wife and mother never for one moment loses the sense of her relationship to her husband and children; the consciousness and the love are there, even among all her engagements.

In the same way, it is not impossible to see how everlasting love can so take and keep possession of our spirits that we too will never for a moment lose the secret consciousness: We are in Christ, kept in Him by His almighty power. Oh, it is possible; we can be sure it is. Our abiding in Jesus is even more than a fellowship of love—it is a fellowship of life. In work or in rest, the consciousness of life never leaves us. And even so can the mighty power of Eternal Life maintain within us the consciousness of its presence. Or rather, Christ, who is our life, himself dwells within us, and by His presence maintains our consciousness that we are in Him.

The second objection has reference to our sinfulness. Christians are so accustomed to looking upon sinning daily as something absolutely inevitable, they regard it as indisputable that no one can keep up abiding fellowship with the Savior; we must sometimes be unfaithful and fail. But it is precisely because we have a sinful nature that abiding in Christ has been ordained for us as our sufficient—and only—deliverance! After all, it is the Heavenly Vine, the living, loving Christ, in whom we have to abide; and His almighty power to hold us fast should be the measure of our expectations! We cannot imagine our Lord giving us the command "Abide in Me" without securing the grace and the power to enable us to perform it! We must remember that we have the Father as the Vinedresser to keep us from falling, and not in a large and general sense, but according to His own precious promise: "Night and day, every moment" (Isaiah 27:2–3). If we will only look to our God as our Keeper we will learn to believe that conscious abiding in Christ every moment, night and day, is indeed what God has prepared for them who love Him.

My beloved fellow Christians, let nothing less than this be your aim. I know that you may not find it easy to attain; there may come more than one hour of weary struggle and bitter failure. Were the church of Christ what it should be—were older believers to younger converts what they should be, witnesses to God's faithfulness, like Caleb and Joshua, encouraging their brethren to go up and possess the land with their good report, "If the Lord delights in us, then He will bring us into this land" (Numbers 14:8), and were the atmosphere which the young believer breathes as he enters the fellowship of the saints that of a healthy, trusting, joyful consecration—abiding in Christ would come as the natural outgrowth of being in Him. But such a great part of the body is in what can only be described as a sickly state that believers who are pressing after this blessing are hindered by the depressing influence of both the thought and the life of others in the body. It is not to discourage that I say this, but to warn, and to urge us to cast ourselves entirely upon the Word of God himself. You may have moments when you are ready to give in to despair. But be of good courage; only believe. He who has put the blessing within your reach will assuredly lead to its possession.

The way in which we receive this blessing may differ. To some it may come as the gift of a moment. In times of revival, in fellowship with other believers in whom the Spirit is working effectually, under the leading of some servant of God who can guide, and sometimes in solitude too it is as if all at once a new revelation comes upon the soul. It sees, as in the light of heaven, the strong Vine holding and bearing the weak branches so securely that doubt becomes impossible. When this happens. we wonder how we could ever have understood the words to mean anything else but this: To abide unceasingly in Christ is the portion of every believer. When the soul sees it and believes it, rejoicing and love will come as the inevitable response.

To others it comes by a slower and more difficult path. Day by day, amid discouragement and difficulty, the soul has to press forward. If this is your situation, hear the Savior say, "Be of good cheer" (John 16:33); this way, too, leads to the rest. Only seek to keep your heart set upon the promise "I the Lord keep it, night and day." Take from His own lips the watchword *"Every moment."* In that, you have the law of His love and the law of your hope. Be content with nothing less. Do not allow your mind to think that the duties and cares, the sorrows and sins of this life, must succeed in hindering the abiding life of fellowship. Take rather the language of faith for the rule of your daily experience: I am persuaded that neither death with its fears, nor life with its cares, nor things present with their pressing claims, nor things to come with their dark shadows, nor height of joy, nor depth of sorrow, nor any other creature, shall be able, for one single moment, to separate us from the love of God which is in Christ Jesus our Lord (see Romans 8:38–39). And it is this love in which He is teaching me to abide. If things look dark and faith would fail, sing again the song of the vineyard: "I the Lord keep it, I water it every moment; Lest any hurt it, I keep it night and day." And be assured that if God the Father keeps the branch night and day, and waters it every moment, a life of continuous and unbroken fellowship with Christ is indeed our privilege.

Day by Day

*The people are to go out each day and gather
enough for that day.*

Exodus 16:4 NIV

Enough for that day: Such was the rule for God's giving and man's working in the gathering of the manna. It is still the law in all the dealings of God's grace with His children. A clear insight into the beauty and application of this arrangement is a wonderful help in understanding how one, who feels himself utterly weak, can have the confidence and the perseverance to hold on brightly through all his earthly years. A patient who had been in a serious accident once asked a doctor: "Doctor, how long will I have to lie here?" The answer, "Only a day at a time," taught the patient a precious lesson. It was the same lesson God recorded for His people of all ages long before: enough for that day.

It was, without doubt, with a view to this and to meet man's weakness that God graciously appointed the change of day and night. If time had been given to man in the form of one long, unbroken day, it would have exhausted and overwhelmed him;

the change of day and night continually replenishes his strength. Children are given only one lesson for the day and in that way master the entire book in time. It would be useless to give the whole book to them at once; so it is with grown men too. Because divisions of time are broken down and divided into small fragments, we can bear them; only the care and the work of each day have to be undertaken—enough for that day only. The rest of the night enables us to make a fresh start with each new morning; the mistakes of the past can be avoided, its lessons improved. And we have only each day to be faithful for the one short day, and long years and a long life take care of themselves without the sense of their length or their weight ever being a burden.

Most sweet is the encouragement to be derived from this truth in the life of grace. Many a soul is upset with the thought as to how it will be able to gather and to keep the manna needed for all its years of travel through such a barren wilderness. It has not learned what unspeakable comfort there is in the word *enough for that day*. That word completely takes away all care for tomorrow. Only today is yours; tomorrow is the Father's. The question "What security do you have that during all the years in which you have to battle the coldness, temptations, or trials of the world, you will always abide in Jesus?" is one you need not, may not ask. Manna, as your food and strength, is given only by the day; to faithfully fill the present is your only security for the future. Accept, enjoy, and fulfill with your whole heart the part you have to perform this day. His presence and grace enjoyed today will remove all doubt as to whether you can entrust tomorrow to Him too.

What great value this truth teaches us to attach to each

single day! We are so easily led to look at life as a great big whole, and to neglect the little today, to forget that the single days do indeed make up the whole, and that the value of each single day depends on its influence on the whole. One day lost is a link broken in the chain, which it often takes more than another day to mend. One day lost influences the next and makes its keeping more difficult. In fact, one day lost may be the loss of what months or years of careful labor had secured. The experience of many a believer would confirm this.

Believer, would you abide in Jesus? Let it be day by day. You have already heard the message of "Moment by Moment"; the lesson of "Day by Day" has even more to teach. Of the moments there are many where there is no direct exercise of the mind on your part; the abiding is in the deeper recesses of the heart, kept by the Father, to whom you entrusted yourself. But this is precisely the work that with each new day has to be renewed for the day—the distinct renewal of surrender and trust for the life of moment by moment. God has gathered up the moments and bound them up into a bundle (1 Samuel 25:29) for the very purpose that we might measure them. As we look forward in the morning, or look back in the evening, and weigh the moments, we learn how to value and how to use them rightly.

As the Father, with each new morning, meets you with the promise of sufficient manna for the day for yourself and those who have to partake with you, meet Him with the bright and loving renewal of your acceptance of the position He has given you in His beloved Son. Accustom yourself to look upon this as one of the reasons for the appointment of day and night. God thought of our weakness and sought to provide for it. Let each day derive its value from your calling to abide in Christ. As its light opens on your waking eyes, accept it on these terms: a day, just one day only, but still a day, given to abide and grow up in Jesus Christ. Whether it be a day of health or sickness, joy or sorrow, rest or work, of struggle or victory, let the main thought with which you receive it in the morning thanksgiving be this: "A day that the Father gave; in it I may, I must become more closely united to Jesus." As the Father asks, "Can you trust Me for just this one day to keep you abiding in Jesus, and Jesus to keep you fruitful?" you are compelled to give the joyful response: "I will trust and not be afraid."

The day's portion, enough for the day, was given to Israel in the morning very early. The portion was for use and nourishment during the whole day, but the giving and the getting of it was the morning's work. This suggests how greatly the power to abide all the day in Jesus depends on the morning hour. "If the firstfruit is holy, the batch is also holy" (Romans 11:16). Hours of intense occupation come during the day in the rush of business or the pressure of deadlines, when only the Father's keeping can ensure the connection with Jesus remains unbroken.

The morning manna fed the Israelites all day; it is only when the believer in the morning secures his quiet time in secret to effectively renew loving fellowship with his Savior that abiding in Christ can be kept up all day. But what cause for thanksgiving that it can be done! In the morning, with its freshness and quiet, the believer can look out upon the day. He can consider its duties and its temptations, and go over them beforehand, as it were, with his Savior, casting all upon Him who has promised to be everything to him. Christ is his manna, his nourishment, his strength, and his life; he can take enough for that day, Christ being his for all the needs the day may bring. In this way the believer can proceed with the assurance that his day will be one of blessing and growth.

And then, as the lesson of the value and the work of the single day is being taken to heart, the learner is unconsciously being led on to perceive the secret of "day by day continually" (Exodus 29:38). The blessed abiding grasped by faith for each day apart is an unceasing and ever-increasing growth. Each day of faithfulness brings a blessing for the next, making both the trust and the surrender easier and more blessed. And so the Christian life grows; as we give our whole heart to the work of each day. And so each day separately, all the day continually, and day by day successively, we abide in Jesus.

The days make up the life; what once appeared too high and too great to attain is given to the soul that was content to take and use "enough for the day, as prescribed for each day" (Ezra 3:4 NIV). Even here on earth the voice is heard: "Well done, good and faithful servant; you have been faithful over a few things, I will make you ruler over many things. Enter into the joy of your master" (Matthew 25:23). Our daily life becomes a wonderful interchange of God's daily grace and our daily praise: "Who daily loads us with His benefits" (Psalm 68:19); "that I may daily perform my vows" (Psalm 61:8). God's reason for daily giving is understood as we see how He gives only enough but also fully enough for each day.

We are encouraged to adopt His way, the way of daily asking and expecting. We begin to number our days not from the sun's rising over the world, or by the work we do or the food we eat, but by the daily renewal of the miracle of the manna—the blessing of daily fellowship with Him who is the Life and the Light of the world. The heavenly life is as unbroken and continuous as the earthly; abiding in Christ each day brings to that day sufficient blessing. And so we learn to abide in Him every day, all through the day.

Lord, help us to see that this is enough—for today and every day to come.

At This Moment

Behold, now is the accepted time; behold,
now is the day of salvation.

2 Corinthians 6:2

Looking at abiding in Christ from our perspective, the thought of living moment to moment is of such central importance that we should speak of it once more. And to all who desire to learn the blessed art of living only a moment at a time, we want to say: The way to learn it is to exercise yourself in living in the present moment. Each time your attention is free to occupy itself with the thought of Jesus—whether it be with time to think and pray, or only for a few passing seconds—let your first thought be to say: "Now, at this moment, I do abide in Jesus." Do not use such time in vain regrets that you have not been abiding fully, or in still more hurtful fears that you will not be able to abide, but rather take the position the Father has given you: "I am in Christ; this is the place God has given me. I accept it; here I rest; I do now abide in Jesus." This is the way to learn to abide continually.

You may be yet so weak as to fear to say of each day, "I am

abiding in Jesus"; but the weakest believer can, each single moment, say, as he agrees to occupy his place as a branch in the Vine, "Yes, I do abide in Christ." It is not a matter of feeling, or a question of growth or strength in the Christian life; rather, it is simply a question of whether or not your will at the present moment desires and agrees to recognize the place you have in your Lord, and to accept it. If you are a believer, you are in Christ. If you are in Christ and wish to stay there, it is your duty to say, though it may be only for a moment, "Blessed Savior, I abide in you now; please keep me now."

It has been well said that in that little word *now* lies one of the deepest secrets of the life of faith. At the close of a conference on the spiritual life, a minister of experience rose and spoke. He said he did not know if he had learned any truth he did not know before, but he had learned how to use correctly what he already knew. He had learned that it was his privilege at each moment, whatever his surrounding circumstances might be, to say, "Jesus saves me *now*." This is the secret of rest and victory. If I can say, "Jesus is to me at this moment all that God gave Him to be—life, strength, and peace"—I only have to hold still, rest, and realize it, and for that moment I have what I need. As my faith sees how I am in Christ and takes the place in Him my Father has provided, my soul can peacefully settle down: Now I abide in Christ.

Believer, when striving to find the way to abide in Christ from moment to moment, remember that the gateway is simple: Abide in Him at this present moment. Instead of wasting effort in trying to get into a state that will last, just remember that it is Christ himself—the living, loving Lord—who alone can keep you, and is waiting to do so. Begin at once and demonstrate faith in Him for the present moment; this is the only way to be kept the next. To attain the life of permanent and perfect abiding is not ordinarily given at once as a possession for the future, it comes step by step. Avail yourself, therefore, of every opportunity to exercise the trust available at the present moment.

Each time you bow in prayer, let there first be an act of simple devotion: "Father, I am in Christ; I now abide in Him." Each time you have, in the midst of busyness, the opportunity of self-recollection, let its first involuntary act be: "I am still in Christ, abiding in Him now." Even when overtaken by sin, and your heart is all disturbed, let your first look be upward as you say: "Father, I have sinned; and yet I come—though I blush to say it—as one who is in Christ. Father, here I am! I can take no other place; of God I am in Christ; I *now* abide in Christ." Yes, Christian, in every possible circumstance, every moment of the day, the voice is calling: "Abide in Me, do it now." And even now, as you are reading this, come at once and enter into the blessed life of always abiding by doing it at once: Do it now.

In the life of David there is a beautiful passage that may help to make this thought clearer (2 Samuel 3:17–18). David had been anointed king in Judah. The other tribes still followed Ish-bosheth, Saul's son. Abner, Saul's chief captain, resolves to lead the tribes of Israel to submit to David, the God-appointed king of the whole nation. He speaks to the elders of Israel: "In time past you were seeking for David to be king over you. *Now then, do it!* For the Lord has spoken of David, saying, 'By the hand of My servant David, I will save My people Israel from the hand of the Philistines and the hand of all their enemies' " (2 Samuel 3:17–18). And they did it; they anointed David a second time to be king, now over all Israel, since they at first had only made him king over Judah (2 Samuel 5:3). This incident is a most instructive type of the way in which a soul is led to the life of entire surrender and undivided allegiance, to full abiding in Christ.

First you have *the divided kingdom*: Judah faithful to the king of God's appointment and Israel still clinging to the king of its own choosing. As a consequence, the nation was divided against itself and had no power to conquer its enemies. What a plain and clear picture of the divided heart that resides in many believers! Jesus is accepted as King in Judah, the place of the holy mount, in the inner chamber of the soul, but the surrounding territory, the everyday life, is not yet under His subjection; more than half the life is still ruled by self-will and its hosts. And so there is no real peace within and no power over one's enemies.

Then there comes *the longing desire* for a better state: "You were seeking for David to be king over you." There was a time, when David had conquered the Philistines, that Israel believed in him; but they had been led astray. Abner appeals to their own knowledge of God's will, which was that David must rule over all. So the believer, when first brought to Jesus, wanted Him to be Lord over all, and had hoped that He alone would be King. But unbelief and self-will came in, and Jesus could not assert His power over his entire life. And yet the Christian is not content. At times he longs, without daring to hope that it can be, for a better time.

Then follows *God's promise*. Abner says, "The Lord has spoken ... By the hand of My servant David, I will save My people ... from the hand of *all* their enemies." He appeals to

God's promise: As David had conquered the Philistines, the nearest enemy in time past, so he alone could conquer those farther off. He would save Israel from the hand of *all* their enemies. This text is a beautiful type of the promise by which the soul is now invited to trust Jesus for victory over every enemy and a life of undisturbed fellowship with Him. "The Lord has spoken"—this is our only hope. On that word rests the sure expectation (Luke 1:70–75): "As *He spoke* . . . That we should be saved from our enemies and from the hand of *all* who hate us, to perform the mercy promised to our fathers and to remember His holy covenant, the oath which He swore . . . That He would grant to us that we, being delivered out of the hand of our enemies, might serve Him without fear, in holiness and righteousness before Him all the days of our life." David reigning over every corner of the land, and leading a united and obedient people on from victory to victory: This is the promise of what Jesus can do for us, as soon as we, exercising faith in God's promise, surrender all to Him and allow our whole life to be kept abiding in Him.

"In time past you were seeking for David to be king over you," spoke Abner, and added, "Now then, do it!" *Do it now* is the message that this story brings to each one of us who longs to give Jesus unreserved supremacy. Whatever the present moment may hold, however unprepared the message finds you, however sad the divided and hopeless state of your life may be, do come and surrender—this very moment. I know that it will take time for the Lord to assert His power and arrange all within you according to His will, time to conquer your enemies and train all your powers for His service. This is not the work of a moment. But there are things that are the work of a moment—of this moment. One is your surrender of all to Jesus, your surrender of yourself entirely to live only in Him. As time goes on, and exercise has made faith stronger and brighter, that surrender may become clearer and more intelligent. But for this you cannot wait. The only way to attain it is to begin at once. *Do it now.* Surrender yourself this very moment to abide wholly, only, always in Jesus. It is the work of a moment. Remember, Christ's renewed acceptance of you is also the work of a moment. Be assured that He has you and holds you as His own, and that each new "Jesus, I do abide in you," meets with an immediate and hearty response from the Unseen One. No act of faith can be in vain. He immediately takes hold of us anew and draws us close to himself. Therefore, as often as the message comes, or the thought of it comes, Jesus says: "Abide in Me, do it at once." Each moment there is the whisper: "Do it now."

Let any Christian begin, then, and he will quickly experience how the blessing of the present moment is passed on to the next. It is the unchanging Jesus to whom he links himself; it is the power of a divine life, in its unbroken continuity, that takes possession of him. The *do it now* of the present moment—although it seems such a little thing—is nothing less than the beginning of the ever-present now, which is the mystery and the glory of eternity. Therefore, Christian, abide in Christ: *Do it now.*

Forsaking All for Him

I have suffered the loss of all things, and count them as rubbish, that I may gain Christ and be found in Him.

Philippians 3:8–9

Wherever there is life, there is continual taking in and giving out, receiving and restoring. The nourishment I take in is given out again in the work I do; the impressions I receive, I express in my thoughts and feelings. The one depends on the other— the giving out ever increases the power of taking in. In the healthy exercise of giving and taking is all the enjoyment of life.

So it is in the spiritual life too. There are Christians who look on its blessing as consisting in the privilege of ever receiving; they do not know how the capacity for receiving is only kept up and enlarged by continual giving up and giving out. For it is only in the emptiness that comes from parting with what we have that divine fullness can flow in. It was a truth our Savior continually insisted on. When He spoke of selling all to secure the treasure, of losing our life to find it, of the hundred-fold that comes to those who forsake all, He was explaining that self-sacrifice is the law of the kingdom for himself as well as for

213

His disciples. If we are really to abide in Christ, and to be found in Him—to have our life always and completely in Him—each of us in our measure must say with Paul, "I count *all things loss* for the excellence of the knowledge of Christ Jesus my Lord . . . that I may gain Christ and be found in Him" (Philippians 3: 8–9).

Let us look at what is to be forsaken and given up. First of all, there is sin. There can be no true conversion without the giving up of sin. And yet, because the young convert is often ignorant of what sin really is, of what the claims of God's holiness are, and to what extent the power of Jesus can enable us to conquer sin, the giving up of sin is at first only partial and superficial. As the Christian life grows, there comes a desire for a deeper and more entire purging out of everything that is unholy. And when the desire to abide in Christ continually, to be always found in Him, becomes strong, the soul is led to see the need of a new act of surrender, in which it accepts afresh its death to sin in Christ, and turns its back on everything that is sin. By the strength of God's Spirit, he appropriates that wonderful power of our nature by which the whole of one's future life can be gathered up and disposed of in one act of the will. In this, the believer yields himself to sin no more—to be only and wholly a servant of righteousness. He does it in the joyful assurance that every sin surrendered is gain indeed and makes room for the inflowing of the presence and the love of Christ.

After parting with unrighteousness, the believer must also give up self-righteousness. Although we contend earnestly against our own works or merits, it is often a long time before we come to really understand what it is to refuse self any place or right in the service of God. Unconsciously we allow the acts of our own mind, heart, and will to freely reign in God's presence. In prayer and worship, in Bible reading and working for God, instead of absolute dependence on the Holy Spirit's leading, self is expected to do a work it never can do. We are slow to learn the lesson "In me (that is, in my flesh) nothing good dwells" (Romans 7:18). As this truth becomes evident and we see how corruption extends to everything that is of our old nature, we understand that there can be no entire abiding in Christ without the giving up of all that is of self in religion. We must give it up to the death, and wait for the breathings of the Holy Spirit to work in us, as only He can, what is acceptable in God's sight.

We all have within us a natural life, with all the powers and gifts given to us by the Creator, which work with all the occupations and interests of the environment that surrounds us. Once you are truly converted, it is not enough that you have a sincere desire to have all these devoted to the service of the Lord. The desire is good, but it cannot teach the way or give the strength to do it acceptably. Incalculable harm has been done to the deeper spirituality of the church by the idea that when we are God's children, the using of our gifts in His service follows as a matter of course. This is not true because for this there is needed very special grace. And the way in which the grace comes is through sacrifice and surrender.

I must see how all my gifts and powers are, even though I am indeed a child of God, still defiled by sin, and under the power of the flesh. I must feel that I cannot proceed at once to use them for God's glory; I must first lay them at Christ's feet, to be accepted and cleansed by Him. *I must feel myself utterly powerless to use them correctly.* I must see that they are very dangerous to me because through them the flesh, the old nature, self, will so easily exert its power. In this conviction I must part with them, giving them entirely up to the Lord. When He has accepted them, and set His stamp upon them, I can receive them back, to hold as His property, to wait on Him for the grace to use them properly day by day, and *to have them act only under His influence.* And so experience proves it true here, too, that the path of entire consecration is the path of full salvation. Not only is what is given up received back again to become doubly our own, but the forsaking all is followed by the receiving of all. We abide in Christ more fully as we forsake all and follow Him. As I count *all things loss* for His sake, I am found in Him.

The same principle holds true for all of the legitimate occupations and possessions we have been entrusted with from God. Such were the fishnets on the Sea of Galilee, the household duties of Martha of Bethany, and the home and the friends of many of Jesus' disciples. Jesus taught them to forsake all for Him. It was no arbitrary command, but the simple application of a law in nature to the kingdom of His grace—that the more perfectly the old occupant is cast out, the more complete can be the possession of the new, and the more entire the renewal of all within.

This principle has an even deeper application. The truly spiritual gifts that are the workings of God's own Holy Spirit within us . . . these surely do not need to be given up and surrendered, do they? They do indeed; the interchange of giving up and taking in is a life process and may not stop for a moment. No sooner does the believer begin to rejoice in the possession of what he has than the inflow of new grace is retarded, and stagnation threatens. It is only into the thirst of an empty soul that the streams of living waters flow. Ever thirsting is the secret of never thirsting.

Each blessed experience we receive as a gift of God must at once be returned back to Him from whom it came, in praise and love, in self-sacrifice and service; only in this way can it be restored to us again, fresh and beautiful with the bloom of heaven. This is the wonderful lesson Isaac on Mount Moriah taught us. Was he not the son of promise, the God-given life, the wonder-gift of the omnipotent One who brings to life the dead? (Romans 4:17). And yet even he had to be given up and sacrificed, that he might be received back again a thousandfold more precious than before. He serves as a type of the only-begotten Son of the Father, whose pure and holy life had to be given up before He could receive it again in resurrection power and could make His people partakers of it. A type, too, of what takes place in the life of each believer, when, instead of resting contently with past experiences or present grace, he presses on, forgetting and giving up all that is behind (Philippians 3:13), and reaches out to the fullest possible apprehension of Christ's life within.

Such surrender of all for Christ, is it a single step, the act and experience of a moment, or is it a course of daily renewal and progressive attainment? It is both. There may be a moment in the life of a believer when he gets a first glimpse, or a deeper insight, of this blessed truth, and when, made willing in the day of God's power, he does indeed gather up the whole of life yet before him into the decision of a moment, and lays himself on the altar as a living and acceptable sacrifice. Such moments have often been the blessed transition from a life of wandering and failure to a life of abiding and divine power. But even then his daily life becomes what the life must be of each one who has no such experience: the unceasing prayer for more light on the meaning of entire surrender, the ever-renewed offering up of all he has to God.

Believer, would you abide in Christ? See here the blessed path. Nature shrinks back from such self-denial and crucifixion in its rigid application to our life. But what nature does not love and cannot perform, grace will accomplish, supplying you with a life full of joy and glory. If you risk yielding yourself up to Christ your Lord, the conquering power of His incoming presence will make it joyous for you to cast out all that before was most precious.

"A hundredfold in this life" (Matthew 19:29): This word of the Master comes true to all who, with wholehearted faithfulness, accept His commands to forsake all. The blessed receiving soon makes the giving up most blessed too. And the secret of a life of close abiding will be seen to be simply this: As I give myself wholly to Christ, I find the power to take Him wholly for myself; and as I lose myself and all I have for Him, He takes me wholly for himself and gives himself wholly to me.

Through the Holy Spirit

The anointing which you have received from Him abides in
you . . . and just as it has taught you, you will abide in Him.

1 John 2:27

How beautiful is the thought of a life always abiding in Christ!
The longer we think of it, the more attractive it becomes. And
yet how often the precious words "Abide in Me" are heard by a
young disciple with a sigh! It is as if he does not understand
what they mean or how such full enjoyment can be reached. He
longs for someone who can make it perfectly clear, and continually reassure him that such abiding is indeed within his reach.
If only this one would listen carefully to the word we have from
John this day; what hope and joy it would bring! It gives us
divine assurance that we have the anointing of the Holy Spirit
to teach us all things, including how to abide in Christ.

Someone may say, "This word does not give me comfort; it
only depresses me more. For it tells of another privilege I do
not know how to enjoy. I do not understand how the teaching
of the Spirit is given, where or how I can discern His voice. If
the Teacher is so unknown, it is no wonder that the promise of

219

His teaching about abiding does not help me much."

Thoughts like these come from an error that is very common among believers. They imagine that the Spirit, in teaching them, must reveal the mysteries of the spiritual life first to their intellect, and afterward in their experience. And God's way is just the opposite of this. What holds true of all spiritual truth is especially true of abiding in Christ: *We must live and experience truth in order to know it.* Life-fellowship with Jesus is the only school for the science of heavenly things. "You do not realize now what I am doing, but later you will understand" (John 13:7 NIV) is a law of the kingdom. It is especially true of the daily cleansing of which it was first spoken, and of the daily keeping.

Receive what you do not comprehend. Submit to what you cannot understand, and accept and expect what appears to reason as a mystery. Believe what looks impossible, and walk in a way you do not know—such are the first lessons in the school of God. "*If you abide* in My word, *you will understand* the truth": in these and other words of God we are taught that there is a habit of mind and life that precedes the understanding of the truth. True discipleship consists in *first* following, and *then* knowing the Lord. The believing surrender to Christ, and submission to His Word to expect what appears most improbable, is the only way to the full blessing of knowing Him.

These principles are especially helpful in regard to the Holy Spirit's teaching. That teaching consists *in His guiding the spiritual life within us to that which God has prepared for us, without our always knowing how.* On the strength of God's promise, trusting in His faithfulness, the believer yields himself to the leading of the Holy Spirit without insisting on having it made clear to the intellect first what He is to do, but consenting to let Him do His work in the soul, and afterward come to know what He has done. Faith trusts the working of the unseen Spirit in the deep recesses of the inner life. And so the word of Christ and the gift of the Spirit are to the believer sufficient guarantee that He will be taught of the Spirit to abide in Christ. By faith he rejoices in what he does not see or feel; he knows and is confident that the blessed Spirit within is doing His work silently but surely, guiding him into a life of full abiding and unbroken communion.

The Holy Spirit is the Spirit of life in Christ Jesus; it is His work, not only to breathe, but also to always foster and strengthen, and so perfect the new life within. And in proportion as the believer yields himself in simple trust to the unseen but most certain law of the Spirit of life working within him, his faith will pass into knowledge. It will be rewarded by the Spirit's light revealing in the Word what has already been accomplished by the Spirit's power in the life.

Apply this now to the promise of the Spirit's teaching us to abide in Christ. The Holy Spirit is indeed the mighty power of God. And He comes to us from the heart of Christ as the bearer of Christ's life, the revealer and communicator of Christ himself within us. In the expression "the fellowship of the Spirit" (Philippians 2:1), we are taught what His highest work is. He is the bond of fellowship between the Father and the Son: By Him they are one. He is the bond of fellowship between all believers: By Him they are one.

Above all, He is the bond of fellowship between Christ and individual believers; He is the life-sap through which Vine and branch grow into real and living oneness: By Him we are one.

And we can be assured of it, that if we believe in His presence and working, if we are careful not to grieve Him because we know that He is in us, and if we wait and pray to be filled with Him, He will teach us how to abide. First guiding our will to a wholehearted clinging to Christ, then energizing our faith into ever-growing confidence and expectation, then breathing into our hearts a peace and joy that pass understanding, He teaches us to abide. Then coming through the heart and life into the understanding, He helps us grasp the truth—not as mere thought, but as the truth which is in Christ Jesus. It comes as a reflection into the mind of the light of what He has already made a reality in the life. "In him was life, and that life was the light of men" (John 1:4 NIV).

In view of such teaching, it is clear that if we would have the Spirit guide us into the abiding life, our first need is quiet, restful faith. Amid all the questions and difficulties that may come up in connection with our striving to abide in Christ, all the longing we may sometimes feel to have a seasoned Christian to help us, and the frequent painful consciousness of failure, ignorance, and helplessness, we need to remember with blessed confidence: *We have the anointing of the Holy One to teach us to abide in Him.* "The anointing which you have received from Him abides in you ... and just as it has taught you, you will abide in Him." Make this teaching of His about abiding a matter of faith.

Believe that as surely as you have Christ, you have His Spirit too. Believe that He will do His work with power, if only you do not hinder Him. Believe that He is working, even when you cannot recognize it. Believe that He will work mightily if you ask this from the Father. *It is impossible to live the life of full abiding without being full of the Holy Spirit*, believe that the fullness of the Spirit is your daily privilege. Be sure to take time in prayer to dwell before the throne of God and the Lamb, from which flows the river of the water of life (Revelation 22:1). It is *there, and only there,* that you can be filled with the Spirit. Cultivate carefully the habit of daily, continually honoring Him by quiet, restful confidence that He is doing His work within. Let faith in His indwelling make you jealous of whatever could grieve Him—the spirit of the world or the actions of self and the flesh. Let your faith seek its nourishment in the Word and all it says of the Spirit, His power, His comfort, and His work.

Above all, let faith in the Spirit's indwelling lead you to look away to Jesus. As we have received the anointing of *Him,* it comes in ever-stronger flow from Him as we are occupied with Christ alone. Christ is the Anointed One. As we look up to Him, the holy anointing comes, the "precious oil poured on the head, running down on the beard, running down on Aaron's beard, down upon the collar of his robes" (Psalm 133:2 NIV). It is faith in Jesus that brings the anointing; then the anointing leads to Jesus and enables us to abide in Him alone.

Believer, abide in Christ, by the power of the Spirit. What do you think? Should such abiding be a fear or a burden? Surely not! If we only knew the graciousness of our Holy Comforter, and the blessing of wholly yielding ourselves to His leading, we would experience the divine comfort of having such a teacher to secure our abiding in Christ. The Holy Spirit was given for this one purpose: that *the glorious redemption and life in Christ might be given and communicated to us with divine power.* We have the Holy Spirit to make the living Christ, in all His saving power and complete victory over sin, ever present within us. It is this that makes Him the Comforter; with Him we need never mourn an absent Christ.

Let us therefore, as often as we read, meditate, or pray about abiding in Christ, count on it as a settled thing that we have the Spirit of God himself within us, teaching, guiding, and working. The Holy Spirit is always at work with secret but divine power in the trusting soul that does not hinder His work by its unbelief. For this reason, we can rejoice in the confidence that we will succeed in our desires to abide in Him if we will only let the Holy Spirit do the work in us.

In Stillness of Soul

In repentance and rest is your salvation, in quietness
and trust is your strength.

Isaiah 30:15 NIV

Rest in the LORD and wait patiently for Him.

Psalm 37:7

Truly my soul silently waits for God.

Psalm 62:1

There is a view of the Christian life that regards it as a sort of partnership, in which God and man each have to do their part. It admits that there is little that man can do, and even that little is defiled with sin; still, the view holds, man must do his utmost; only then can he expect God to do His part. To those who think this way, it is extremely difficult to understand what Scripture means when it speaks of our being still and doing nothing, of our resting and waiting to see the salvation of God. It appears to them a perfect contradiction when we speak of this quietness and ceasing from all effort as the secret of the

225

most productive activity of man. And yet this is just what Scripture does teach.

The explanation of the apparent mystery is to be found in this: When God and man are spoken of as working together, it is not in the usual sense of a partnership between two partners who each contribute out of their individual reserves their share to a mutual project. The relationship between a believer and Christ is a very different one. Here, cooperation is founded on subordination. As Jesus was entirely dependent on the Father for all His words and all His works, so the believer can do nothing of himself. What he can do of himself is altogether sinful. He must therefore cease entirely from his own doing and wait for the working of God in him. As he ceases from self-effort, faith assures him that God is working in him to complete the work; what God does is to renew, sanctify, and awaken all his energies to their highest power.

So as the believer yields himself as a truly passive instrument in the hand of God, and works with renewed confidence in God's almighty power rather than his own, in that proportion will he experience the deepest possible expression of the Christian life. Passivity does not mean inactivity; it means that as we live out our Christian responsibilities, we do not trust in our own strength but in God's at work within us.

Among the lessons to be learned of those who are studying the blessed art of abiding in Christ, there is none more needful and more profitable than cultivating stillness of soul. In it alone can we produce a teachable spirit, to which the Lord will reveal His secrets. To the meek He shows His ways. This spirit was exhibited so beautifully by three women in the New Testament. It was evident in Jesus' mother, whose only answer to the most wonderful revelation ever made to a human being was, "I am the Lord's servant, May it be to me as you have said" (Luke 1:38 NIV); and as mysteries multiplied around her, it is written of her: "Mary kept all these things and pondered them in her heart" (Luke 2:19). In Mary of Bethany, who "sat at Jesus' feet and heard His word" (Luke 10:39), and who showed in anointing Him for His burial how she had understood the mystery of His death better than His disciples had, we also see this spirit of meekness. She wanted to be still and learn from the One who had the words of life. We also see a meek and quiet spirit in the sinful woman who sought the Lord in the house of the Pharisee, with tears that spoke more than words (Luke 7:37–38). It is *a soul silent before God* that is best prepared for knowing Jesus, and for holding on to the blessings He bestows. It is when the soul is hushed in silent awe and worship before the Holy Presence revealed within that the still, small voice of the blessed Spirit will be heard.

Therefore, beloved Christian, as often as you seek to better understand the blessed mystery of abiding in Christ, let this be your first thought: "My soul, *wait silently* for God alone; for my expectation is from Him" (Psalm 62:5). Do you hope to realize the wondrous union with the Heavenly Vine? Then know that flesh and blood cannot reveal it to you, but only the Father in heaven. You only have to acknowledge your own ignorance and impotence; the Father will delight to give you the teaching of the Holy Spirit. If your ear is open, and your thoughts are brought into subjection, and your heart is prepared in silence to wait upon God and to hear what He speaks, then He will reveal to you His secrets.

One of the first secrets revealed will be deeper insight into the truth that as you sink low before Him in nothingness and helplessness, in a silence and stillness of soul that seeks to catch the faintest whisper of His love, teachings will come to you that you never heard before because of the rush and noise of your own thoughts and efforts. You will learn how your best work is to listen, hear, and believe what He promises; to watch, wait, and see what He does; and then, by faith, worship, and obedience, to yield yourself to the One who works mightily in you.

One would think that no message could be more beautiful or welcome than this: that we may rest and be quiet, and that our God will work for us and in us. And yet how far this is from being the case! How slow many are to learn that quietness is blessing, that quietness is strength, that quietness is the source of the highest activity—the secret of all true abiding in Christ! Let us try to learn it and to watch out for whatever interferes with it. The dangers that threaten the soul's rest are many.

There is a depleting of energy that comes from entering needlessly and too deeply into the interests of this world. Every one of us has his divine calling; and within the circle pointed out by God himself, interest in our work and its surroundings is a duty. But even here the Christian needs to be watchful and sober-minded. We need a holy self-control in regard to things not absolutely imposed upon us by God. If abiding in Christ is really our first aim, we must beware of all needless entertainment. We must watch even in lawful and necessary things against the wondrous power these have to keep the soul so occupied that there remains little power or zest for fellowship with God. Then there is the restlessness and worry from care and anxiety about earthly things; these eat away the life of trust and keep the soul like a troubled sea. There the gentle whispers of the Holy Comforter cannot be heard.

No less hurtful is the spirit of fear and distrust in spiritual things; with its apprehensions, it never really hears what God has to say. Above all, though, is the unrest that comes from seeking in our own way and in our own strength the spiritual blessing that comes only from above. *The heart occupied with its own plans and efforts for doing God's will and securing the blessing of abiding in Jesus will fail continually.* God's work is hindered by our interference. He can do His work perfectly only when the soul ceases from its work. He will do His work mightily in the soul that honors Him by expecting Him to work both in intent and fulfillment.

Last of all, even when the soul seeks to enter the way of faith, there is the impatience of the flesh, which forms its judgment of the life and progress of the soul not according to the divine but a human standard.

In dealing with all this, and so much more, blessed is the man who learns the lesson of stillness, and fully accepts God's Word: "In quietness and confidence shall be your strength." Each time he listens to the word of the Father, or asks the Father to listen to his words, he does not dare to begin his Bible reading or prayer without first pausing and waiting, until the soul is hushed in the presence of the Eternal Majesty. Under a sense of the Divine nearness, the soul, feeling how self is always ready to assert itself and intrude even into the holiest of all with its thoughts and efforts, yields itself in a quiet act of self-surrender to the teaching and working of the Holy Spirit. It is still and waits in holy silence, until all is calm and ready to receive the revelation of the divine will and presence. Its reading and prayer then become a waiting on God with ear and heart open, cleansed to receive fully only what He says.

"Abide in Christ!" Let no one think that he can do this if he does not have his daily quiet time, his seasons of meditation and waiting on God. In these a habit of soul must be cultivated, in which the believer goes out into the world and its distractions with the peace of God that surpasses all understanding, guarding the heart and mind (Philippians 4:7). It is in such a calm and restful soul that the life of faith can take root deeply, the Holy Spirit can give His blessed teaching, and the Father can accomplish His glorious work.

May each one of us learn every day to say, "Truly my soul silently waits for God." And may every feeling of difficulty in attaining this only cause us to look to Him and trust the One whose presence makes even a storm to be calm. Cultivate quietness as a means to abiding in Christ, and expect the ever-deepening quietness and calm of heaven in the soul as the fruit of abiding in Him.

In Affliction and Trial

Every branch that bears fruit He prunes,
that it may bear more fruit.

John 15:2

In the whole plant world there is not a tree to be found that so suits the image of man in his relationship to God as the vine. No other plant has fruit and juice that are so full of spirit, so alive and stimulating. But there is also none that has such a natural tendency toward evil, that is, growth that loves to run into wood that is utterly worthless except for the fire. Of all plants, the vine most needs the pruning knife to be used unsparingly and unceasingly. Also, none is so dependent on cultivation and training. But even with all these problems, no other plant yields a richer reward to the Vinedresser. In His wonderful parable, the Savior refers to this need of pruning the vine, and the blessing it brings. In this dark world, often so full of suffering and sorrow for believers, we can take comfort in His words about pruning, knowing that He means it for our good.

What treasures of teaching and comfort to the bleeding branch in its hour of trial: "Every branch that bears fruit *He prunes,* that it may bear more fruit." This is how He prepares

His people, who are prone when trial comes to be shaken in their confidence and to be moved away from abiding in Christ; in each affliction we need to hear the voice of a messenger that encourages us to abide even closer. Yes, believer, especially in times of trial, abide in Christ.

Abide in Christ! This is *the Father's object* in sending the trial. In a storm the tree puts down deeper roots into the soil; in a hurricane the inhabitants of the house stay inside and rejoice in its shelter. Through suffering the Father leads us to enter more deeply into the love of Christ. Our hearts are continually prone to wander from Him; prosperity and enjoyment all too easily satisfy us, dull our spiritual perception, and make us unfit for full communion with God. It is an unspeakable mercy that the Father comes with His affliction and makes the world around us dark and unattractive. This leads us to feel more deeply our sinfulness, and for a time we lose our joy in what was becoming so threatening to our spiritual life. He does this in the hope that when we have found our rest in Christ in time of trouble, we will learn to choose abiding in Him as our best option. Then when the affliction is removed, His hope for us is that we will have grown more firmly in Him, so that in prosperity He will still be our only joy. He has set His heart on this to the point that although He has no pleasure in afflicting us, He will not hold back even the most painful correction if He can thereby guide His beloved child to come home and abide in the beloved Son. Christian, pray for grace to see in every trouble, small or great, the Father pointing you to Jesus, and saying, "Abide in Him."

Abide in Christ; in this way you will become *partaker of all the rich blessings God designed for you* in the affliction. The purposes of God's wisdom will become clear to you, your assurance of His unchangeable love will become stronger, and the power of His Spirit will fulfill in you the promise "God disciplines us for our good, that we may share in his holiness" (Hebrews 12:10 NIV). Abide in Christ, and your cross becomes the means of fellowship with His Cross, providing access into its mysteries—the mystery of the curse that He bore for you, of the death to sin in which you partake with Him, and of the love in which, as sympathizing High Priest, He descended into all your sorrows. Abide in Christ; for by conforming to your blessed Lord in His sufferings, a deeper experience of the reality and the tenderness of His love will be yours.

Abide in Christ; in the fiery furnace, one like the Son of Man will be seen as never before and the burning away of the dross and the refining of the gold will be accomplished. Then Christ's own likeness will be reflected in you. If you abide in Christ, the power of the flesh will be put to death, and the impatience and self-will of the old nature will be humbled to make room for the meekness and gentleness of Christ. A believer may pass through a lot of affliction and, sadly, receive little blessing from it all. Abiding in Christ is the secret to receiving all the benefits that the Father meant for us to have from such experiences.

Abide in Christ; in Him you will find *sure and abundant consolation.* Comfort is often the first priority with the afflicted, and the profit of the affliction only of secondary interest. But our heavenly Father loves us so much that though our real and abiding profit is His first object of interest, He does not forget to comfort us too. When He comforts, it is that He may turn the believer's aching heart to Christ to receive the blessing of fellowship with Him. When He refuses to comfort us, His object is still the same. It is in making us partakers of His holiness that true comfort comes. The Holy Spirit is the Comforter, not only because He can suggest comforting thoughts of God's love, but far more, because He makes us holy and brings us into close union with Christ and the Father.

In Christ, the heart of the Father is revealed, and there can be no higher comfort than to rest in the Father's arms. *In Him* the fullness of the Divine Love is revealed, combined with the tenderness of a mother's compassion—and what can comfort like this? *In Him* you see a thousand times more given to you than you have lost; see how God only took from you so that you might have room to take from Him what is so much better. *In Him* suffering is consecrated and becomes the foretaste of eternal glory; in suffering the Spirit of God and of glory rests on us. Believer, would you have comfort in affliction? Then abide in Christ.

If you want to *bear more fruit* you must abide in Him. Not a vine is planted but the owner thinks of the fruit, and the fruit only. Other trees may be planted for ornament, for shade, or for wood, but the vine is planted *only for the fruit*. And of each vine the vinedresser is continually asking how it can bring forth more fruit, much fruit. If we can learn to abide in Christ in times of affliction, we will bear more fruit. The deeper experience of Christ's tenderness and the Father's love will urge you to live to His glory. Another benefit of surrender of self and self-will in suffering is that it will prepare you to sympathize with the misery of others; the softening that comes from such experiences will enable you to become, as Jesus was, the servant of all. The thought of the Father's desire for fruit in the pruning will help you to yield yourself afresh, and more than ever, to

Him, and to say that now you have but one object in life: making known and conveying His wonderful love to others. You will learn the art of forgetting self, and, even in affliction, using this separation from ordinary life to plead for the welfare of others. When you see affliction coming, meet it in Christ; when it has come, feel that you are more in Christ than in the affliction, for He is closer to you than affliction ever can be; and when it is passing, still abide in Him. Let the one thought of the Savior, as He speaks of the pruning, and the one desire of the Father, as He does the pruning, be yours: "Every branch that bears fruit He prunes, that it may bear *more fruit*."

In this way, your times of affliction become your times of choicest blessing—preparation for rich fruitfulness. Led into closer fellowship with the Son of God, and a deeper experience of His love and grace, you are established in the blessed confidence that He and you belong entirely to each other. You will find that you are more completely satisfied with Him and more wholly given up to Him than ever before. With your own will crucified, and your heart brought into deeper harmony with God's will, you will be a cleansed vessel that is suitable for the Master's use, prepared for every good work (2 Timothy 3:17).

True believer, try to learn this important truth, that in affliction your first, your only, calling that will be blessed is to abide in Christ. Spend much time with Him alone. Beware of the comfort and the distractions that friends so often bring. Let Jesus Christ be your chief companion and comforter. Delight yourself in the assurance that closer union with Him and more abundant fruit through Him are sure to be the results of trial because it is the Vinedresser himself who is doing the pruning. He will ensure the fulfillment of the desire of the soul that yields itself lovingly to His work.

That You May Bear Much Fruit

He who abides in Me, and I in him, bears much fruit; By this
My Father is glorified, that you bear much fruit.

John 15:5, 8

We all know what fruit is—the produce of the branch that refreshes and nourishes men. The fruit is not for the branch, but for those who come to carry it away. As soon as the fruit is ripe, the branch gives it up, to begin again its work of benevolence, and to prepare its fruit for another season. A fruit-bearing tree does not live for itself, but entirely for those to whom its fruit brings refreshment and life. And so the branch's whole existence is for the sake of the fruit, while its object and glory is to make the heart of the vinedresser glad.

What a beautiful image of the believer who is abiding in Christ! He not only grows in strength as his union with the Vine becomes progressively surer and firmer but he also bears fruit, much fruit to God's glory. He has the power to offer to others something to eat and by which they may live. Among all who surround him he becomes like a tree of life, of which they can taste and be refreshed. He is in his circle a center of life and blessing simply because he abides in Christ; he receives from Him the Spirit and the life that he can then impart to others. If you would bless others, learn to abide in Christ; and if you do abide, you will indeed be a blessing. As surely as the branch abiding in a fruitful vine bears fruit, so surely, *much more surely*, will a soul abiding in Christ with His fullness of blessing be made a blessing.

The reason for this is easily understood. If Christ, the Heavenly Vine, has taken the believer as a branch, then He has pledged himself, in the very nature of things, to supply the sap, spirit, and nourishment to make it bear fruit. The soul needs to concern itself with only one thing—to abide closely, fully, and entirely in Him. Christ will give the fruit. He works all that is needed to make the believer a blessing.

Abiding in Him, you receive from Him *His Spirit of love and compassion toward sinners*, which makes you want to see them blessed. By nature the heart is full of selfishness. Even in the believer, his own salvation and happiness is too often his only object. But abiding in Jesus, you come into contact with His infinite love, and its fire begins to burn within your heart; you see the beauty of love; you learn to look upon loving, serving, and saving your fellowmen as the highest privilege a disciple of Jesus can have. Abiding in Christ, your heart learns to feel the wretched condition of sinners still in darkness, and what dishonor is done to God by their alienation from Him. With Christ you begin to bear the burden of souls, the burden of sins not your own. As you are more closely united to Him, some measure of that passion for souls that urged Him to Calvary begins to breathe within you, and you are ready to follow His footsteps, to forsake the heaven of your own happiness and devote your life to win the souls Christ has taught you to love. The very spirit of the Vine is love, and this spirit of love streams into the branch that abides in Him.

The desire to be a blessing is just the beginning. As you begin to work, you quickly become conscious of your own weakness and the difficulties in your way. You realize that souls are not saved at your bidding. You become discouraged, and are tempted to relax your effort. But by abiding in Christ you receive *new courage and strength for the work.* Believing what Christ teaches, that it is *He* who *through you* will give His blessing to the world, you understand that you are only a weak instrument through which the hidden power of Christ does its work. You find that His strength may be perfected and made glorious in your weakness.

It is a great step when the believer fully consents to his own weakness, and the abiding consciousness of it, and so works faithfully on, fully assured that his Lord *is working* through him. He rejoices that the excellence of the power is of God, and not of him (2 Corinthians 4:7). Realizing his oneness with his Lord, he no longer considers his own weakness, but counts on the power of Him whose hidden workings make all the difference. It is this secret assurance that gives brightness to his look, a gentle firmness to his tone, and perseverance to all his efforts, all effective means of influencing those he is seeking to win. He goes forth in the spirit of one who knows that victory is assured; for this is the victory that overcomes, even our faith (1 John 5:4). He no longer considers it humility to say that God cannot bless his unworthy efforts. He claims and expects a

239

blessing because it is not he, but Christ within, that will accomplish it.

The great secret of abiding in Christ is the deep conviction that we are nothing, and He is everything. As this is learned, it no longer seems strange to believe that our weakness need not be a hindrance to His saving power. The believer who yields himself wholly to Christ for service in the spirit of a simple, childlike trust will most certainly bear much fruit. He will not fear to claim his share in the wonderful promise: "He who believes in Me, the works that I do he will do also; and *greater works* than these he will do, because I go to My Father" (John 14:12). He no longer thinks that He cannot have a blessing or be fruitful in order that he may be kept humble. He sees that the most heavily laden branches bow down the lowest! Abiding in Christ, he has agreed that, as is true in the arrangement between all vines and branches, any fruit will be to the glory of the Heavenly Vinedresser alone.

Let us learn two lessons. If we are abiding in Jesus, let us begin to work. Let us first seek to influence those around us in daily life. Let us accept distinctly and joyfully our holy calling, that we are even now to live as servants of the love of Jesus to our fellowmen. Our daily life must have for its object the making of an impression favorable to Jesus. When you look at the branch, you see at once the likeness to the Vine. We must live so that something of the holiness and the gentleness of Jesus may shine out in us. We must live to represent Him. As was the case with Him while on earth, the life must prepare the way for the teaching.

What the church and the world both need is this: men and women full of the Holy Spirit and of love, who, as living examples of the grace and power of Christ, witness for Him and for His power on behalf of those who believe in Him. Living so, with our hearts longing to have Jesus glorified in the souls He is seeking after, let us offer ourselves to Him for practical expressions of mercy. There is work to be done in our own homes. There is work among the sick, the poor, and the outcast. There is work in a hundred different paths that the Spirit of Christ opens up through those who allow themselves to be led by Him. There is work perhaps for us in ways that have not yet been opened up by others. Abiding in Christ, let us work. Let us work not like those who are content if they simply follow the expectations of our society and take some share in Christian work. No; let us work as those who are growing more like Christ because they are abiding in Him, and who, like Him, count the work of winning souls to the Father the very joy and glory of heaven begun on earth.

The second lesson is: If you work, abide in Christ. This is one of the blessings of work if done in the right spirit—it will deepen your union with your blessed Lord. It will discover your weakness and throw you back on His strength. It will stir you to pray more; and in prayer for others is the time when the soul, forgetful of itself, unconsciously grows deeper into Christ. Prayer will make clearer to you the true nature of branch-life, its absolute dependence, and at the same time its glorious sufficiency independent of all else, because it is only dependent on Jesus.

If you work, abide in Christ. There are temptations and dangers. Work for Christ has sometimes drawn believers away from Christ and taken the place of fellowship with Him. Work can sometimes present a form of godliness without the power.

As you work, abide in Christ. Let a living faith in Christ working in you be the secret spring of all your work; this will inspire in you both humility and courage. Let the Holy Spirit of Jesus dwell in you as the Spirit of His tender compassion and His divine power. Abide in Christ, and offer every part of your nature freely and unreservedly to Him to sanctify it for himself. If Jesus Christ is really to work through us, it will require an entire consecration of ourselves to Him that is renewed daily. But we understand now, this is what abiding in Christ means; this is what constitutes our highest privilege and happiness. To be a branch bearing much fruit—nothing less, nothing more— may this be our only joy.

So Will You Have Power in Prayer

*If ye abide in Me, and My words abide in you, you shall ask
what you desire, and it shall be done for you.*

John 15:7

Prayer is both one of the means and one of the fruits of union with Christ. As a means it is of great importance. All the things of faith, all the pleadings of desire, all the yearnings after a fuller surrender, all the confessions of shortcoming and of sin, all the exercises in which the soul gives up self and clings to Christ, find their utterance in prayer. In each meditation on abiding in Christ, as some new feature of what Scripture teaches concerning this blessed life is understood, the first impulse of the believer is to look up to the Father and pour out his heart, to ask Him for the full understanding and the full possession of what has been revealed in the Word. And it is the believer who is not content with this spontaneous expression of his hope, but who takes time in secret prayer to wait until he has received what he has seen, who will really grow strong in Christ.

However weak the soul's first abiding, its prayer will be heard, and it will find prayer one of the best means of abiding more abundantly.

But it is not so much as a means but as a fruit of abiding that the Savior mentions it in the parable of the Vine. He does not think of prayer as we too often do—exclusively as a means of getting blessing for ourselves. Rather, He sees prayer as one of the primary channels of influence by which, through us as workers together with God, the blessings of Christ's redemption are dispensed to the world. He sets before himself and us the glory of the Father, in the extension of His kingdom, as the object for which we have been made branches; and He assures us that if we will only abide in Him, we will be Israels, having power with God and man. Ours will be the effectual, fervent prayer of a righteous man, availing much, like Elijah's prayer for ungodly Israel (James 5:16–18). Such prayer will be the fruit of our abiding in Him and the means of bearing much fruit.

To the Christian who is not abiding completely in Jesus, the difficulties connected with prayer are often so great that they rob him of the comfort and the strength it could bring. Under the guise of humility, he asks how one so unworthy could expect to have influence with the Holy One. He thinks of God's sovereignty, His perfect wisdom and love, and cannot see how his prayer can really have any distinct effect. He prays, but it is more because he cannot rest without prayer than from a loving faith that the prayer will be heard. But what a blessed release from such questions and perplexities is given to the soul who is truly abiding in Christ! He realizes more and more how it is in real spiritual unity with Christ that we are accepted and heard. The union with the Son of God is a life union; we are indeed one with Him—our prayer ascends as His prayer. It is because we abide in Him that we can ask what we desire and it is given to us.

There are many reasons why this must be so. One is that abiding in Christ, and having His words abiding in us, teaches us to pray *in accordance with the will of God*. As we abide in Christ our self-will is kept down, and the thoughts and wishes of the old nature are brought into captivity to the thoughts and wishes of Christ; like-mindedness to Christ grows in us and as a result all our works and desires come into harmony with His. There is deep and frequent heart-searching to see whether the surrender is complete, fervent prayer to the heart-searching Spirit that nothing may be kept back. Everything is yielded to the power of His life in us so that it may exercise its sanctifying influence even on ordinary wishes and desires. His Holy Spirit breathes through our whole being. Without our being conscious how, our desires, as the breathings of the divine life, are brought into conformity with the divine will, and are fulfilled. Abiding in Christ renews and sanctifies the will; we then ask what we will, and it is given to us.

In close connection with this is the thought that abiding in Christ teaches the believer in prayer *only to seek the glory of God*. In promising to answer prayer, Christ's one thought (see John 14:13) is this, "that the Father may be glorified in the Son." In His intercession on earth (John 17), this was His one desire and plea; in His intercession in heaven, it is still His chief object. As the believer abides in Christ, the Savior breathes this desire into him. The thought *only the glory of God* becomes more and more the keynote of the life hidden in Christ. At first this subdues, quiets, and makes the soul almost afraid to entertain a wish, lest it should not be to the Father's glory. But when His glory has finally been accepted, and everything yielded to it, it comes with mighty power to enlarge the heart and open it to the vast possibilities in the area of God's glory. Abiding in Christ, the soul learns not only to desire but also to spiritually discern what will be for God's glory. One of the first conditions of acceptable prayer is fulfilled in it when, as the fruit of its union with Christ, the whole mind is brought into harmony with that of the Son as He said, "Father, glorify Your name" (John 12:28).

Abiding in Christ, we can freely use *the name of Christ*. Asking in the name of another means that person has authorized me and sent me to ask. The person doing the asking wants the favor done for him. Believers often try to think of the name of Jesus and His merits, and to talk themselves into the faith that they will be heard, while they painfully acknowledge how little faith they have in His name. They are not living wholly in Jesus' name. This is obvious because it is only when they begin to pray that they want to take up His name and use it. But this is not what Scripture teaches. The promise "Whatever you ask in My name" (John 14:13) cannot be separated from the command "Whatever you do in word or deed, *do all in the name* of the Lord Jesus" (Colossians 3:17).

If the name of Christ is to be at my disposal, so that I may have the full command of it for all I desire, it must be because I first put myself at His disposal, so that He has free and full command of me. It is abiding in Christ that gives us the right and power to use His name with confidence. To Christ, the Father refuses nothing. Abiding in Christ, I come to the Father as one with Him. His righteousness, as well as His Spirit, is in me; the Father sees the Son in me, and gives me my petition. It is not—as so many think—by a sort of imputed act that the Father looks upon us as if we were in Christ, even when we are not, in fact, in Him. No; the Father wants to *see* us living in Him; in this way our prayer really will have power to prevail. Abiding in Christ not only renews the will to pray in the right spirit but also secures the full power of His merits to us.

Abiding in Christ also works in us *the faith that can obtain an answer.* "According to your faith let it be to you" (Matthew 9:29); this is one of the laws of the kingdom. "Believe that you receive them, and you will have them" (Mark 11:24). This faith rests upon and is rooted in the Word, but is something infinitely higher than the mere logical conclusion: God has promised, therefore I will obtain. No; faith, as a spiritual act, depends upon the words abiding in us as living power, and so upon the state of the whole inner life. Without fasting and prayer (Mark 9:29), without humility and a spiritual mind (John 5:44), without wholehearted obedience (1 John 3:22), there cannot be this living faith. But as the soul abides in Christ, and grows into the consciousness of its union with Him, and sees how it is only Jesus who makes its petition acceptable, it dares to claim an answer because it knows that it is one with Him. It was by faith it learned to abide in Him; as the fruit of that faith, it rises to even greater faith in all that God has promised to be and to do. It learns to breathe its prayers in deep, quiet, confident assurance: We know we have the petition we ask of Him.

Abiding in Christ keeps us in the place where *the answer can be given.* Some believers pray earnestly for blessing, but when God comes and looks for them to bless them, they are not to be found. They did not realize that the blessing must not only be asked, but also waited for, and received in prayer. Abiding in Christ is the place for receiving answers. If the answer came outside of Him it would be dangerous in that we would only spend it on our own pleasures (James 4:3). Many of the richest answers—for spiritual grace, for example, or for power to work and to bless others—can only come in the form of a larger experience with God in what He makes Christ to us. The fullness is *in Him*; abiding in Him is the condition for power in prayer because the answer is treasured up and given in Him.

Believer, abide in Christ, for there in the abiding is the school of prayer—mighty, effectual, answered prayer. Abide in Him, and you will learn what to so many is a mystery: *The secret of the prayer of faith is the life of faith*—the life that abides in Christ alone.

Continue in His Love

As the Father loved Me, I also have loved you;
continue in My love.

John 15:9

Blessed Lord, enlighten our eyes to see clearly the glory of this wondrous word. Open to our meditation the secret chamber of your love, so that our souls may enter in, and find there their everlasting dwelling place. How else will we comprehend a love "which passes knowledge" (Ephesians 3:19)?

Before the Savior speaks the word that invites us to continue in His love, He first tells us what that love is. What He says of it gives power to His invitation and makes the thought of not accepting it an impossibility: "As the Father loved me, I also have loved you!"

"As the Father loved me" . . . How can we rightly comprehend this love? Lord, teach us. God is love; love is His very being. Love is not an attribute, but the very essence of His nature, the center around which all His glorious attributes revolve. It is because He is love that He is the Father, and that there is a Son. Love needs an object to give itself away to, in whom it can lose itself, with whom it can make itself one. Because God is love, there must be a Father and a Son. The love of the Father to the Son is that divine passion that finds delight in the Son and declares of Him, "This is My beloved Son, in whom I am well-pleased" (Matthew 3:17). Divine love is a burning fire; in all its intensity and infinity it has but one object and one joy: the only begotten Son. When we gather together all the attributes of God—His infinity, His perfection, His immensity, His majesty, His omnipotence—and consider them as only rays of the glory of His love, we still fail to grasp what that love must be. It is a love that passes knowledge.

And yet this love of God to His Son must serve as the glass in which you are to learn how Jesus loves you. As one of His redeemed ones you are His delight, and all His desire is to you, with the longing of a love that is stronger than death, and which many waters cannot quench. His heart yearns for you, seeking your fellowship and your love. If it were needed, He would die again to possess you. As the Father loved the Son, and could not live without Him—this is how Jesus loves you. His life is bound up in yours; you are to Him inexpressibly more indispensable and precious than you can ever know. You are one with Him. "As the Father loved me, I also have loved you." What love!

It is an eternal love. From before the foundation of the world—God's Word teaches us this—the purpose had been formed that Christ should be the head of His church, that He should have a body in which His glory could be shown. In that eternity He loved and longed for those who had been given to Him by the Father; and when He came and told His disciples that He loved them, it was not with a love of earth and of time, but with the love of eternity. And it is with that same infinite love that His eye still rests upon each of us here seeking to abide in Him. In each expression of that love there is the very power of eternity. "I have loved you with an everlasting love" (Jeremiah 31:3).

It is also a perfect love. It gives all, and holds nothing back. "The Father loves the Son, and has given all things into His hand" (John 3:35). And in the same way, Jesus loves His own; all He has is theirs. When it was needed, He sacrificed His throne and crown for you; He did not count His own life and blood too dear to give for you. His righteousness, His Spirit, His glory, even His throne—all are yours. This love holds nothing back, but, in a manner that no human mind can grasp, makes you one with itself. O wondrous love! For Christ to love us even as the Father loved Him, and to offer us this love as our everyday dwelling is truly amazing.

His is a gentle and most tender love. As we think of the love of the Father to the Son, we see in the Son everything so infinitely worthy of that love. But when we think of Christ's love to us, there is nothing but sin and unworthiness to meet the eye. And the question inevitably comes: How can that love within the heart of God with all His perfections be compared to the love that rests on sinners? Can it indeed be the same love? Praise be to God, we know it is so. The nature of love is always the same, however different the objects of it might be. Christ knows of no other law of love but that with which His Father loved Him. Our sinfulness only serves to call out more distinctly the beauty of His love, such love as could not be seen even in heaven. With tender compassion He bows to our weakness, with inconceivable patience He bears with our slowness, with the gentlest loving-kindness He meets our fears and our failures. It is the love of the Father to the Son, beautified and glorified in its condescension, in its exquisite adaptation to our needs.

It is an unchangeable love. "Having loved His own who were in the world, He loved them to the end" (John 13:1). "The mountains shall depart and the hills be removed, but My kindness shall not depart from you" (Isaiah 54:10). The promise with which love begins its work in the soul is this: "I will not leave you until I have done what I have spoken to you" (Genesis 28:15). And just as our wretchedness was what first drew it to us, so our sin, which so often grieves His love, and which may cause us to fear and doubt, is only a new motive for love to hold us even more tightly. And why is this so? We can give no other reason than this: "As the Father loved me, I also have loved you."

And now we need to look at the implications of this tremendous love. For God's love suggests the *motive*, the *measure*, and the *means* by which we can yield ourselves to wholly abide in Him.

This love definitely supplies a motive. Only look and see how this love stands, pleads, and prays. Gaze on the divine form, the eternal glory, the heavenly beauty, and the tenderly pleading gentleness of Crucified Love as it stretches out its pierced hands and asks, "Will you not abide with Me? Will you not come and abide in Me?" It points you up to the eternity of love from which it came to seek you. It points you to the Cross and all it has carried to prove the reality of its affection, and to win you for itself. It reminds you of all it has promised to do for you, if you will only yield yourself unreservedly into its arms. It asks you if, so far as you have come to dwell with it and taste its blessing, it has done well by you. And with a divine authority, mingled with such inexpressible tenderness that one might almost think he heard the tone of reproach in it, it says, "Soul, as the Father has loved me, I also have loved you: continue in My love." Surely there can be but one answer to such pleading: Lord Jesus Christ, here I am! From now on your love will be the only home of my soul; in your love alone will I abide.

His love is not only the motive but also the measure of our surrender to abide in it. Love gives all, but also asks all. It does so not because it begrudges us what has been given, but because without this it cannot get possession of us to fill us with itself. In the love of the Father and the Son, it was so. In the love of Jesus to us, it was so. In our entering into His love to abide there, it must be so; our surrender to it must have no other measure than its surrender to us. If only we could understand how the love that calls us has infinite riches and fullness of joy for us, and that what we give up for its sake will be rewarded a hundredfold in this life! It is love with height and depth and length and breadth that passes knowledge (Ephesians 3:18–19)! If we could grasp even a part of its knowledge, all thought of sacrifice or surrender would pass away, and our souls would be filled with wonder at the unspeakable privilege of being loved with such love, of being allowed to come and abide in it forever.

And if doubt again suggests the question: But is it possible that I can always abide in His love? Then listen how such love itself supplies the only means for abiding in Him: It is faith in that love that will enable us to abide in it. If this love is so divine, such an intense and burning passion, then surely I can depend on it to keep me in its grasp. Surely all my unworthiness and frailty can be no hindrance to such love. If this love, being divine, has infinite power at its command, I surely have a right to trust that it is stronger than my weakness and that with its almighty arm it will hold me in its arms and allow me to wander no more. I see how this is the one thing my God requires of me. Treating me as a reasonable being endowed with the wondrous power of willing and choosing, He cannot force all this blessing on me, but waits until I give the willing consent of my heart. And the token of this consent He has, in His great kindness, ordered faith to be—that faith by which utter sinfulness casts itself into the arms of love to be saved, and utter weakness entrusts itself to be kept and made strong. What Infinite Love! The love with which the Father loved the Son! Love with which the Son loves us!

I can trust you; I do trust you. O keep me abiding in you, my loving Savior.

Abide As Christ Abides in the Father

*As the Father loved Me, I also have loved you; continue in My
love . . . you will abide in My love, just as I . . . abide
in my Father's love.*

John 15:9–10

Christ taught His disciples that to abide in Him was to abide in
His love. The hour of His suffering is near, and He cannot
speak much more to them. No doubt they have many questions
to ask Him about His love and their abiding in Him. He antic-
ipates and meets their wishes, and gives them His *own life* as
the best expression of His command. As example and rule for
abiding in His love, they only have to look to His abiding in
the Father's love. In the light of His union with the Father, their
union with Him will become clear. *His life in the Father is the
law of their life in Him.*

The thought is so high that we can hardly take it in, and yet
it is so clearly revealed that we dare not neglect it. Do we not
read in John 6:57, "As I live because of the Father, *even so* he

255

who feeds on Me will live because of me"? And the Savior prays so distinctly (John 17:22–23), "that they may be one *just as* We are one: I in them, and You in Me." The blessed union of Christ with the Father and His life in Him is the only rule of our thoughts and expectations in regard to living and abiding in Him.

Think first of *the origin* of that life of Christ in the Father. They were *one*—one in life and one in love. In this, His abiding in the Father had its root. Though dwelling here on earth, He knew that He was one with the Father, that the Father's life was in Him, and His love on Him. Without this knowledge, abiding in the Father and His love would have been utterly impossible for Christ. In the same way it is only in this knowledge that you can abide in Christ and His love. Know that you are one with Him—one in the unity of nature. By His birth He became man and took on your nature so that He might be one with you. By your new birth you become one with Him and are made partaker of His divine nature. The link that binds you to Him is as real and close as the one that bound Him to the Father—the link of a divine life. Your claim on Him is as sure as was His on the Father. Your union with Him is just as close.

And as it is the union of a divine life, it is one of an infinite love. In His life of humiliation on earth He tasted the blessing and strength of knowing himself to be the object of an infinite love, and He dwelt in it all through His days; from His own example He invites you to learn that in this the secret of your rest and joy can be found. You are one with Him: Yield yourself now to be loved by Him; let your eyes and heart open up to the love that shines and presses in on you on every side. Abide in His love.

Think also of *the form* of that abiding in the Father and His love that is to be the law of your life: "I have kept My Father's commandments and abide in His love" (John 15:10). His was a life of subjection and dependence and yet was most blessed. To our proud, self-seeking nature the thought of dependence and subjection suggests the idea of humiliation and servitude; but in the life of love lived by the Son of God, and to which He invites us, they are the secret to enjoying great blessing. The Son is not afraid of losing anything by giving up all to the Father, for He knows that the Father loves Him and can have no interest apart from that of the beloved Son. He knows that as complete as the dependence on His part so is the sharing on the part of the Father of all He possesses. Therefore, when He said, "The Son can do nothing of Himself, but what He sees the Father do"; He adds at once, "for whatever He (the Father) does, the Son also does in like manner. For the Father loves the Son, and shows Him all things that He Himself does" (John 5:19–20).

The believer who studies this life of Christ as the pattern and the promise of what his life may be learns to understand how "Without Me you can do nothing" (John 15:5) is the forerunner of "I can do all things through Christ who strengthens me" (Philippians 4:13). We learn to glory in weaknesses, to delight in hardships and difficulties for Christ's sake, for "when I am weak, then I am strong" (2 Corinthians 12:10). The apostle Paul rises above the ordinary tone in which so many Christians speak of their weakness. They are seemingly content to merely tolerate their state, while Paul sees much more; he has learned from Christ that in the life of divine love the emptying of self and the sacrifice of our will is the surest way to have all we could wish or want. Dependence, subjection, and self-sacrifice are for the Christian, as for Christ, the blessed path of life. Just as Christ lived through and in the Father, even so the believer lives through and in Christ.

Think of the *glory* of this life of Christ in the Father's love. Because He gave himself wholly to the Father's will and glory, the Father crowned Him with glory and honor. He acknowledged Him as His only representative; He made Him partaker of His power and authority; He exalted Him to share His throne as God. And even so will it be with him who abides in Christ's love. If Christ finds us willing to trust ourselves and our interests to His love, if in that trust we give up all care for our own will and honor, if we make it our glory to exercise and confess absolute dependence on Him in all things, if we are content to have no life but in Him, *He will do for us what the Father did for Him.* He will bestow His glory on us: As the name of our Lord Jesus Christ is glorified in us, we are glorified in Him (see 2 Thessalonians 1:12).

He acknowledges us as His true and worthy representatives; He entrusts us with His power; He admits us to His counsels as He allows our intercession to influence His rule of His church and the world; He makes us the vehicles of His authority and His influence over humankind. His Spirit knows no other dwelling than this, and seeks no other instruments for His divine work. What a blessed life of love awaits the soul that abides in Christ's love, even as He abides in the Father's!

Take and study Jesus' relationship to the Father as a pledge of what your own abiding can become. As blessed, as mighty, as glorious as was His life in the Father, so yours can be in Him! Let this truth, accepted under the teaching of the Spirit by faith, remove every element of fear that regards abiding in Christ a burden. In the light of His life in the Father, let it be from now on a blessed rest in union with Him, an overflowing fountain of joy and strength. To abide in His love—His mighty, saving, keeping, satisfying love, even as He did in the Father's love—can never be a work we have to perform; it must be with us as it was with Him, the result of the spontaneous outflow of a life from within.

All we need to do is to take time to study the divine image of this life of love set before us in Christ. We need to be quiet before God, gazing upon Christ's life in the Father until the light from heaven falls on it, and we hear the voice of our Beloved whispering gently to us the teaching He gave to the disciples. Soul, be still and listen; let every thought be hushed until the word has entered your heart: "Child, I love you, just as the Father loved Me. Abide in My love, even as I abide in the Father's love. Your life on earth in Me is to be the perfect counterpart of mine in the Father."

And if the thought comes: Surely this is too high for me; can it really be true? You must remember that the greatness of the privilege is justified by the greatness of the object He has in view. *Christ was the revelation of the Father on earth.* He could only be this because there was the most perfect unity, the most complete communication of all that the Father had to the Son. He could be His revelation because the Father loved Him, and He lived in that love. *Believers are the revelation of Christ on earth.* They can only be this when there is perfect unity; by this unity the world can know that He loves them. They are His representatives, His revelation to the world that Christ loves them with the infinite love that gives itself and all it has.

Lord, show us your love. Help us know with all the saints the love that passes knowledge. Lord, show us in your own blessed life what it is to abide in your love. And the sight will so win us that it will be impossible for us to seek, even for one single hour, any other life than the life of abiding in your magnificent love.

Obeying His Commandments

If you keep My commandments, you will abide in My love, just as I have kept My Father's commandments and abide in His love.

John 15:10

How clearly we are taught here the place that good works are to occupy in the life of the believer! Christ as the beloved Son was in the Father's love. He kept His commandments, and so *abode* in the Father's love. So the believer, without works, receives Christ and is in Him; he keeps the commandments and so *abides* in Christ's love. When the sinner, in coming to Christ, seeks to prepare himself by works, the voice of the Gospel sounds, "Not of works." Once in Christ, however, lest the flesh should abuse the word "Not of works," the Gospel lifts its voice as loudly to say, "Created in Christ Jesus *for good works*" (Ephesians 2:9–10). To the sinner out of Christ, works may be his greatest hindrance, keeping him from union with the Savior. To the believer in Christ, works are his strength and blessing, for

261

by them faith is made perfect (James 2:22), the union with Christ is cemented, and the soul is established and more deeply rooted in the love of God. "If anyone loves Me, he will keep My word; and My Father will love him" (John 14:23). "If you keep My commandments, you will abide in My love."

The connection between keeping the commandments and abiding in Christ's love is easy to understand. Our union with Jesus Christ is not something of the intellect or sentiment, but a real, vital union in heart and life. The Holy Spirit breathes the holy life of Jesus, with His feelings and disposition, into us. The believer's calling is to think, feel, and will what Jesus thought, felt, and willed. Such a believer desires to be a partaker not only of the grace but also of the holiness of his Lord; or rather, he sees that holiness is the chief beauty of grace. To live the life of Christ means to him to be delivered from the life of self; the will of Christ is to him the only path of liberty from the slavery of his own self-will.

To the casual believer there is a great difference between the promises and the commands of Scripture. The former he counts his comfort and his food; but to the one who is really seeking to abide in Christ's love, the commands become no less precious. As much as the promises, they are the revelation of divine love, serving as guides into a deeper experience of the divine life; they are blessed helpers in the path to a closer union with the Lord. The harmony of our will with His will is one of the chief elements of our fellowship with Him. The will is the central faculty in the Divine as well as in human beings. The will of God is the power that rules the moral as well as the natural world.

How could there be fellowship with Him without delight in

His will? Of course, if salvation is to the sinner nothing but personal safety, then he can be careless or afraid of doing God's will. But as soon as Scripture and the Holy Spirit reveal to him the true meaning of salvation—the restoration to communion with God and conformity to Him—he realizes that there is no law more natural or more beautiful than this: Keeping Christ's commandments is the way to abide in Christ's love. His inmost soul approves when he hears his beloved Lord make the larger measure of the Spirit, with the manifestation of the Father and the Son in the believer, entirely dependent upon the keeping of His commandments (John 14:15–16, 21, 23).

There is another thing that opens to the sinner a deeper insight and secures a still more cordial acceptance of this truth. It is this: In no other way did Christ himself abide in the Father's love. In the life that Christ led on earth, obedience was a solemn reality. The dark and awful power that led humankind to revolt from God tempted Him too. To Him, as with all men, its offers of self-gratification were not matters of indifference; to refuse them, He had to fast and pray. He suffered, being tempted. He spoke very distinctly of *not* seeking to do His own will. This was a surrender He had to make continually. He made the keeping of the Father's commandments the distinct object of His life, and so did He abide in His love. He plainly tells us, "I do nothing of Myself; but as My Father has taught Me, I speak these things. And He who sent Me is with Me. The Father has not left Me alone, for I always do those things that please Him" (John 8:28–29). In this way He opened to us the only path to a blessed life on earth in the love of heaven; and when, as from our vine, His Spirit flows in the branches, keeping His commands is a sure sign of the life He inspires.

Believer, if you would abide in Jesus, be very careful to keep His commandments. Keep them in the love of your heart. Do not be content to have them in the Bible for reference, but have them transferred to the fleshy tables of your heart by careful study, by meditation and prayer, by a loving acceptance, and by the Spirit's teaching. Do not be content with the knowledge of some of the commands, those most commonly received among Christians, while others remain unknown and neglected. Surely, with your New Covenant privileges, you would not want to be behind the Old Testament saints who spoke so fervently: "Therefore *all* your precepts concerning *all* things I consider to be right" (Psalm 119:128). Be assured that there is still much of your Lord's will that you do not yet understand.

Make Paul's prayer for the Colossians yours, praying it for yourself and all believers: "that you may be filled with the knowledge of His will in all wisdom and spiritual understanding" (Colossians 1:9); and likewise, "labor fervently in prayers" as did wrestling Epaphras, "that you may stand perfect and complete in all the will of God" (Colossians 4:12). Remember that this is one of the great elements of spiritual growth—a deeper insight into the will of God concerning you. Do not imagine that entire consecration is the end; it is only the beginning of the truly holy life!

See how Paul, after having taught believers to lay themselves upon the altar as whole and holy burnt offerings to their God (Romans 12:1), immediately proceeds in verse 2 to tell them that true altar-life is becoming "transformed by the renewing of your mind, that you may prove what is that good and acceptable and perfect will of God." The progressive renewal of the Holy Spirit leads to growing like-mindedness to Christ; then comes a delicate power of spiritual perception—a holy instinct—by which the soul knows to recognize the meaning and the application of the Lord's commands to daily life in a way that remains hidden to the ordinary Christian. Keep the commandments of Christ dwelling richly within you; hide them within your heart, and you will taste the blessing of the man whose "delight is in the law of the Lord, and in His law he meditates day and night" (Psalm 1:2). Love will assimilate the commands into your inmost being as food from heaven. They will no longer come to you as a law standing outside and against you, but as the living power that has transformed your will into perfect harmony with all your Lord requires.

Keep them through strict obedience in your life, making it your solemn vow not to tolerate even a single sin. "I have sworn and confirmed that I will keep Your righteous judgments" (Psalm 119:106). Labor earnestly in prayer so that you may stand perfect and complete in all the will of God. Ask for the discovery of every secret sin—anything that is not in perfect harmony with the will of God. Walk faithfully and tenderly in the light you have, and yield yourself in an unreserved surrender to obey all that the Lord has spoken. When Israel took that vow, "All that the Lord has spoken we will do" (Exodus 19:8), all too soon they broke it. But the new covenant gives us the grace to make the vow and to keep it too (see Jeremiah 31). Be careful about disobedience even in little things. Disobedience dulls the conscience, darkens the soul, and deadens our spiritual energies. Therefore, keep the commandments of Christ with implicit obedience; be a soldier that asks for nothing but the orders of the commander.

And if even for a moment the commandments appear

grievous, just remember whose they are. They are the commandments of Him who loves you. They are all love; they come from His love and they lead to His love. Each new surrender to keep the commandments, each new sacrifice in keeping them, leads to deeper union with the will, the spirit, and the love of the Savior. The double reward promised in Scripture will be yours—a fuller entrance into the mystery of His love, a greater conformity to His own blessed life. And you will learn to prize these words as among your choicest treasures: "If you keep My commandments, you will abide in My love, just as I have kept My Father's commandments and abide in His love."

That Your Joy May
Be Full

*These things I have spoken to you that My joy may remain in
you, and that your joy may be full.*

John 15:11

Abiding fully in Christ is a life of exquisite and overflowing
happiness. As Christ gets more complete possession of the soul,
it enters into the joy of its Lord. His own joy, the joy of heaven,
becomes its own in full measure, as an ever-abiding portion.
Just as joy on earth is everywhere connected with the vine and
its fruit, so joy is an essential characteristic of the life of the
believer who fully abides in Christ, the Heavenly Vine.

We all know the value of joy. It alone is the proof that what
we have really satisfies the heart. As long as duty, or self-
interest, or other motives influence me, no one can know what
the object of my pursuit or possession is really worth to me.
But when it gives me joy, and they see me delight in it, they
know that to me at least it is a treasure. So there is nothing
quite so attractive as joy, no preaching so persuasive as the sight

267

of hearts made glad. This makes gladness such a strong element in Christian character. There is no proof of the reality of God's love and the blessing He bestows, which people so quickly feel the strength of, as when the joy of God overcomes all the trials of life. And for the Christian's own welfare, joy is just as indispensable; the joy of the Lord is his strength (see Nehemiah 8:10), and confidence, courage, and patience find their inspiration in joy. With a heart full of joy no work can make us weary and no burden can depress us; God himself is our strength and song.

Let us hear what the Savior says about the joy of abiding in Him. He promises us *His own joy*: "My joy." As the whole parable refers to the life His disciples should have in Him after He ascended to heaven, the joy is that of His resurrection life. This is clear from other words of His in John 16:22: "I will see you again and your heart will rejoice, and your joy no one will take from you." It was only with the Resurrection and its glory that the power of the never-changing life began, and only in it that the never-ceasing joy could arise. With it was fulfilled the word: "Therefore God, even Your God, has anointed You with the oil of gladness more than Your companions" (Hebrews 1:9). The day of His crowning was the day of the gladness of His heart. That joy of His was the joy of a work fully and forever completed, the joy of the Father's presence regained, and the joy of souls redeemed. These are the elements of His joy, and abiding in Him makes us partakers of them.

The believer shares so fully Christ's victory and His perfect redemption that his faith can without ceasing sing the conqueror's song: "Thanks be to God who always leads us in triumph in Christ" (2 Corinthians 2:14). As the fruit of this, there is the joy of undisturbed dwelling in the light of the Father's love. And then, with this joy in the love of the Father, as a love received, we experience the joy of loving souls, as love going forth and rejoicing over the lost. Whether we look backward and see the work He has done, or upward and see the reward He has in the Father's love that passes knowledge, or forward in anticipation of continual joy experienced as sinners are brought home, His joy is ours. With our feet on Calvary, our eyes on the Father's face, and our hands helping sinners home, we have His joy as our own.

And then He speaks of this joy as *abiding*—a joy that is never to cease or be interrupted for a moment: "That My joy may remain in you." "Your joy no one will take from you." This is what many Christians cannot understand. Their view of the Christian life is that it is a succession of changes, sometimes joy and sometimes sorrow. And they appeal to the experiences of a man like the apostle Paul as proof of how much there may be of weeping, sorrow, and suffering. They have not noticed how Paul gives the strongest evidence to this unceasing joy. He understood the paradox of the Christian life as the combination at one and the same moment of all the bitterness of earth and all the joy of heaven.

He writes, "As sorrowful, yet *always rejoicing*" (2 Corinthians 6:10): These precious words teach us how the joy of Christ can overrule the sorrow of the world, can make us sing even while we weep, and can maintain in the heart, even when cast down by disappointment or difficulties, a deep consciousness of a joy that is unspeakable and full of glory (1 Peter 1:8). There is only one condition: "*I will see you again* and your heart will rejoice, and your joy no one will take from you." The presence of Jesus, distinctly manifested, cannot help but give joy. How can the soul not rejoice and be glad when it is abiding in Him consciously? Even when weeping for the sins and the souls of others, there is a fountain of gladness that springs up in us when we recognize His power and love to save.

And He wants His own joy abiding in us to be *full*. Jesus spoke three times of this full joy on His last night with the disciples. Once here in the parable of the Vine: "*These things I have spoken* to you that your joy may be *full*" (John 15:11); and every deeper insight into the wonderful blessing of being the branch of such a Vine confirms His Word. Then He connects it in John 16:24 with our prayers being answered: "*Ask and you will receive*, that your joy may be *full*." To the spiritual mind, answered prayer is not only a means of obtaining certain blessings, but something infinitely higher. It is a token of our fellowship with the Father and the Son in heaven, of their delight in us, and our having been admitted and having a voice in that wonderful interchange of love in which the Father and the Son hold counsel and decide the daily guidance of the children on earth.

To a soul abiding in Christ, who longs for manifestations of His love and knows to take an answer to prayer in its true spiritual value—as a response from the throne to all its utterances of love and trust—the joy it brings is truly beyond words. The word of Jesus is found true: "Ask and you will receive, that your joy may be full." And then the Savior says, in His high-priestly prayer to the Father (John 17:13), "*These things I speak . . .* that they may have My joy *fulfilled* in themselves." It is the sight of the great High Priest entering the Father's presence for us, ever living to pray and carry on His blessed work in the power of an endless life (see Hebrews 7:16) that removes every possible cause of fear or doubt and gives us the assurance and experience of a perfect salvation.

Let the believer who seeks, according to the teaching of John 15, to possess the full joy of abiding in Christ, and according to John 16, the full joy of prevailing prayer, press forward to John 17. Let him listen there to those amazing words of intercession spoken on his behalf, asking that his joy might be full. Let him, as he listens to those words, learn about the love that pleads even now for him in heaven without ceasing; let him take in the glorious objectives being pleaded for, and realize that by His all-prevailing pleading they are being accomplished. If the believer can do these things, Christ's joy will be fulfilled in him.

Christ's own joy, abiding joy, fullness of joy—this is the reward of the believer who abides in Christ. Why is it that this joy has so little power to attract? The reason, simply stated, is this: People, yes, even God's children, do not believe in it. Instead of looking upon abiding in Christ as the happiest life that ever can be led, it is regarded as a life of self-denial and of sadness. They forget that any self-denial and the sadness are the result of *not* abiding. To those who finally yield themselves unreservedly to abide in Christ for a bright and blessed life, their faith comes true—the joy of the Lord is theirs. The difficulties all arise from our refusal to surrender to full abiding.

Child of God, who seeks to abide in Christ, remember what the Lord says. At the close of the parable of the Vine He adds these precious words: "*These things* I have spoken to you that My joy may remain in you, and that your joy may be full." Claim the joy as part of the branch-life—not the first or main part, but the blessed proof of the sufficiency of Christ to satisfy every need of the soul. Be happy. Cultivate gladness. If there are times when it comes by itself, and the heart feels the unutterable joy of the Savior's presence, praise God for it and seek to maintain it. If at other times feelings are dull, and the experience of joy is not what you would wish, still praise God *for the life of unutterable blessing to which you have been redeemed.* In this, too, the word holds good: "According to your faith let it be to you" (Matthew 9:29). As you claim all the other gifts in Jesus, be sure to claim this one too—not for your own sake, but for His and the Father's glory. "*My joy* in you"; "that *My joy* may *remain* in you"; "*My joy fulfilled* in themselves"—these are Jesus' own words. It is impossible to take Him wholly and heartily, and not to get His joy too. Therefore, "Rejoice in the Lord always. Again I will say, rejoice!" (Philippians 4:4).

Showing Love to Fellow Believers

This is My commandment, that you love one another as I have loved you.

John 15:12

"As the Father loved me, I also have loved you; continue in My love" (John 15:9). God became man; divine love began to run in the channel of a human heart; it became the love of man to man. The love that fills heaven and eternity is to be seen daily here in the life of earth and of time.

"This is My commandment," the Savior says, "That you love one another as I have loved you." He sometimes spoke of commandments, but love, which is the fulfilling of the law, is the all-including one and therefore is called His commandment—the new commandment. It is to be the great evidence of the reality of the new covenant, of the power of the new life revealed in Jesus Christ. It is to be the one convincing and indisputable token of discipleship: "*By this all will know* that you are My disciples" (John 13:35); "That they also may be one

273

in Us, *that the world may believe*" (John 17:21); "That they may be made perfect in one, and *that the world may know* that You have sent Me, and have loved them as You have loved me" (v. 23). To the believer seeking perfect fellowship with Christ, the keeping of this commandment is both the blessed proof that he is abiding in Him and the path to a fuller, more perfect union with Him.

Let us try to understand how this is so. We know that God is love and that Christ came to reveal this, not as a doctrine but as a life. His life, in its wonderful self-abasement and self-sacrifice, was, above everything, the embodiment of divine love, which showed humankind in a way they could understand, how God loves. In His love to the unworthy and the ungrateful, in humbling himself to walk among men as a servant, in giving himself up to death, He lived and acted out the life of divine love that was in the heart of God. He lived and died to show us the love of the Father.

And now, just as Christ was to show forth God's love, believers are to show forth to the world the love of Christ. *They are to prove to others that Christ loves them, and in loving fills them with a love that is not of earth. They, by living and by loving just as He did,* are to be perpetual witnesses to the love that gave itself to die. Christ loved in such a way that even the Jews cried out at Bethany, "See how He loved him!" (John 11:36). Christians are to live so that men are compelled to say, "See how these Christians love one another." In their daily interactions with one another, Christians are "made a spectacle to the world, both to angels and to men" (1 Corinthians 4:9); and in the Christlikeness of their love to one another they are to prove what manner of spirit they are. In all the diversity of character, creed, language, or station in life, Christians are to prove that love has made them members of one body and of one another, and has taught them each to forget and to sacrifice self for the sake of the other. Their life of love is the primary evidence of Christianity, the proof to the world that God sent Christ and that He has shed abroad in them the same love with which He loved Him. Of all the evidences of Christianity, this is the most powerful and the most convincing.

This love of Christ's disciples to one another occupies a central position between their love for God and their love for their fellowmen. It is the test of their love to God, whom they cannot see. The love to one unseen may so easily be a mere sentiment, or even an imagination; but in the face-to-face dealings with God's children, love to God is really called into practice and shows itself in deeds that the Father accepts as done to himself. This is the only way that love for God can be proved to be true. Love to fellow believers is the flower and fruit of the root, unseen in the heart, of love to God. And this fruit again becomes the seed of love to all humankind; interaction with one another is the school in which believers are trained and strengthened to love their fellowmen who are as yet outside of Christ, not simply with cordiality that rests on points of agreement, but with the holy love that takes hold of the most unworthy, and bears with the most disagreeable for Jesus' sake. It is love to one another as disciples that is brought to the forefront as the link between love to God alone and to people in general.

In Christ's interaction with His disciples, this brotherly love finds the law of its conduct. As we study His forgiveness toward His friends—with the seventy times seven (Matthew 18:22) as its only measure—and look to His unwearied patience and His infinite humility, seeing the meekness and lowliness with which He seeks to win for himself a place as their servant who is wholly devoted to their interests, we can accept with gladness His command, "You should do as I have done" (John 13:15). Following His example, each lives not for himself but for the other. The law of kindness is on the tongue, for love has vowed that no unkind word will ever cross its lips. It not only refuses to speak but also not even to hear or think evil; the name and character of fellow Christians becomes even more important to protect than our own. My own good name I may leave to the Father; but my brother's or sister's my Father has entrusted to me. In gentleness and loving-kindness, in courtesy and generosity, in self-sacrifice and benevolence, in its life of blessing and of beauty, divine love, which has been shed abroad in the believer's heart (Romans 5:5), should shine out as it was displayed in the life of Jesus.

What is your response to such a glorious calling—to love like Christ? Does your heart leap at the thought of the unspeakable privilege of showing forth the likeness of eternal love? Or do you instead sigh at the thought of the inaccessible height of perfection to which you are called to climb? Christian, do not sigh at what is in fact the highest token of the Father's love, that He has called us to be like Christ in our love, just as He was like the Father in His love. Understand that the One who gave the command to abide in Him, gave the assurance that we only have to abide in Him to be able to love like Him. Accept the command as a new motive for fully abiding in Christ.

Regard abiding in Him more than ever as an abiding in His love. Rooted and grounded daily in a love that passes knowledge, you receive of its fullness and learn to love. With Christ abiding in you, the Holy Spirit pours out the love of God in your heart (Romans 5:5), and you love your fellow believers, even the most trying and unlovable, with a love that is not your own, but the love of Christ in you. And the command for you to love them is changed from a burden into a joy, if you can keep it linked, as Jesus linked it, to the command about His love for you: "Abide in my love; love one another as I have loved you" (John 15:10, 12).

"This is my commandment, that you love one another as I have loved you." This is some of the "much fruit" that Jesus promised we will bear—indeed, a cluster of the grapes of Eshcol, with which we can prove to others that the land of promise is indeed a good land (Deuteronomy 1:24–25). Let us try in all simplicity and honesty to translate the language of high faith and heavenly enthusiasm into the plain prose of daily conduct, so that all can understand it. Let our temperament be under the control of the love of Jesus: *He can* make us gentle and patient. Let the vow that not an unkind word about others shall ever be heard from our lips be laid trustingly at His feet. Let the gentleness that refuses to take offense, that is always ready to excuse, and to think and hope the best, mark our behavior with everyone.

Let the love that seeks not its own (1 Corinthians 13:5), but is always ready to wash others' feet (John 13), or even to give its life for them (John 15:13), be our aim as we abide in Jesus. Let our life be one of self-sacrifice, always studying the welfare of others, finding our highest joy in blessing others. And let us, in studying the divine art of doing good, yield ourselves as obedient learners to the guidance of the Holy Spirit. By His grace, the most commonplace life can be transformed with the brightness of heavenly beauty, as the infinite love of the divine nature shines out through our frail humanity.

"Abide in my love, and love as I have loved." Is this possible? Of course! We have the new holy nature, which grows ever stronger as it abides in Christ the Vine, and it can love as He did. Every discovery of evil in our old nature, every longing desire to obey the command of our Lord, every experience of the power and the blessing of loving with Jesus' love will urge us to accept with fresh faith our Lord's words: "Abide in Me, and I in you"; "Continue in My love."

That You Might Not Sin

In Him there is no sin. Whoever abides in Him does not sin.

1 John 3:5–6

"You know," the apostle John said in verse 5, "that He was manifested to take away our sins," and thereby indicated salvation from sin as the great object for which the Son was made man. The connection shows clearly that the "taking away" has reference not only to the Atonement and freedom from guilt but also to deliverance from the power of sin, so that the believer no longer practices it. It is Christ's personal holiness that constitutes His power to accomplish this purpose. He admits sinners into life-union with himself; the result is that their life becomes like His. "*In Him* there is no sin. Whoever abides *in Him* does not sin." As long as the believer abides, and as far as he abides, he does not sin. Our holiness of life has its roots in the personal holiness of Jesus. "If the root is holy, so (also) are the branches" (Romans 11:16).

The question at once arises: How is this consistent with what the Bible teaches about the continuing corruption of our human nature, or with what John tells us in 1 John 1:8, 10—

that if we say we have no sin, or have not sinned, we deceive ourselves and call God a liar? It is this passage that, if we look at it carefully, will teach us to understand our current text correctly. Note the difference in the two statements (v. 8), "If we say that *we have no sin*," and (v. 10), "If we say that *we have not sinned.*" The two expressions cannot be equivalent; the second would then be merely a repetition of the first. *Having sin* in verse 8 is not the same as *practicing sin* in verse 10. *Having sin* means having a sinful nature.

The holiest believer must each moment confess that he has sin within him—namely, the flesh, in which dwells "no good thing" (Romans 7:18). Sinning or *practicing sin* is something very different: It is yielding to the indwelling sinful nature and falling into actual transgression. And so we have two admissions that every true believer must make. The one is that he still has sin within him (v. 8); the second is that sin has in former times broken out into sinful actions (v. 10).

No believer can make either statement: "I have no sin in me," or "I have in time past never sinned." If we say we have no sin at present, or that we have not sinned in the past, we deceive ourselves. But although we *have sin*, we need not confess that we are presently *practicing sin*; the confession of actual sinning refers to the past. It may, as appears from 1 John 2:2, be in the present also, but it is not *expected* to be. And so we see how the deepest confession of sin in the past (as Paul acknowledged his having been a persecutor of the church), and the deepest consciousness of still having a vile and corrupt nature in the present may coexist with humble but joyful praise to Him who keeps us from stumbling as we abide in Him.

But how is it possible that a believer, having sin in him—

sin of such intense vitality, and such terrible power as we know the flesh to have—can yet *not be practicing sin*? The answer is: "In Him there is no sin. He that abides in Him does not sin." When abiding in Christ becomes close and unbroken, so that the soul lives from moment to moment in perfect union with the Lord his keeper, He does, indeed, keep down the power of the old nature to such an extent that it does not regain dominion over him. We have seen that there are degrees in abiding. With most Christians the abiding is so weak and intermittent that sin continually obtains supremacy and brings the soul into subjection. The divine promise given to faith is: "Sin shall not have dominion over you" (Romans 6:14). But accompanying the promise is the command: "Do not let sin reign in your mortal body" (Romans 6:12).

The believer who claims the promise in full faith has the power to obey the command, and sin is kept from overpowering him. Ignorance of the promise, unbelief, or carelessness, however, opens the door for sin to reign. And so the life of many believers is a course of continual stumbling and sinning. But when a believer seeks full admission into a life of continual, permanent abiding in Jesus, the Sinless One, then the life of Christ can keep him from actual transgression. "In Him there is no sin. Whoever abides in Him does not sin." Jesus does save such a believer from his sin—not by the removal of his sinful nature, but by keeping him from yielding to it.

I have read of a young lion that could only be awed or kept down by the eye of his keeper. With the keeper anyone could come near the lion, and he would crouch—his savage nature still unchanged, thirsting for blood—trembling at the keeper's feet. You might even put your foot on his neck so long as the keeper was with you. But to approach him without the keeper would be instant death. In the same way, we can *have sin* and yet *not practice sin.* The evil nature, the flesh, is unchanged in its rebellion against God, but the abiding presence of Jesus keeps it under control. In faith the believer can entrust himself to the keeping, the indwelling, of the Son of God; as he abides in Him, he can count on Jesus to be there for him. It is union and fellowship with the Sinless One that is the secret of a holy life: "In Him there is no sin. Whoever abides in Him does not sin."

And now another question arises: Admitting that complete abiding in the Sinless One will keep us from sinning, is such abiding possible? May we hope to be able to so abide in Christ, even for one day, that we may be kept from actual transgressions? If the question is fairly stated and considered it will suggest its own answer. When Christ commanded us to abide in Him, and promised us such rich fruit-bearing to the glory of the Father, and such mighty power in our intercession, could He mean anything but the healthy, vigorous, complete union of the branch with the Vine? When He promised that as we abide in Him He would abide in us, could He mean anything else but that His dwelling in us would be a reality of divine power and love? Is not this way of saving from sin most glorifying to Him?

By keeping us on a daily basis humble and helpless in our consciousness of our evil nature, watchful and active in the knowledge of its terrible power, dependent and trustful in the remembrance that only His presence can keep the lion down—this gives all glory to Him and not to ourselves. O let us believe that when Jesus said, "Abide in Me, and I in you," He meant that, while we were not to be freed from the world and its tribulation, from the sinful nature and its temptations, we were at least to have this blessing fully secured to us—the grace to abide wholly, only, in our Lord. Abiding in Jesus makes it possible to keep from actual sinning; and Jesus himself makes it possible to abide in Him.

Dear Christian, I am not surprised if you find the promise of the text almost too high. Do not, however, let your attention be diverted by the question as to whether it would be possible to be kept for your whole life, or for so many years, without sinning. Faith only has to deal with the present moment. Ask this: Can Jesus at the present moment, as I abide in Him, keep me from those actual sinful acts that have been the stain and weariness of my daily life? You must say, "Surely He can." Take Him then at this present moment and say, "Jesus keeps me now; Jesus saves me now." Yield yourself to Him by earnest, believing prayer to be kept by His own abiding in you—and go into the next moment, and the succeeding hours, with this trust continually renewed. As often as the opportunity occurs in the moments between your activities, renew your faith in an act of devotion: Jesus keeps me now; Jesus saves me now. Let failure and sin, instead of discouraging you, only urge you to seek even more your safety by abiding in the Sinless One.

Abiding is a grace in which you can grow wonderfully, if you will but make a complete surrender, and then persevere with ever-increasing expectations. Regard it as *His* work to keep you abiding in Him and *His* work to keep you from sinning. It is indeed your work to abide in Him; but this is only possible because it is *His* work as the Vine to bear and hold you, the branch. Gaze upon *His holy human nature as something He prepared for you to be partaker of with himself,* and you will see that there is something even higher and better than being kept from sin—that is, the restraining from evil. There is the positive and larger blessing of now being a vessel purified and cleansed, filled with His fullness, and made a channel for showing forth His power, His blessing, and His glory.

He Is Your Strength

All authority has been given to Me in heaven and on earth.

Matthew 28:18

Be strong in the Lord and in the power of His might.

Ephesians 6:10

My strength is made perfect in weakness.

2 Corinthians 12:9

No truth is more generally admitted among sincere Christians than that they are utterly weak. Yet there is no truth more generally misunderstood and abused than this. Here, as elsewhere, God's thoughts are high above ours (Isaiah 55:8).

The Christian often tries to forget his weakness, but God wants us to remember it, and to feel it deeply. Christians want to conquer their weakness and to be freed from it; God wants us to rest and even rejoice in it. Christians mourn over their weakness, while Christ teaches His servants to say, "I take pleasure in infirmities; most gladly will I boast in my infirmities" (2 Corinthians 12:9–10). Christians think their weakness is the greatest hindrance in their life and service to God; but God tells us that rather than being a hindrance, our weakness is actually the secret of strength and success. It is our weakness, heartily accepted and continually realized, that gives us our claim and access to the strength of Him who has said, "*My strength* is made perfect *in weakness.*"

When our Lord was about to take His seat upon the throne, one of His last statements was "All authority has been given to Me in heaven and on earth." Just as taking His place at the right hand of the power of God was something new and true—a real advance in the history of the God-man—so was His assuming all power and authority for heaven and earth. Omnipotence was now entrusted to the man Christ Jesus, so that from then on it might put forth its mighty energies through the channels of human nature. Here He connected this revelation of what He was to receive with the promise of the share that His disciples would have in it: When I am ascended, you will receive power from on high (Luke 24:49; Acts 1:8). It is in the power of the omnipotent Savior that the believer must find his strength for life and for work.

The disciples found this principle to be true. During ten days in the Upper Room they worshiped and waited at the foot-stool of His throne. They gave expression to their faith in Him as their Savior, their adoration of Him as their Lord, their love for Him as their Friend, and their devotion and readiness to work for Him as their Master. Jesus Christ was their one object of thought, of love, of delight. In such worship and devotion their souls grew up into intense communion with Him upon the throne, and when they were prepared, the baptism of power came. It was power within and power around them.

The power came to qualify them for the work to which they had yielded themselves—of testifying by life and word to their unseen Lord. With some the main testimony was to be that of a holy life, revealing heaven and the Christ from whom holiness came. The power came to set up the kingdom within them, to give them victory over sin and self, and to equip them by living experience to testify to the power of Jesus on the throne to make men live in the world as saints. Others were to give themselves up entirely to speaking in the name of Jesus. But all needed and all received the gift of power to prove that Jesus had received the kingdom of the Father. All power in heaven and earth was indeed given to Him, and by Him imparted to His people just as they needed it, whether for a holy life or effective service. They received the gift of power to prove to the world that the kingdom of God, to which they professed to belong, was "not in word but in power" (1 Corinthians 4:20). By having power within, they also had power around them, outside of themselves. For even those who would not yield themselves to the power of God felt its reality (Acts 2:43; 4:13; 5:13).

And what Jesus was to these first disciples, He is to us too. Our whole life and calling as disciples find their origin and their guarantee in the words: "All authority is given to Me in heaven and on earth." What He does in and through us, He does with almighty power. What He claims or demands, He works himself by that same power. All He gives, He gives with power and authority. Every blessing He bestows, every promise He fulfills, every grace He works—all is to be with power. Everything that comes from Jesus on the throne of power is to bear the stamp of power. The weakest believer may be confident that in asking to be kept from sin, to grow in holiness, to bring forth much fruit, he may count upon these his petitions being fulfilled with divine power. The power is in Jesus; Jesus is ours with all His fullness. It is in us, members of His body, that the power is to work and to be made known.

And if we want to know how the power is bestowed, the answer is simple: Christ gives His power in us by giving His life to us. He does not, as so many believers imagine, take the frail life He finds in them, and impart a little strength to help them in their frailty. No; it is in giving His own life to us that He gives us His power. The Holy Spirit came down to the disciples directly from the heart of their exalted Lord, bringing down into them the glorious life of heaven into which He had entered. And so His people are still taught to be strong in the Lord and in the power of His might (Ephesians 6:10). When He strengthens them, it is not by taking away the sense of weakness, and giving in its place the feeling of strength. Not at all.

Rather, in a very wonderful way He leaves and even increases the sense of utter impotence; along with it He gives them the consciousness of strength in Him. "We have this treasure in earthen vessels, that the excellence of the power may be of God and not of us" (2 Corinthians 4:7). The weakness and the strength are side by side; as the one grows, the other does, too, until his disciples understand the saying, "When I am weak, then am I strong; I boast in my infirmities, that the power of Christ may rest upon me" (2 Corinthians 12:9–10).

The believing disciple learns to look upon Christ on the throne, Christ the Omnipotent, as his life. He studies that life in its infinite perfection and purity, in its strength and glory; it is eternal life dwelling in a glorified man. And when he thinks of his own inner life, and longs for holiness, to live a life well-pleasing to God, or for power to do the Father's work, he looks up, and, rejoicing that Christ is his life, he confidently acts on the assurance that Christ's life will work mightily in him all he needs. In things both small and great, in being kept from sin from moment to moment, or in the struggle with some special difficulty or temptation, *the power of Christ* is the measure of his expectation. He lives a truly joyous and blessed life, not because he is no longer weak, but because, being utterly helpless, he consents and expects to have the mighty Savior work in him.

The lessons these thoughts teach us for practical life are simple but very precious. The first is that all our strength is in Christ, laid up and waiting for our use, according to the measure in which it finds the channels open. But whether its flow is strong or weak, whatever our experience of it may be, there it is in Christ: all authority in heaven and earth. Let us take time to study this. Let us get our minds filled with the thought: So that Jesus might be to us a perfect Savior, the Father gave Him all power and authority. That is the qualification that fits Him for our needs—having all the power of heaven that triumphs over all the powers of earth, including those in our heart and life.

The second lesson is: This power flows into us as we abide in close union with Him. When the union is weak, undervalued or undercultivated, the inflow of strength will be weak. On the other hand, when our union with Christ is praised as our highest good, and everything is sacrificed for the sake of maintaining it, His power will work in us: His strength "is made perfect in (our) weakness." Our one care must therefore be to abide in

Christ as our strength. Our one duty is to be strong in the Lord and in the power of His might.

Let our faith be expanded to appropriate the exceeding greatness of God's power in them that believe, *even that power* of the risen and exalted Christ by which He triumphed over every enemy (Ephesians 1:19–21). Let our faith consent to God's wonderful arrangement: nothing but weakness in us *as our own*, all the power in Christ, and yet within our reach as surely as if it were in us. Let our faith go beyond self and its life daily into the life of Christ, placing our whole being at His disposal for Him to work in us. Let our faith, above all, confidently rejoice in the assurance that He will, with His almighty power, perfect His work in us. As we abide in Christ, the Holy Spirit will work mightily in us, and we too will be able to sing, "The Lord is *my strength* and song" (Isaiah 12:2). "*I can do all things* through Christ who strengthens me" (Philippians 4:13).

It Is Not in Ourselves

In me (that is, in my flesh) nothing good dwells.

Romans 7:18

To have life in himself is the prerogative of God alone, and of the Son, to whom the Father has also given it. To seek life, not in itself, but in God, is the highest honor of the creature. To live in and to himself is the folly and guilt of sinful man; to live to God in Christ is the blessing of the believer. To deny, to hate, to forsake, and to lose his own life: such is the secret of the life of faith. "It is no longer I who live, but Christ lives in me" (Galatians 2:20); "Not I, but the grace of God which was with me" (1 Corinthians 15:10): This is the testimony of each one who has found out what it is to give up his own life and to receive instead the blessed life of Christ within. There is no path to true life, to abiding in Christ, other than the way taken by our Lord before us—through death.

At the beginning of the Christian life, very few see this truth. In the joy of pardon, they feel compelled to live for Christ and trust that with the help of God they will be able to do so. They are still ignorant of the terrible struggle of the flesh against

God and its absolute refusal in the believer to be subject to the law of God. They do not know that nothing but death, the absolute surrender to death of all that is of the old nature, will do if the life of God is to be manifested in them with power. But bitter experience of failure soon teaches them the insufficiency of what they know about Christ's power to save; deep heart-longings are awakened to know Him better. He lovingly points them to His Cross. He tells them that in the same way they exercised faith in His death as their substitute, and found their title to life, so there they will also enter into its fuller experience. He asks them if they are willing to drink of the cup He drank of—to be crucified and to die with Him. He teaches them that in Him they are indeed already crucified and dead, for at conversion they became partakers of His death. But what they need now is to give a full and intelligent consent to what they received before they understood it, by an act of their own choice to die with Christ.

This demand of Christ's is one of unspeakable solemnity. Many a believer shrinks back from it, having a hard time understanding it. For he has become so accustomed to a life of continual stumbling that he barely desires, and still less expects, deliverance. Holiness, perfect conformity to Jesus, unbroken fellowship with His love, can scarcely be counted distinct articles of his creed. Where there is not intense longing to be kept to the utmost from sinning, and to be brought into the closest possible union with the Savior, the thought of being crucified with Him can hardly be welcome. The only impression it makes is that of suffering and shame; such a Christian is content that Jesus bore the Cross and so won for him the crown he hopes to wear. But how differently the believer who is really seeking to abide fully in

Christ looks upon it. Bitter experience has taught him how, both in the matter of entire surrender and simple trust, his greatest enemy in the abiding life is *self.* First it refuses to give up its will; then again, by its working, it hinders God's work.

Unless this life of self, with its willing and working, can be displaced by the life of Christ, with *His* willing and working, abiding in Him will be impossible. And then comes the solemn question from Him who died on the cross: "Are you ready to give up self, even to the point of death?" You, a living person born of God, are already in Me; you are already dead to sin and alive to God, He explains. But are you ready now, in the power of this death, to give up self entirely to death on the cross, to be kept there until your self-will is conquered? The question is a heart-searching one. Am I prepared to say that my old self will no longer have a word to say; that it will not be allowed to have a single thought, however natural, not a single feeling, however gratifying, not a single wish or work, however right?

Is this really what He requires? Is not our nature God's handiwork, and may not our natural powers be sanctified to His service? They may and must indeed. But perhaps you have not yet seen how the only way they can be sanctified is that they be taken out from under the power of self and brought under the power of the life of Christ. Do not think that this is a work that you can do because you earnestly desire it and are one of His redeemed ones. No, there is no way to the altar of consecration but through death.

As you yielded yourself a sacrifice on God's altar as one alive from the dead (Romans 6:13; 7:1), so each power of your nature—each talent, gift, and possession that is really to be holiness to the Lord—must be separated from the power of sin and self, and laid on the altar to be consumed by the fire that is ever burning there. It is in the slaying of self that the wonderful powers with which God has fitted you to serve Him can be set free for a complete surrender to God and offered to Him to be accepted, sanctified, and used. And though, as long as you are in the flesh, there is no thought of being able to say that self is dead; yet when the life of Christ is allowed to take full possession, self can be so kept in its crucified place, and under its sentence of death, that it will have no dominion over you. Jesus Christ becomes your second self.

Believer, would you truly and fully abide in Christ? Then prepare yourself to part forever from self and not to allow it, even for a single moment, to have anything to say in your inner life. If you are willing to entirely give up self, and to allow Jesus Christ to become your life within you, inspiring all your thinking, feeling, and acting, in things temporal and spiritual, He is ready to take charge. In the fullest and widest sense the word *life* can have, He will be *your life*, extending His interest and influence to each one of the thousand things that make up your daily life. To do this He asks only one thing: Come away, out of self and its life; abide in Christ and He will be your life. The power of His holy presence will cast out the old life.

To this end give up self at once and forever. If you have never yet dared to do it, for fear you might fail, do it now, in view of the promise Christ gives you that His life will take the place of your old life. Try to realize that though self is not dead, you are indeed dead *to* self. Self is still strong and living, but it has *no power over you*. You, your renewed nature—you, your new self, born again in Jesus Christ from the dead—are indeed dead to sin and alive to God (Romans 6:11). Your death in

Christ has freed you completely from the control of self; it has no power over you, except as you, in carelessness or unbelief consent to yield to its usurped authority. Come and accept by faith the glorious position you have in Christ. Be of good courage, only believe; do not fear to take the irrevocable step, and to say that you have, once and for all, given up self to the death for which it has been crucified in Christ (Romans 6:6). And trust Jesus the Crucified One to hold self to the Cross and to fill its place in you with His own blessed resurrection life.

In this faith, abide in Christ! Cling to Him; rest on Him; hope in Him. Renew your consecration daily; daily accept afresh your position as one ransomed from your tyrant, and now in turn made a conqueror. Daily look with holy fear on the enemy, self, which struggles to free itself from the cross. Be aware that it seeks to allure you into giving it some little liberty, or else stands ready to deceive you by its profession of willingness now to do service for Christ. Remember, self that seeks to serve God is more dangerous than self that refuses to obey God. Look upon it with holy fear, and hide yourself in Christ; in Him alone is your safety. Abide in Him; He has promised to abide in you. He will teach you to be humble and watchful. He will teach you to be happy and trustful.

Bring every interest of your life, every power of your nature, all the unceasing flow of thought, will, and feeling that makes up life, and trust Him to take the place that self once filled so easily and so naturally. Jesus Christ will indeed take possession of you and dwell in you; and in the restfulness, peace, and grace of the new life, you will have unceasing joy at the wondrous exchange that has been made—the coming out of self to abide in Christ alone.

The Guarantee of the New Covenant

Jesus has become the guarantee of a better covenant.

Hebrews 7:22

Scripture speaks of the old covenant as not being faultless; God complains that Israel did not continue in it and so He disregarded them (Hebrews 8:7–9). The problem was that the old covenant did not secure its apparent object of uniting Israel and God: Israel had forsaken Him, and He had as a consequence disregarded Israel. Therefore, God promises to make a new covenant, free from the faults of the first, and able to accomplish its purpose. If it were to accomplish its end, it would need to secure God's faithfulness to His people, and His people's faithfulness to God. And the terms of the new covenant expressly declare that these two objects will be attained. "I will put My laws into their mind"; in this way God seeks to secure their unchanging faithfulness to Him. "Their sins and their lawless deeds I will remember no more" (see Hebrews 8:10–12); this will be the means of assuring His unchanging faithfulness to

297

them. A pardoning God and an obedient people: These are the two parties who are to meet and be eternally united in the new covenant.

The most beautiful provision of this new covenant is that of the guarantee in whom its fulfillment on both parts is assured. Jesus was made the guarantee of the better covenant. To man He became the guarantee that God would faithfully fulfill His part, so that man could confidently depend upon God to pardon, accept, and never again forsake them. And to God He likewise became the guarantee that man would faithfully fulfill his part, so that God could bestow on him the blessing of the covenant. The way in which He fulfills His office is this: As one with God, and having the fullness of God dwelling in His human nature, Christ Jesus personally guarantees to men that God the Father will do what He has promised. As one with us, and having taken us up as members into His own body, He is a guarantee to the Father that His interests will be cared for. All that man must be and do is secured in Christ. It is the glory of the new covenant that it has in the Person of the God-man its living guarantee, its everlasting security. And it can be easily understood how, in proportion as we abide in Him as the guarantee of the covenant, its objects and its blessings will be realized in us.

We will understand this best if we consider it in the light of one of the promises of the new covenant: "I will make an everlasting covenant with them, that *I will not turn away from doing them good*; but I will put My fear in their hearts so that *they will not depart from Me*" (Jeremiah 32:40).

With what wonderful condescension the infinite God here bows to our weakness! He is the Faithful and Unchanging One, whose word is truth; and yet to show more abundantly to the heirs of the promise how unchanging is His counsel, He binds himself in the covenant to remain faithful: "I will make an everlasting covenant, that I will not turn away from doing them good." Blessed is the man who has thoroughly appropriated this and finds his rest in the everlasting covenant of the Faithful One!

But in a covenant there are two parties. And what if man becomes unfaithful and breaks the covenant? Provision must be made, if the covenant is to be well ordered in all things and sure, that this cannot happen. Man can never undertake to give such an assurance but God provides for this too. He not only undertakes in the covenant that He will never turn from His people but also pledges to put His fear in their hearts so that they will not depart from Him. In addition to His own obligations as one party in the covenant, He undertakes for the other party too: "I will put My Spirit within you and cause you to walk in My statutes, and *you will keep* My judgments and do them" (Ezekiel 36:27). Blessed is the man who understands this part of the covenant as well! He sees that his security is not in the covenant that he makes with his God, for he would likely break it continually. He finds that a covenant has been made in which God stands good, not only for himself, but also for all humankind. He grasps the blessed truth that his part in the covenant is to accept what God has promised to do, and to expect the sure fulfillment of God's plan to secure the faithfulness of His people: "I will put My fear in their hearts so that *they will not depart from Me.*"

It is here that the blessed work of the Guarantor comes in to secure the covenant, appointed of the Father to see to its maintenance and perfect fulfillment. To Christ Jesus the Father has said, "I will give You as a covenant to the people" (Isaiah 42:6). And the Holy Spirit testifies, "All the promises of God in Him are Yes, and in Him Amen, to the glory of God through us" (2 Corinthians 1:20). The believer who abides in Him has divine assurance for the fulfillment of every promise of the covenant.

Christ was made the guarantee of a better covenant. It is as our Melchizedek that Christ is this guarantee (see Hebrews 7). Aaron and his sons passed away; of Christ it is witnessed that *He ever lives.* He is a priest in the power of an *endless life.* Because He *continues forever,* He has an unchangeable priesthood. And because He *ever lives* to make intercession, He can "save to the uttermost" all who come to Him (Hebrews 7:25). It is because Christ is the Ever-Living One that His guarantee of the covenant is so effectual. He ever lives to make intercession and can therefore save completely. Every moment the unceasing pleadings rise up from His holy presence to the Father, the unceasing pleadings that secure for His people the powers and the blessings of the heavenly life. And every moment from Him flows out the mighty influences of His unceasing intercession toward His people, continually conveying to them the power of the heavenly life. As guarantee with us for the Father's favor, He never ceases to pray and present us before Him; as guarantee with the Father for us, He never ceases to work and reveal the Father within us.

The mystery of the Melchizedek priesthood, which the Hebrews were not able to receive (Hebrews 5:10–14), is the mystery of resurrection life. It is in the Resurrection that the glory of Christ as guarantee for the covenant consists: He ever lives. He performs His work in heaven in the power of a divine, omnipotent life. He ever lives to pray; there is not a moment that as our guarantee His prayers do not ascend to secure the Father's fulfillment of the covenant to us. He performs His work on earth in the power of that same life; there is not a moment that His answered prayers—the powers of the heavenly world—do not flow downward to secure for His Father our fulfillment of the New Covenant. In the life that is eternal there are no breaks, never a moment's interruption; each moment has the power of eternity in it. He every moment lives to pray. Every moment He lives to bless. He can, therefore, save to the uttermost, completely and perfectly.

Believer, come and see here how the possibility of abiding in Jesus every moment is secured by the very nature of this ever-living priesthood of your guarantee. Moment by moment, as His intercession rises up, its effectiveness descends. And because Jesus stands good for fulfilling the covenant—"I will put My fear in their hearts so that they will not depart from me"—He cannot afford to leave you a single moment to yourself. He dare not do so, or He fails in His undertaking. Your unbelief may fail to realize the blessing, but He cannot be unfaithful. If you will consider Him, and the power of that endless life after which He was made and serves as High Priest, your faith will arise to believe that an endless, ever-continuing, unchangeable life of abiding in Jesus awaits you.

It is as we see what Jesus is, and is to us, that abiding in Him will become the natural and spontaneous result of our knowledge of Him. If His life unceasingly, moment by moment, rises to the Father for us and descends to us from the Father, then to abide moment by moment is easy, even simple. Each moment of conscious communion with Him let us say, "Jesus, our guarantor, keeper, ever-living Savior, in whose life I live, I abide in you." Each moment of need, darkness, or fear, we still say, "Great High Priest, in the power of an endless, unchangeable life, I abide in you." And for the moments when direct and distinct communion with Him must give way to necessary earthly activities, we can trust Him to be our guarantee. His unceasing priesthood, with its divine effectiveness and the power with which He saves to the uttermost, will keep us abiding in Him still.

The Glorified One

Your life is hidden with Christ in God. When Christ who is our life appears, then you also will appear with Him in glory.

Colossians 3:3–4

The one who abides in Christ, the Crucified One, learns what it is to be crucified with Him, and in Him to be dead to sin. The one who abides in Christ, the Risen and Glorified One, becomes a partaker of His resurrection life and the glory He is now crowned with in heaven. Unspeakable are the blessings that flow out of our union with Jesus in His glorified life.

This life is a life of *perfect victory and rest*. Before His death, the Son of God had to suffer and struggle, could be tempted and troubled by sin and its assaults. But as the Risen One, He has triumphed over sin; and, as the Glorified One, His humanity has participated in the glory of Deity. The believer who abides in Him as such is led to see how the power of sin and the flesh are indeed destroyed; the consciousness of complete and everlasting deliverance becomes increasingly clear, and blessed rest and peace—the fruit of such a conviction that victory and deliverance are an accomplished fact—take possession of the life. Abiding in Jesus, in whom he has been raised and set in heavenly places (Ephesians 2:6), such a believer receives that glorious life streaming from the Head through every member of the body.

This life is a life in *the full fellowship of the Father's love and holiness.* Jesus often gave prominence to this thought with His disciples. His death was a return to the Father. He prayed: "O Father, glorify Me together *with Yourself,* with the glory which I had *with You* before the world was" (John 17:5). As the believer, abiding in Christ the Glorified One, seeks to realize and experience what His union with Jesus on the throne implies, he understands how the unclouded light of the Father's presence is His highest glory and blessing, and in Christ it is the believer's portion too. He learns the sacred art of always, in fellowship with His exalted Head, dwelling in the secret place of the Father's presence. When Jesus was on earth, temptation could still reach Him, but in glory that is done away with. Everything is holy there and in perfect harmony with the will of God. And so the believer who abides in Him experiences the awesome fact that in this high fellowship his spirit is sanctified into growing harmony with the Father's will. The heavenly life of Jesus is the power that casts out sin for him.

This life is a life of *loving goodness and activity.* Seated on His throne, Christ dispenses His gifts, bestows His Spirit, and never ceases to lovingly watch and work for those who are His. The believer cannot abide in Jesus the Glorified One without feeling himself stirred and strengthened to work; the Spirit and the love of Jesus breathe into him the will and the power to be a blessing to others. Jesus went to heaven with the objective of obtaining power there to bless abundantly. As the Heavenly

Vine, He does this work only through the medium of His people as His branches. Therefore, whoever abides in Him, the Glorified One, bears much fruit, because he receives of the Spirit the power of his exalted Lord's eternal life. The humblest believer can become the channel through which the fullness of Jesus, who has been exalted to be a Prince and a Savior, flows out to bless those around him.

There is one more thought in regard to this life of the Glorified One, and ours in Him. It is a life of *wondrous expectation and hope.* Christ sits at the right hand of God, *waiting in expectation* till all His enemies are made His footstool (Hebrews 10:13), looking forward to the time when He will receive His full reward, when His glory will be known to all, and His beloved people will be with Him forever in that glory. The hope of Christ is also the hope of His redeemed: "I will come again and receive you to Myself; that where I am, there you may be also" (John 14:3). This promise is as precious to Christ as it ever can be to us. The joy of meeting is surely no less for the coming Bridegroom than for the waiting bride. The life of Christ in glory is one of longing expectation; the full glory only comes when His beloved people are with Him.

The believer who abides closely in Christ will share with Him in this spirit of expectation. Not so much for the increase of personal happiness, but from the spirit of enthusiastic allegiance to his King, he longs to see Him come in His glory, reigning over every enemy, the full revelation of God's everlasting love. "Till He comes" is the watchword of every truehearted believer. "When Christ who is our life appears, then you also will appear with Him in glory" (Colossians 3:4).

There may be serious differences in the understanding of

His promised coming. To one it is plain as day that He is coming very soon in person to reign on earth, and that imminent coming is his hope and his stay. To another, who loves his Bible and his Savior just as much, the coming can mean nothing but the Judgment Day—the solemn transition from time to eternity, the close of history on earth, the beginning of heaven; and the thought of that manifestation of his Savior's glory is his joy and his strength. It is Jesus, Jesus coming again, Jesus taking us to himself, Jesus adored as Lord of all, that is important; He is the sum and the center of the whole church's hope.

It is by abiding in Christ the Glorified One that the believer can fully anticipate, in true spiritual longing, His coming, which alone brings true blessing to the soul. There is an interest in the study of the end times, and such schools sadly are often better known by their contentions about opinions and condemnation of believers who do not agree with them than by the meekness of Christ's character. It is only the humility that is willing to learn from those who may have other gifts and deeper revelations of the truth than we, the love that always speaks gently and tenderly of those who do not see as we do, and the heavenly character that shows that the Coming One is indeed already our life, that will persuade either the church or the world that our faith is not in the wisdom of men but in the power of God.

To testify of the Savior as the Coming One, we must be abiding in and bearing His image as the Glorified One. Not the correctness of the views we hold, nor the earnestness with which we advocate them, will prepare us for meeting Him, but only our abiding in Him. Only then can our manifestation in glory with Him be what it is meant to be: a transfiguration, a breaking out and shining forth of the indwelling glory that only awaited the day of revelation.

Blessed is the life "hidden with Christ in God, set in the heavenly places in Christ," abiding in Christ the glorified! Once again the question comes: Can a frail child of dust really dwell in fellowship with the King of Glory? And again the blessed answer has to be given: To maintain that union is the very work for which Christ has all power and authority in heaven and on earth at His disposal. The blessing will be given to him who will trust his Lord for it, the one who in faith and confident expectation continually yields himself to be wholly one with Him. It was an act of wondrous though simple faith by which the soul first yielded itself to the Savior. That faith grows up to gain clearer insight and a surer hold on God's truth that we are one with Him in His glory. In that same wondrously simple but wondrously mighty faith, the soul learns to abandon itself entirely to the keeping of Christ's almighty power and the merits of His eternal life. Because it knows that it has the Spirit of God dwelling within to communicate all that Christ is, it no longer looks upon it as a burden or even an effort, but allows God's divine life to have its way, to do its work; its faith is the increasing abandonment of self, the expectation and acceptance of all that the love and the power of the Glorified One can perform. In that faith, unbroken fellowship is maintained and growing conformity to His image realized. As with Moses, the fellowship makes us partakers of the glory, and our lives begin to shine with a brightness not of this world.

What a blessed life! *It is* ours, for Jesus is ours. We have the possession within us in its hidden power, and we have the prospect before us in the manifestation of its full glory. May our daily lives be the bright and blessed proof that a hidden power dwells within, preparing us for the glory to be revealed. May our abiding in Christ the Glorified One be our strength to live to the glory of the Father, our enabling to share in the glory of the Son.

And now,
little children,
abide in Him,
that when He appears, we may have
confidence and not be ashamed
before Him at His coming.
1 John 2:28

LIVING A PRAYERFUL LIFE

◆

Introduction

Knowing the origin of this book and the reason why it was written will help the reader better understand its teaching.

It came out of a ministers' conference at Stellenbosch, South Africa, April 11–14, 1912. Professor de Vos, of our Dutch Reformed Theological Seminary, had written a letter to our church ministers concerning the low spiritual state that marked the church in general and which ought to lead us to inquire how far the statement included our church as well. What was said about the lack of spiritual power in the book *The State of the Church* called for deep searching of the heart, since Professor de Vos thought the statement was true. He suggested we come together and in God's presence find the cause of the lack. He wrote: "If we but study the conditions in all sincerity, we will have to acknowledge that our unbelief and our sins are the cause of our lack of spiritual power, and that this condition is one that places us guilty before God and grieving God's Holy Spirit."

His invitation met with a hearty response. Our four theological professors, together with more than two hundred ministers, missionaries, and theological students, met on the basis of the above statement as the keynote of our meeting. From the very first message, there was a tone of confession as the only way to repentance and restoration. Then opportunity was given for testimony as to what the sins might be

311

that made the life of the church so ineffectual. Some began to mention failures in conduct, in presentation of doctrine, or in service that they had seen in other ministers. Soon it was felt that this was not the right approach; each must acknowledge his personal guilt.

The Lord led us gradually to the sin of prayerlessness as one of the deepest roots of the problem. No one could claim to be free from this. Nothing so reveals a defective spiritual life in a minister or a congregation as the lack of believing and unceasing prayer. Prayer is the pulse of the spiritual life. It is the great means by which ministers and laypeople alike receive the blessing and power of heaven. Persevering and believing prayer preludes strong and abundant life.

When the spirit of confession began to prevail, the question came up as to whether it would be possible to gain victory over all that had in the past hindered our prayer life. In smaller sessions held previously, many had been anxious to make a new beginning and yet doubted that they would be able to maintain a prayer life consistent with what they saw in the Word of God. Though they often made the attempt, they had utterly failed. They did not dare to promise the Lord that they would live and pray as He would have them do, because they felt such a thing was impossible. Such confessions gradually led to the revelation that the only power to be found for a new prayer life was in an entirely new relationship to the Savior. As we see in Him the Lord who saves us from sin—even the sin of prayerlessness—our faith yields itself to a life of closer intimacy with Him. Then a life in His love and fellowship will make prayer the natural expression of our inner life. Before we parted, many testified that they were returning with new light and new hope of finding in Jesus Christ strength for a renewed prayer life.

Many felt that this was only the beginning. Satan, who had so long prevailed in the place of prayer, would do his utmost again to tempt us to yield to the power of the flesh and the world. Nothing but the teaching and fellowship of Christ himself could give power to remain faithful.

The need was expressed for a statement of the truths dealt with at the conference to remind those present of what they had learned and what might help them in their new endeavor after the prayer life so essential to a minister's success. It was also needed for those who were not able to attend, and for the church elders, who had in many cases had a deep interest in hearing the purpose for which their ministers had gathered.

Early copies of the book were sent out with the thought that if the leaders of the church could see that in spiritual work *everything depends upon prayer,* and that God himself helps those who wait on Him, it could truly be a day of hope for our church. It was also intended for all believers who longed for a life of complete separation to the Lord. For all who desired to pray more and pray more effectively, it pointed to the glory of God in the personal place of prayer and the way that power can rest upon the soul.

When first asked to have the book translated into English, I felt that its composition had been too hurried and its tone, because of the close connection with the meetings that had preceded these, too colloquial to make it desirable. My own limited strength made it impossible for me to think of rewriting it. When, however, my friend the Rev. W. M. Douglas asked permission to translate it, I consented. If God has a message through the book to any of His servants, I would count it a privilege to tell what He has done here in our church as an encouragement for what He might do in other churches.

I close with my greetings to all ministers of the gospel and church members who may read these pages. The grace of God has wrought among us conviction of sin, confession of deep need and helplessness, and then given us the vision and the faith for what Jesus Christ can do for those who fully trust Him. I pray that He will also give many who read these pages the courage to meet with their co-workers and to seek for and obtain that full fellowship with God in prayer that is the very essence of the Christian life. It has been said, "Only the prayerless are too proud to own up to prayerlessness." Let us believe that many hearts are waiting for the call inviting them to united and wholehearted confession of sin as the only way to a return and restoration of God's favor and the experience of answers to prayer.

I wish to add one more word in regard to the Pentecostal prayer meetings held throughout our church. These have had an interesting and important place in our work. At the time of the great revival in America and Ireland in 1858, and the years following, some of our elder ministers issued a circular urging the churches to pray that God might visit us too. In 1860 revival broke out in various parishes. And in April 1861 there was a deep interest shown in this practice of prayer in one of our oldest congregations. During the week preceding Pentecost Sunday, the minister, who ordinarily preached only once on a Sunday, announced that there would be a public prayer meeting in the church in the afternoon. The occasion was one of extraordinary interest, and many hearts were deeply touched. One result was that the minister suggested that the ten days between Ascension and Pentecost Sunday should be observed by daily prayer meetings. This took place the following year. Such blessing was received that all the neighboring congregations adopted the idea, and now for fifty years these ten days of prayer have been observed throughout the whole church. Each year notes were distributed outlining the subjects of the messages and prayer. As a result, Christians throughout our whole church have been educated in the knowledge of what God's Word teaches regarding the Holy Spirit, and have been stirred to seek His blessed leading and yield themselves to it. These ten days have often led to special effort with the unconverted and the beginnings of revival. They have been the means of untold blessing in leading ministers and people to recognize the place that the Holy Spirit ought to have as the executive of the Godhead in the heart of believers, in dealing with souls, and in consecration to the service of the kingdom. Much is still lacking of the full knowledge and power of the Holy Spirit, but we feel that we cannot be sufficiently grateful to God for what He has done through leading us to dedicate these days to special prayer for His Holy Spirit to work.

I have written about this with the thought that some will not only be glad to know of it but they also will unite in the same observance in their congregations.

—Andrew Murray

Part One

The Prayer Life

Chapter 1

The Sin of Prayerlessness

If conscience is to do its work and the contrite heart is to feel its proper remorse, it is necessary for each individual to confess his sin by name. The confession must be intensely personal. In a meeting of ministers, probably no single sin should be acknowledged with deeper shame than the sin of prayerlessness. Each one of us needs to confess that we are guilty of this.

Why is prayerlessness such a serious sin? At first it would seem to be merely a weakness. So much is said about lack of time and all sorts of distractions that the deep guilt of the situation is not recognized. From now on, let us acknowledge prayerlessness as the sin that it is.

1. *It is a reproach to God.* The holy and most glorious God invites us to come to Him, to converse with Him, to ask Him for the things we need, and to experience the depth of blessing there is in fellowship with Him. He has created us in His own image and has redeemed us by His own Son, so that in conversation with Him we should find our greatest delight.

What use do we make of this heavenly privilege? How many of us admit to taking a mere five minutes for prayer! The claim is that there is no time. The reality is that a heart desire for prayer is lacking. Many do not know how to spend half an hour with God! It is not that they absolutely do not pray; they may pray every day—but they have no joy in prayer. Joy is the sign that God is everything to you.

If a friend comes to visit, there is time. We make time—even at the cost of something else—for the sake of enjoying pleasant conversation with our friend. Yes, there is time for everything that truly interests us, but time is scarce to practice fellowship with God and to enjoy being with Him! We find time for someone who can be of service to us; but day after day, month after month passes, and for many there is no time to spend even one hour with God.

We must acknowledge that we disrespect and dishonor God when we say we cannot find time for fellowship with Him. If this sin begins to appear ordinary to us, we must cry out to God: "O God, be merciful to me, and forgive me this awful sin of prayerlessness."

2. *It is the cause of a deficient spiritual life.* Prayerlessness is proof that for the most part our life is still under the power of the flesh. Prayer is the pulse of life; by it the doctor can diagnose the condition of the heart. The sin of prayerlessness proves to the ordinary Christian or minister that the life of God in the soul is mortally sick and weak.

Much is said and many complaints are made about the failure of the church to fulfill her calling, to exercise an influence on her members, to deliver them from the power of the world, and to bring them to a life of holy consecration to God. Much is also said about the church's indifference to the millions for whom Christ died who depend upon her to make known to them His love and salvation. Why is it that thousands of Christian workers in the world have no greater influence than they do? I venture to say that it is because of prayerlessness. With all their zeal for study and work in the church, in spite of all their faithfulness in preaching and encouragement of the people, they lack the prayer that brings the Spirit and power from on high. The sin of prayerlessness is the root cause of a powerless spiritual life.

3. *The church suffers great loss as a result of the prayerlessness of their minister.* A minister's business is to train believers for a life of prayer. How can a leader do this if he himself understands little about the art of conversing with God and of receiving from the Holy Spirit each day abundant grace for himself and for his work? A minister cannot lead a congregation higher than he is himself. He cannot with enthusiasm point out a way or explain a work in which he himself neither walks nor lives.

How many thousands of Christians know next to nothing of the blessedness of prayer fellowship with God! How many know something of it and long to know more, but the preaching of the Word does not urge it of its hearers. The reason is no doubt that the minister understands little about the secret of powerful prayer himself, and so does not give it the place in his service that in the nature of the case and in the will of God is indispensably necessary. What a difference we would notice in our congregations if ministers could see the sin of prayerlessness in its proper light and be delivered from it!

4. *It is impossible to preach the gospel to all men—as we are commanded by Christ to do—as long as this sin is not acknowledged and dealt with.* Many feel that the greatest need of missions is finding men and women who will give themselves to the Lord for the salvation of souls. It has also been said that God is eager and able to deliver and bless the world He has redeemed if His people are willing and ready to cry

to Him day and night. But how can congregations be brought to that place without our ministers recognizing that the indispensable thing is not preaching, pastoral visitation, or church activity, but fellowship with God in prayer?

Oh, that all thought and work and expectation concerning the kingdom might drive us to the acknowledgment of prayerlessness as sin! *God, help us to see it! Deliver us from it through the blood and power of Jesus! Teach every minister of the Word what a glorious place he can occupy if he is first delivered from his lack of prayer, so that with courage and joy, in faith and perseverance, he can go on with God.*

May the Lord lay the burden of the sin of prayerlessness so heavy on our hearts that we may not rest until it is taken far from us through the name and power of Jesus.

A Witness From America

In 1898 two members of the presbytery of New York attended the Northfield Conference for the deepening of the spiritual life. They returned to their work with the fire of a new enthusiasm as they endeavored to bring about a revival in the entire presbytery. In a meeting they held, the chairman was led to ask the group about their prayer life: "Brethren," he said, "let us today make confession before God and each other. It will do us good. Will everyone who spends half an hour each day with God in connection with His work, raise your hand?" One hand was raised. He made a further request: "All who spend fifteen minutes in this way, raise your hand." Less than half of the hands went up. Then he said, "Prayer is the working power of the church of Christ, and half of the workers make hardly any use of it! All who spend five minutes a day hold up your hand." All hands went up, but one man came later with the confession that he was not sure if he spent five minutes in prayer every day. "It is," said he, "a terrible revelation of how little time I spend with God."

Chapter 2

The Cause of Prayerlessness

In an elders' prayer meeting, one brother asked: "What is the cause of so much prayerlessness? Is it unbelief?"

The answer was: "Certainly; but what is the cause of unbelief?" The disciples asked the Lord Jesus: "Why could we not cast the devil out?" His answer was: "Because of your unbelief." He added: "Howbeit, this kind goes out only by prayer and fasting." If the life is not one of self-denial—of fasting (letting the world go) and of prayer (laying hold of heaven)—faith cannot be exercised. In a life lived according to the flesh and not according to the Spirit, we find the origin of the prayerlessness of which we complain. As we left the meeting, one brother said to me, "The whole difficulty is that we wish to pray in the Spirit and at the same time walk after the flesh. This is impossible."

If one is sick and desires healing, it is of prime importance that the true cause of the sickness be discovered. This is always the first step toward recovery. If the root problem is not recognized, and attention is directed toward the wrong cause or to secondary problems, healing is out of the question. In like manner, it is of utmost importance for us to obtain correct insight into the cause of the sad condition of deadness and failure in our private place of prayer, which should be a blessed place. Let us seek to fully recognize the root of this problem.

Scripture teaches us that there are only two conditions possible for the Christian: one is to walk according to the Spirit and the other is to walk according the flesh. These two powers are in irreconcilable conflict with each other. So most Christians—even though they may be born again through the Spirit and have received the life of God—still continue to live their life not according to the Spirit but according to the flesh. Paul wrote to the Galatians: "Are you so foolish? After beginning with the Spirit, are you now trying to attain your goal by human effort?" (Galatians 3:3). Their service lay in fleshly outward performances. They did not understand that where the flesh is permitted to influence service to God, it soon results in open sin.

So he mentions as the work of the flesh not only grave sins such as adultery, murder, and drunkenness but also the more ordinary sins of daily life: anger, strife, and arguing. Then he exhorts: "Live by the Spirit, and you will not gratify the desires of the sinful nature. . . . Since we live by the Spirit, let us keep in step with the Spirit" (Galatians 5:16, 25). The Spirit must be honored not only as the author of a new life but also as the leader and director of our entire walk. Otherwise we are what the apostle calls "carnal" or fleshly.

The majority of Christians have little understanding in this matter. They have no real knowledge of the deep sinfulness and godlessness of the carnal nature to which they unconsciously yield. "God . . . condemned sin in sinful man" (Romans 8:3)—through the cross of Christ. "Those who belong to Christ Jesus have crucified the sinful nature with its passions and desires" (Galatians 5:24). The flesh cannot be improved or sanctified. "The sinful mind is hostile to God. It does not submit to God's law, nor can it do so" (Romans 8:7). There is no means of dealing with the flesh except as Christ dealt with it, bearing it to the cross. "We know that our old self was crucified with him" (Romans 6:6); so we by faith also crucify it and regard it and treat it daily as a cursed thing that finds its rightful place on the cross.

It is unfortunate that so many Christians seldom think or speak seriously about the deep and immeasurable sinfulness of the flesh. Paul said, "I know that nothing good lives in me, that is, in my sinful nature" (Romans 7:18). The man who truly believes this may well cry out: "I see another law at work in the members of my body. . . . What a wretched man I am! Who will rescue me from this body of death?" (Romans 7:23–24). Happy is the one who can go a step further and say: "Thanks be to God—through Jesus Christ our Lord! . . . Through Christ Jesus the law of the spirit of life set me free from the law of sin and death" (Romans 7:25; 8:2).

Oh, that we would understand God's supreme grace toward us: The flesh was put on the cross; the Spirit dwells in the heart and controls the life.

This spiritual life is too little understood or sought after; yet it is literally what God has promised and will accomplish in those who unconditionally surrender themselves to Him for this purpose.

Here, then, we see this deep root of sin as the cause of the prayerless life. The flesh can say prayers well enough, calling itself religious for so doing, and thus satisfy the conscience. But the flesh has no desire or strength for the prayer that strives after an intimate knowledge of God, that rejoices in fellowship with Him, and that continues to lay hold of His strength. So, finally, it comes to this: the flesh must be denied and crucified.

The Christian who is still carnal (fleshly) has neither the disposition nor the strength to follow after God. He remains satisfied with his prayer of habit or custom. But the glory and the blessedness of secret prayer is a hidden thing to him, until one day his eyes are opened, and he begins to see that the flesh in its disposition to turn away from God is the arch-enemy that makes powerful prayer impossible.

At a conference I spoke on the subject of prayer and used strong words about the enmity of the flesh as a cause of prayerlessness. After my talk, the minister's wife said that she thought I had spoken too strongly. She also regretted that she had too little desire for prayer, but she knew her heart was sincerely set on seeking God. I showed her what the Word of God said about the flesh, and that everything that prevents the reception of the Spirit is a secret work of the flesh. Adam was created to have fellowship with God and enjoyed it before his fall. But after the Fall, immediately there came a deep-seated aversion to God, and Adam fled from Him. This incurable aversion is characteristic of the unregenerate nature and the chief cause of our unwillingness to surrender ourselves to fellowship with God in prayer. The following day that woman told me that God had opened her eyes. She confessed that the enmity and unwillingness of the flesh was the hidden hindrance in her defective prayer life.

Do not seek to find in circumstances the explanation for this prayerlessness over which we mourn. Seek it where God's Word declares it to be—in the hidden aversion of the heart to a holy God.

When a Christian does not yield completely to the leading of the Spirit—and such a surrender is certainly the will of God and the work of His grace—he lives, without knowing it, under the power of the flesh. This life in the flesh manifests itself in many different ways. It appears

- in the hastiness of spirit or the anger that so unexpectedly arises in you;
- in the lack of love for which you have so often blamed yourself;
- in the over-pleasure found in eating and drinking, about which at times your conscience has chided you;
- in seeking after your own will and honor, confidence in your own wisdom and power, and pleasure in the world, of which you are sometimes ashamed before God.

All this is life "after the flesh." "You are still worldly" (1 Corinthians 3:3). If there is strife or quarreling among us, we are still worldly. Perhaps this text disturbs you at times; you do not have full peace and joy in God.

Take time to answer the question: "Have I found here the cause of my prayerlessness, of my powerlessness to effect any change in the matter? I live in the Spirit; I have been born again, but I do not walk after the Spirit—the flesh rules over me. The carnal (fleshly) life cannot possibly pray in the spirit with power. God forgive me. My carnal life is obviously the cause of my shameful prayerlessness.

The Storm Center on the Battlefield

Mention was made in a conference of the expression "strategic position," used so often in reference to the great strife between the kingdom of heaven and the powers of darkness.

When a general chooses the place from which he intends to strike his enemy, he pays most attention to those points that he thinks most important in the fight. On the battlefield of Waterloo, there was a farmhouse that Wellington immediately saw as the key to the situation. He did not spare his troops in his endeavor to hold that point: the victory depended on it. And so it happened as he predicted it would. It is the same in the conflict between the believer and the powers of darkness. The place of private prayer is the key, the strategic position, where decisive victory is obtained.

The Enemy uses all his power to lead the Christian—and above all, the minister—to neglect prayer. Satan knows that however admirable the sermon may be, however attractive the service, however faithful the pastoral visitation, none of these things can damage him or his kingdom if prayer is neglected. When the church closes herself in to the power of the prayer meeting, and the soldiers of the Lord have received on their knees "power from on High," then the powers of darkness will be shaken and souls will be delivered. In the church, on the mission field, with the minister and his congregation, everything depends on the faithful exercise of prayer.

During the week of conference, I found the following illustration in *The Christian*:

> Two persons quarrel over a certain point. We call them Christian and Apollyon. Apollyon notices that Christian has a certain weapon that would give him a sure victory. They meet in deadly strife, and Apollyon resolves to take away the weapon from his opponent and destroy it. For the moment, the main cause of the strife has become subordinate to: who will gain possession of the weapon on which

everything depends? It is of vital importance to get hold of it.

So it is in the conflict between Satan and the believer. God's child can conquer anything and everything by prayer. Is it any wonder that Satan does his utmost to snatch that weapon from the Christian or hinder him in the use of it?

How does Satan stand in the way of prayer? He hinders it by the temptation to postpone or curtail it; by bringing in wandering thoughts and all sorts of distractions; and through unbelief and hopelessness. Happy is the prayer hero who, through it all, takes care to hold fast to his weapon and use it regularly. Like our Lord in Gethsemane, the more violently the Enemy attacked, the more earnestly He prayed, and He did not stop until He had obtained the victory. After naming all the other parts of the armor, Paul adds, "And pray in the Spirit on all occasions with all kinds of prayers and requests. With this in mind, be alert and always keep on praying for all the saints" (Ephesians 6:18). Without prayer, the helmet of salvation, the shield of faith, and the Sword of the Spirit (God's Word) have no power. All depend on prayer. *God, teach us to believe and hold fast to prayer!*

— *Chapter 3* —

The Fight Against Prayerlessness

As soon as the Christian becomes convinced of his sin in this matter, his first thought is that he must begin to strive, with God's help, to gain the victory over it. But soon he finds that his striving is worth little. The discouraging thought comes over him: he cannot continue faithful! At conferences on the subject of prayer during the past years, many a minister has said openly that it seemed impossible for him to attain to such a strict life.

Recently I received a letter from a minister well known for his ability and devotion:

> As far as I am concerned, it does not seem to help me to hear too much about the life of prayer, about the strenuous exertion for which we must prepare ourselves, and about all the time and trouble and endless effort it will cost us. These things discourage me—I have heard them so often. Time after time I have put them to the test, and the result has always been sadly disappointing. It does not help me to be told: "You must pray more, and hold a closer watch over yourself, and become altogether a more earnest Christian."

My reply to him was as follows: "I think in all I said at the conference or elsewhere, I have never mentioned exertion or struggle, because I am so entirely convinced that our efforts are futile unless we first learn how to abide in Christ by a simple faith."

My correspondent said further: "The message I need is this: 'See that your relationship to your living Savior is what it ought to be. Live in His presence, rejoice in His love, rest in Him.'" A better message could not be given, if it is only rightly understood. *See that your relationship to the living Savior is what it ought to be.* But this is exactly what will make it possible for you to live the life of prayer.

We must not comfort ourselves with thoughts of standing in a right relationship to the Lord Jesus while the sin of prayerlessness has any power over us and while we, along with the whole church, complain about our weak life that makes us unfit to pray for ourselves, for the church, or for missions as we should. But if we first recognize that a right relationship to the Lord Jesus above all else includes prayer, with both the desire and power to pray according to God's will, then we have something that gives us the right to rejoice in Him and to rest in Him.

This incident points out how naturally discouragement is the result of self-effort, and so blocks out all hope of improvement or victory. Indeed, this is the condition of many Christians when called on to persevere in prayer as intercessors. They feel it is something entirely beyond their reach: they do not have the power for the self-sacrifice and consecration necessary for such prayer. And they shrink from the effort and struggle that will, they assume, make them unhappy. They have tried in the power of the flesh to conquer the flesh—a wholly impossible thing. They have endeavored by Beelzebub to cast out Beelzebub—and this will never happen. It is Jesus alone who can subdue the flesh and the devil.

We have spoken of a struggle that will certainly result in disappointment and discouragement. This is the effort made in our own strength. But there is another struggle that will certainly lead to victory. The Scripture speaks of "the good fight of faith," that is to say, a fight that springs from and is carried on by faith. We must secure a right concept of faith and stand fast in our faith. Jesus Christ is the author and finisher of faith. When we come into right relationship with Him, we can be sure of His help and power. Just as earnestly as we must in the first place say, "Do not strive in your own strength. Cast yourself at the feet of the Lord Jesus and wait upon Him in the sure confidence that He is with you and works in you"; so do we in the second place say, "Strive in prayer; let faith fill your heart—so will you be strong in the Lord and in the power of His might."

An illustration will help us to understand this: A devoted Christian woman who conducted a large Bible class with zeal and success, once came troubled to her minister. In her earlier years she had enjoyed much blessing in her place of private prayer, in fellowship with the Lord, and in His Word. But this fellowship had gradually been lost, and whatever she did, she could not regain it. The Lord had blessed her work, but the joy had gone out of her life. The minister asked what she had done to regain the lost blessing. "I have done everything that I could think of," she said, "but all was in vain."

He then questioned her about her experience in connection with her conversion. She gave an immediate and clear answer: "At first I spared no pains in my attempt to become better and to free myself from sin, but it was all useless. At last I began to understand that I must lay aside all my efforts and simply trust the Lord Jesus to bestow on me His life and peace; and He did it."

"Why, then," said the minister, "do you not try this again? As you go to pray, however cold and dark your heart may be, do not try in your own might to force yourself into the right attitude. Bow before Him and tell Him that He sees in what a poor state you are and that your only hope is in Him. Trust Him with a childlike trust to have mercy upon you and then wait upon Him. With such trust you are in a right relationship to Him. You have nothing; He has everything." Some time later she told the minister that his advice had helped her; she had learned that faith in the love of the Lord Jesus is the only method for getting into fellowship with God in prayer.

Do you see that there are two kinds of warfare? The first is when we seek to conquer prayerlessness in our own strength. In that case my advice to you is: "Give up your restlessness and effort; fall helpless at the feet of the Lord Jesus; He will speak the word, and your soul will live." If you have done this, I give you the second message: "This is only the beginning. It will require deep earnestness, the exercise of all your power, and a watchfulness of the entire heart— eager to detect the least backsliding. Above all, it will require surrender to a life of self-sacrifice, which God desires to see in us and that He will work out for us."

Chapter 4

How to Be Delivered from Prayerlessness

The greatest stumbling block in the way of victory over prayerlessness is the secret feeling that we will never obtain the blessing of being delivered from it. Often we have tried, but in vain. Old habits, the power of the flesh, and our surroundings with their varied attractions and distractions, have been too strong for us. What good does it do to attempt what our heart assures us is out of our reach? The change needed in the entire life is too great and too difficult. If the question is put: "Is a change possible?" our sighing heart says, "For me it is entirely *im*possible!" Do you know why we answer like that? It is simply because we have heard the call to prayer as the voice of Moses and as a command of the law. Moses and his law have never given anyone the power to obey.

Do you really long for the courage to believe that deliverance from a prayerless life is possible for you and may become a reality? Then you must learn the great lesson that such a deliverance is included in the redemption that is in Christ Jesus, that it is one of the blessings of the new covenant that God himself will impart to you through Christ Jesus. As you begin to understand this, you will find that the exhortation "Pray without ceasing" conveys a new meaning. Hope begins to spring up in your heart that the Spirit—who has been bestowed on you to cry constantly, "Abba, Father"—will make a true life of prayer possible for you. Then you will hearken not in the spirit of discouragement but in the gladness of hope to the voice that calls you to repentance.

Many a person has turned to his place of prayer under bitter self-accusation that he has prayed so little, and he has resolved for the future to live in a different manner. Yet no blessing has come—there has not been the strength to continue faithful, and the call to repentance has had no power because his eyes were not fixed on the Lord Jesus. If he had only understood, he would have said, "Lord, you see how cold and dark my heart is. I know that I must pray, but I feel I cannot do so. I lack the urgency and desire to pray."

He did not know that at that same moment the Lord Jesus in His tender love was looking down upon him and saying, "You cannot pray. You feel that all is cold and dark. Why not give yourself over into my hands? Only believe that I am ready to help you in prayer. I long to pour my love into your heart so that you, in the consciousness of weakness, may confidently rely on me to bestow the grace of prayer. Just as I will cleanse you from all other sins, so also will I deliver you from the sin of prayerlessness—only do not seek the victory in your own strength. Bow before me as one who expects everything from his Savior. Let your soul keep silence before me, however lame you feel your state is. Be assured of this: I will teach you how to pray."

Many will acknowledge: "I see my mistake. I had not

thought that the Lord Jesus must deliver and cleanse me from this sin also. I had not understood that He was with me every day as I prayed, ready in His great love to keep and to bless me, however sinful and guilty I felt myself to be. I had not supposed that just as He will give all other grace in answer to prayer, so, first and most of all, He will bestow the grace of a praying heart. What folly to think that all other blessings must come from Him, but that prayer, on which everything else depends, must be obtained by personal effort! Thank God, I have begun to comprehend: The Lord Jesus himself is in my prayer closet, watching over me and holding himself responsible to teach me how to approach the Father. He only asks that I, with childlike confidence, wait upon Him and glorify Him.

Have we forgotten this truth? From a defective spiritual life, nothing better can be expected than a defective prayer life. It is vain for us to endeavor to pray more or better while we remain in a state of spiritual drought. *It is an impossibility.* It is essential that we experience that "he who is in Christ Jesus is a new creature: old things have passed away; behold, all things are become new." This is literally true for the man who understands and experiences what it is to be in Christ.

Our whole relationship to the Lord Jesus must be a new thing. I must believe in His infinite love, which longs to have communion with me every moment and to keep me in the enjoyment of His fellowship. I must believe in His divine power, which has conquered sin and will truly keep me from it. I must believe in Him who, as the great Intercessor, through the Spirit, will inspire each member of His body with joy and power for communion with God in prayer. My prayer life must be brought entirely under the control of Christ and His love. Then for the first time prayer will become what it really is: the natural and joyous breathing of the spiritual life, by which the heavenly atmosphere is inhaled and then exhaled in prayer.

Do you see that when this faith possesses us, the call to a life of prayer that pleases God will be a welcome call? The cry "Repent of the sin of prayerlessness" will not be responded to by a sigh of helplessness or by the unwillingness of the flesh. The voice of the Father will be heard as He sets before us a widely opened door and receives us into blessed fellowship with himself. Prayer for the Spirit's help to pray will no longer be in fear of an effort too great for our own power. Instead, it will be merely falling down in utter weakness at the feet of the Lord Jesus to find there that victory comes through the might and love that stream from His countenance.

Perhaps the question arises in our mind: *Will this continue?* Fear follows, "You know how often you have tried and been disappointed." But now faith finds strength, not in the thought of what you will do, but in the changeless faithfulness and love of Christ, who once again helps and assures you that those who wait on Him shall not be ashamed.

If fear and hesitation still remain, I pray that you by the mercies of God in Jesus Christ and by the unspeakable faithfulness of His tender love, dare to cast yourselves at His feet. Only believe with your whole heart—there is deliverance from the sin of prayerlessness. "If we confess our sins, he is faithful and just and will forgive us our sins and purify us from all unrighteousness" (1 John 1:9). In His blood and grace there is complete deliverance from all unrighteousness and from all prayerlessness. Praise His name forever!

How Deliverance from Prayerlessness Might Continue

What we have said about deliverance from the sin of prayerlessness also applies to answer the question "How may the experience of deliverance be maintained?" Redemption is not granted to us piecemeal, as something of which we may use a part from time to time. It is bestowed as a fullness of grace stored up in the Lord Jesus, which may be enjoyed in new fellowship with Him every day. It is so necessary that this great truth be driven home and fixed in our minds that I will say it again: Nothing can preserve you from carelessness or make it possible for you to persevere in living, powerful prayer, except daily close fellowship with Jesus our Lord.

He said to His disciples: "Trust in God; trust also in me. . . . Believe me when I say that I am in the Father and the Father is in me. . . . Anyone who has faith in me will do what I have been doing. He will even do greater things than these, because I am going to the Father" (John 14:1, 11–12).

The Lord wanted to teach His disciples that all they had

learned from the Old Testament concerning the power and holiness and love of God must now be transferred to Him. They must not believe merely in certain written documents but in Him personally. They must believe that He was in the Father, and the Father in Him, in such a sense that they had one life and one glory. All they knew about God they would find in Christ. He laid great emphasis on this, because it was only through such faith in Him and His divine glory that they could do the works that He did, and even greater works. This faith would lead them to know that just as Christ and the Father are one, so also they were in Christ, and Christ was in them.

It is this intimate, spiritual, personal, uninterrupted relationship to the Lord Jesus that manifests itself powerfully in our lives, and especially in our prayer lives. All the glorious attributes of God are in our Lord Jesus Christ. What does this mean?

1. *God's omnipresence* with which He fills the world and every moment is present in everything. Like the Father, so now our Lord Jesus is everywhere present, above all with each of His redeemed ones. This is one of the greatest and most important lessons our faith must grasp. We can clearly understand this from the example of our Lord's disciples. What was the peculiar privilege of these disciples who were always in fellowship with Him? It was uninterrupted enjoyment of the presence of the Lord Jesus. Because of this they were extremely sorrowful at the thought of His death. They would be deprived of that presence; He would be with them no longer. Under these circumstances, how did the Lord Jesus comfort them? He promised that the Holy Spirit from heaven should work in them such a sense of the fullness of His life and of His personal presence that He would be even

more intimately near and have more unbroken fellowship with them than they experienced while He was on the earth.

This great promise is now the inheritance of every believer, although so many know little about it. Jesus Christ, in His divine personality, in that eternal love that led Him to the cross, longs to have fellowship with us every moment of the day and to keep us in the enjoyment of that fellowship. This ought to be explained to every new convert: "The Lord loves you so much that He would have you near Him without a break so that you may experience His love." Every believer who has felt his powerlessness for a life of prayer, of obedience, and of holiness must learn this. This alone will give us power as intercessors to conquer the world and to win souls for our Lord.

2. *The omnipotence of God.* God's power is wonderful! We see it in creation; we see it in the wonders of redemption recorded in the Old Testament. We see it in the wonderful works of Christ that the Father wrought in Him, and above all, in Christ's resurrection from the dead. We are called on to believe in the Son just as we believe in the Father. Yes, the Lord Jesus, who in His love is so unspeakably near us, is the Almighty One with whom nothing is impossible. Whatever may be in our hearts or flesh that will not bow to His will, He can and will conquer. Everything that is promised in God's Word, and all that is our inheritance as children of the new covenant, the almighty Jesus can bestow upon us. When I bow before Him in prayer, I am in contact with the eternal, unchanging power of God. When I commit myself for the day to the Lord Jesus, I may rest assured that His eternal, almighty power takes me under its protection and accomplishes everything for me.

If only we would take time for the hidden place of prayer,

so that we might experience in full the presence of Jesus! What a blessed life would be ours through faith—an unbroken fellowship with an omnipresent and almighty Lord.

3. *The holy love of God.* This means that with His whole heart He offers all His divine attributes for our service and is prepared to impart himself to us. Christ is the full revelation of God's love. He is the Son of that love—the gift of His love—the power of His love. This Jesus, who on the cross gave overwhelming proof of His love by His death and the shedding of His blood so as to make it impossible for us not to believe in that love, is He who comes to meet us in the place of private prayer. There He gives positive assurance of unbroken fellowship with Him as our inheritance. Through Him it will become our experience. The holy love of God that sacrificed everything to conquer sin and bring it to nothing comes to us in Christ to save us from sin.

Think about our Lord's words: "Believe me when I say that I am in the Father and the Father is in me. [And] you know him, for he lives with you and will be in you" (John 14:11, 17). Those words are the secret of the life of prayer. Take time in your place of prayer to bow down and worship. Wait on Him until He reveals himself, takes possession of you, and goes with you to show you how a person may live and walk in abiding fellowship with Him.

Do you long to know how you may always experience deliverance from the sin of prayerlessness? Here you have the secret. Believe in the Son of God; give Him time in your quiet place of prayer to reveal himself in His ever-present nearness as the Eternal, Almighty One, the Eternal Love who watches over you. Then you will experience something that you possibly have not known before: It has not entered into the heart of man what God can do for those who love Him.

Chapter 6

The Blessing of Victory

If we are delivered from the sin of prayerlessness and understand how this deliverance may continue to be experienced, what will be the fruit of our liberty? He who grasps this truth will seek after this freedom with renewed enthusiasm and perseverance. His life and experience will show that he has obtained something of unspeakable worth. He will be a living witness of the blessing found in victory.

1. *The blessedness of unbroken fellowship with God.* Think of the confidence in the Father that will replace the reproach and self-condemnation that characterized our lives before. Think of the deep consciousness we will have that God's almighty grace has effected something in us, proving that we bear His image and are fitted for a life of communion with Him. In spite of the conviction of our own unworthiness, think how we may live as children of the King in communion with our Father, and how we may manifest something of the character of our Lord Jesus that He had when He was on earth. Think how the hour of prayer may become the happiest time in our whole day, and how God may use us there to share in carrying out His plans, making us a fountain of blessing to the world around us.

2. *The power we may have for the work to which we are*

called. The preacher will learn to receive his message from God through the power of the Holy Spirit and to deliver it in that power to his congregation. He will know where he can be filled with the love and zeal that will enable him in his pastoral visiting to meet and help each individual in a spirit of compassion. He will be able to say with Paul: "I can do all things through Christ who strengthens me." We are more than conquerors through him that loved us. We are ambassadors for Christ, calling all men to be reconciled to God. These are not dreams or pictures of a vain imagination. God has given Paul as an example, so that though we may differ from him in our gifts or calling, by experience we may know the all-sufficiency of grace that can do all things for us as it did for him.

3. *The prospect that opens before us the future:* to be consecrated as intercessors in the work of bearing in our hearts the needs of the entire church and of the world. Paul sought to stir men to pray for all the saints, and he tells us what a burden he had for those who had not yet seen his face. In his personal presence he was subject to conditions of time and place, but in the Spirit he had power in the name of Christ to pray for blessing on those who had not yet heard of the Savior. In addition to his life in connection with men here on earth, near or far, he lived another life—one of love and of power in prayer, which he continually exercised. We can hardly conceive of the power God will bestow when we are freed from the sin of prayerlessness and pray with the boldness that reaches heaven in the almighty name of Christ to bring down blessing.

What a prospect! Ministers and missionaries brought by God's grace to pray with full faith and joy! What a difference it would make in our preaching, in our prayer meetings, in our fellowship with others! What power would fall in a prayer room, sanctified by communion with God and His love through Christ. What influence would be exercised on believers, urging them forward in the work of intercession. How great this influence would be felt throughout the church and among the unsaved. Who knows how God might use us for His church throughout the whole world! Is it not worthwhile to sacrifice everything and to beseech God without ceasing to give us full victory over the prayerlessness that has brought us shame?

Why do I write these things and extol so highly the blessedness of victory over "the sin that so easily besets us," and which has so robbed us of the power that God intended for us? Let me answer this. I know all too well what weak concepts we have concerning the promises and the power of God. I see how prone we are to backsliding, to limiting God's power, and to deeming it impossible for Him to do greater things than we have seen. It is a glorious thing to get to know God in a new way in our prayer time. That, however, is only the beginning. It is something still greater and more glorious to know God as the All-Sufficient One and to wait on His Spirit to open our hearts and minds to receive the great things, the new things that He longs to bestow on those who wait for Him.

God's purpose is to encourage faith in His children, His servants, so that they understand and rely upon the unspeakable greatness and omnipotence of God, so that they take literally, in a childlike spirit, this word: "Now to him who is able to do immeasurably more than all we ask or imagine, according to his power that is at work within us, to him be glory in the church and in Christ Jesus throughout all generations, for ever and ever! Amen" (Ephesians 3:20–21). Oh, that we knew what a great and glorious God we have!

You may ask: "May not this note of certain victory become a snare and lead to levity and pride?" Undoubtedly. That which is the highest and best on earth is always liable to abuse. How then can we be saved from this? Through nothing more than true prayer, which brings us into contact with God. The holiness of God, sought for in persistent prayer, will cover our sinfulness. The omnipotence and greatness of God will cause us to acknowledge our unworthiness. Fellowship with God in Jesus Christ will lead us to realize that there is in us no good thing, and that we can have fellowship with God only as our faith causes us to humble ourselves as Christ humbled himself.

Prayer is not merely coming to God to ask something of Him. It is, above all, fellowship with God and being brought under the power of His holiness and love, until He takes possession of us and stamps our entire nature with the lowliness of Christ, which is the secret of all true worship.

In Christ Jesus we draw near to the Father just as those who have died with Christ and have entirely given up their own life, like those in whom He lives and who He enables to say: "Christ lives in me." What we have said about the work that the Lord Jesus does in us to deliver us from prayerlessness is true not only of the beginning of the life of prayer and of the joy that a new experience of power to pray causes us but also for the whole life of prayer day by day. Through Him we have access to the Father. In this, as in the whole spiritual life, Christ is all. They saw no man but Jesus.

May God strengthen us to believe that there is certain victory prepared for us and that the blessing will be more than the heart of man has conceived! God will do this for those who love Him.

This does not come to us all at once. God has great patience with His children. He bears with us in fatherly patience at our slow progress. Let each child of God rejoice in all that God's Word promises. The stronger our faith, the more earnestly will we persevere to the end.

Chapter 7

The More Abundant Life

Our Lord spoke this word concerning the more abundant life when He said that He had come to give His life for His sheep: "I have come that they may have life, and have it to the full" (John 10:10). A man may have life, and still through lack of nourishment or through illness there may be no abundance of life or power. This was the distinction between the Old Testament and the New. In the former there was life under the law but not the abundance of grace of the New Testament. Christ had given life to His disciples, but they could receive the abundant life only through His resurrection and the gift of the Holy Spirit.

All true Christians have received life from Christ. The majority, however, know nothing about the more abundant life that He is willing to bestow. Paul speaks constantly of this. He says about himself that the grace of God was exceedingly abundant: "I can do all things through Christ who strengthens me. Thanks be to God, who always causes us to triumph in Christ. We are more than conquerors through him that loved us."

We have spoken of the sin of prayerlessness, the means of deliverance, and how to be kept free from it. What has been said on these points is all included in that expression of

Christ: "I have come that they may have life, and have it to the full" (John 10:10). It is of utmost importance for us to understand this more abundant life, because for a true life of prayer it is necessary that we walk in an ever-increasing experience of that overflowing life.

It is possible for us to begin this conflict against prayerlessness in dependence on Christ, looking to Him to be assisted and kept in it, and still be disappointed. This is the time when prayerlessness must be looked upon as the one sin against which we must strive. It must be recognized as part of the whole life of the flesh and as being closely connected with other sins that spring from the same source. We forget that the flesh and all its affections, whether manifested in the body or the soul, must be regarded as crucified and be handed over to death. We must not be satisfied with a weakened life, but must seek an abundant life. We must surrender ourselves entirely so that the Spirit may take full possession of us and manifest His life in us so that our spiritual being will be completely transformed.

What is it that particularly constitutes this abundant life? We cannot too often repeat it or in different ways too often explain it: the abundant life is nothing less than Jesus having full mastery over our entire being through the power of the Holy Spirit. As the Spirit makes known in us the fullness of Christ and the abundant life that He gives, it will be done chiefly in three aspects:

1. *As the Crucified One.* Not merely as the One who died for us to atone for our sins, but as He who has taken us up with himself on the cross to die with Him, and who now works out in us the power of His cross and death. You have true fellowship with Christ when you can say: "I have been crucified with Christ. He, the Crucified One, lives in me."

The feelings, the disposition that was in Him, His lowliness and obedience even to death on the cross—these were what He referred to when He said of the Holy Spirit: "He shall take of mine, and shall show it unto you"—not as an instruction, but as childlike participation of the same life that was in Him.

Do you desire the Holy Spirit to take full possession of you so as to cause the crucified Christ to dwell in you? This is exactly the purpose for which He has been given, and this He will surely accomplish in all who yield themselves to Him.

2. *As the Risen One.* The Scripture frequently mentions the resurrection in connection with the wonder-working power of God by which Christ was raised from the dead and from which comes the assurance of "his incomparably great power toward us who believe. That power is like the working of his mighty strength, which he exerted in Christ when he raised him from the dead" (Ephesians 1:19–20). Do not pass over these words too quickly. Read them again. No matter how powerless and weak you feel, recognize the truth that the omnipotence of God is working in you; and if you believe, will give you daily a share in the resurrection of His Son.

Yes, the Holy Spirit can fill you with the joy and victory of the resurrection of Christ as the power of your daily life right in the midst of the trials and temptations of this world. Let the cross humble you to the death of self. God will work out the heavenly life in you through His Spirit. How little we have understood that it is entirely the work of the Holy Spirit to make us partakers of the crucified and risen Christ and to conform us to His life and death!

3. *As the Glorified One.* The glorified Christ is He who

baptizes with the Holy Spirit. When the Lord Jesus himself was baptized with the Spirit, it was because He had humbled himself and offered himself to take part in John's baptism of repentance—a baptism for sinners—in the Jordan River. Even so, when He took upon himself the work of redemption, He received the Holy Spirit to fit Him for His work from that hour until on the cross "He offered himself without spot to God." Do you want this glorified Christ to baptize you with the Holy Spirit? Then offer yourself to Him for His service to further His great work of making known to sinners the love of the Father.

God help us to understand what a great thing it is to receive the Holy Spirit with power from the glorified Jesus! It means a willingness—a longing of the soul—to work for Him and if need be to suffer for Him. You have known and loved your Lord, you have worked for Him and have had blessing in that work, but the Lord has more than that to bestow. By the power of the Holy Spirit, He can so work in us, in our brothers and sisters around us, and in the ministers of the church so as to fill our hearts with adoring wonder and praise.

Have you grasped this truth? The abundant life is neither more nor less than the full life of Christ as the Crucified One, the Risen One, and the Glorified One, who baptizes with the Holy Spirit and reveals himself in our hearts and lives as Lord of all within us.

Not long ago I read an interesting thought: "Live in what must be." Do not live limited by your human imagination of what is possible. Live in the Word—in the love and infinite faithfulness of the Lord Jesus. Even though it goes slowly, with many a faltering step, the faith that always thanks

Him—not for experiences but for the promises on which it can rely—goes on from strength to strength, ever increasing in the blessed assurance that God himself will perfect His work in us.

Chapter 8

The Example of Our Lord

The connection between the prayer life and the Spirit life is close and indissoluble. Not only do we receive the Spirit through prayer, but also a continuous prayer life is indispensable to the Spirit life. Only as I give myself continually to prayer can I expect to be led continually by the Spirit.

This was very evident in the life of our Lord. A study of His life will give us a picture of the power of prayer.

Consider His baptism. When He was baptized and prayed, heaven was opened, and the Holy Spirit came down upon Him. Christ's surrender of himself to the sinner's baptism in the Jordan was also a surrender of himself to the sinner's death. God desired to crown that surrender with the gift of His Spirit for the work that He would accomplish. But this could not have taken place had He not prayed. In the fellowship of worship the Spirit was bestowed upon Him to lead Him out into the desert to spend forty days in prayer and fasting. Mark 1:32–35 says, "That evening after sunset the people brought to Jesus all the sick and demon-possessed. The whole town gathered at the door. Very early in the morning, while it was still dark, Jesus got up, left the house and went off to a solitary place, where he prayed."

The work of the day and evening had exhausted Him. In His healing of the sick and casting out devils, power had gone out of Him. While others slept, He went away to pray and to renew His strength in communion with His Father. He needed this time with God—otherwise He would not have been ready for the new day. The holy work of delivering souls demands constant renewal through fellowship with God.

Think of the calling of the apostles as recorded in Luke 6:12–13: "One of those days Jesus went out to a mountainside to pray, and spent the night praying to God. When morning came, he called his disciples to him and chose twelve of them, whom he also designated apostles." It is clear that if anyone wants to do God's work, he must take time for fellowship with Him to receive His wisdom and power. The dependence and helplessness we all experience opens the way to give God an opportunity to reveal His power. Choosing the apostles who would follow Christ's example was of great importance for the work of the early church. It had God's blessing and seal, and the stamp of prayer was on it.

Read Luke 9:18, 20: "Once when Jesus was praying in private and his disciples were with him, he asked them, 'Who do the crowds say I am?' Peter answered, 'The Christ of God.'" The Lord had prayed that the Father might reveal to them who He was. It was in answer to that prayer that Peter said, 'The Christ of God'; and the Lord then said: 'This was not revealed to you by man, but by my Father in heaven'" (Matthew 16:17). This great confession was the fruit of prayer.

Read on in Luke 9:28–36: "He took Peter, John and James with him and went up onto a mountain to pray. As he was praying, the appearance of his face changed. . . . A voice came from the cloud, saying, 'This is my Son, whom I have chosen; listen to him.' " Christ desired that for the strengthening of their faith God might give them assurance from heaven that He was the Son of God. Jesus' prayer that who He was might be revealed to His disciples was answered on the Mount of Transfiguration.

Does it not become even more clear that what God wills to accomplish on earth needs prayer as its indispensable condition? There was only one way for Christ and so for believers: a heart and mouth open toward heaven in believing prayer will certainly not be put to shame.

Read Luke 11:1–13: "One day Jesus was praying in a certain place. When he finished, one of his disciples said to him, 'Lord, teach us to pray.' " And then He gave them that inexhaustible prayer: "Our Father, who art in heaven . . ." In this He showed what was going on in His heart when He prayed that God's name might be hallowed, His kingdom come, His will be done, and all of this "on earth as it is in heaven." How will this ever come to pass? It will come about through prayer. The Lord's Prayer has been uttered through the ages by countless millions to their unspeakable comfort. But do not forget: it was born out of the prayer of our Lord Jesus. He had been praying himself and therefore was able to give the answer in the form of a prayer.

John 14:16 says, "I will ask the Father, and he will give you another Counselor." The entire dispensation of the New Testament, with the wonderful outpouring of the Holy Spirit, is the outcome of the prayer of the Lord Jesus. It is as though God had impressed on the gift of the Holy Spirit this seal: in answer to the prayer of the Lord Jesus, and later of His disciples, the Holy Spirit will surely come. But it will be in answer to prayer like that of our Lord, in which He took time to be alone with God, and in that prayer offered himself wholly to God.

Read John 17, the high-priestly, most holy prayer! Here the Son prays first for himself that the Father will glorify Him by giving Him power for the cross, by raising Him from the dead, and by setting Him at His right hand. These great things could not take place except through prayer. Prayer had the power to obtain them.

Afterward He prayed for His disciples that the Father might preserve them from the Evil One, keep them from the world, and sanctify them. Further on He prayed for all those who through the Word might believe on Him, that all might be one in love even as the Father and the Son are one. This prayer gives us a glimpse into the remarkable relationship between the Father and the Son. It teaches us that all the blessings of heaven come and continue to come through the prayer of Him who is at God's right hand and prays for us. But it teaches us also that all these blessings must in the same manner be desired and asked for by us. The whole nature and glory of God's blessings consist in this: they must be obtained in answer to prayer by hearts entirely surrendered to Him and by hearts that believe in the power of prayer.

Now we look at the most stunning instance of all: in Gethsemane, according to His habit, our Lord consulted and arranged with the Father the work He had to do on earth. First, He besought Him in agony and blood to allow the cup to pass from Him. When He understood that this could not be, He prayed for strength to drink the cup and surrendered himself with the words: "Your will be done." He was able to meet the Enemy full of courage, and in the power of God gave himself over to death on the cross. *He prayed.*

Why have God's children so little faith in the glory of prayer as the great power for subjecting our own wills to that of God as well as for the confident carrying out of the work of God in spite of our great weakness? Learn from our Lord Jesus how impossible it is to walk with God, obtain God's blessing or leading, or do His work joyously and fruitfully apart from close, unbroken fellowship with the One who is our living fountain of spiritual life and power.

Think over this simple study of the prayer life of our Lord Jesus. Then with prayer for the leading of the Holy Spirit, endeavor to learn from God's Word about the life that the Lord Jesus Christ bestows upon every Christian and then supports. It is nothing other than the life of daily prayer. Let every minister of the gospel recognize how entirely useless it is to attempt to do the work of the Lord in any other way than the way He did it. Let us as layworkers believe that we are set free from the ordinary business of the world, that we may above everything have time, in our Savior's name and by His Spirit and in oneness with Him, to ask for and obtain blessing for the world.

Chapter 9

The Holy Spirit and Prayer

Is it not unfortunate that our thoughts about the Holy Spirit are so often coupled with grief and self-reproach? Yet He bears the name of Comforter [Counselor, in the NIV] and is given to lead us to find in Christ our highest delight and joy. Sadder still is the fact that He who dwells within us to comfort us is often grieved by us because we will not permit Him to accomplish His work of love. All this prayerlessness in the church must be a source of inexpressible pain to the Holy Spirit. Surely the low energy and utter helplessness so often found in us is because we do not permit the Holy Spirit to lead us.

God grant that our meditation on the work of the Holy Spirit may cause rejoicing and the strengthening of our faith!

The Holy Spirit is the Spirit of prayer. He is called in Zechariah 12:10 "a spirit of grace and supplication." Twice in Paul's epistles there is a remarkable reference to Him in the matter of prayer: "For you did not receive a spirit that makes you a slave again to fear, but you received the Spirit of sonship. And by him we cry, 'Abba, Father'" (Romans 8:15, emphasis added). "Because you are sons, God sent the Spirit of his Son into our hearts, the Spirit who calls out, '*Abba,* Father'" (Galatians 4:6, emphasis added). Have you ever meditated on the words *Abba, Father*? In that name our Savior offered His greatest prayer to the Father, accompanied by the total surrender and sacrifice of His life and love. The Holy Spirit is given for the express purpose of teaching us right from the very beginning of our Christian life to utter that word in childlike trust and surrender. In one of these passages we read, "We cry", in the other, "the Spirit calls." What a wonderful blending of the divine and the human cooperation in prayer. What proof that God has done His utmost to make prayer as natural and effectual as the cry of a child to an earthly father when he says, "Abba, Father."

And is it not proof that the Holy Spirit is often a stranger in the church when prayer for which God has made such provision is regarded as a task and a burden? Does not this teach us to look for the deep root of prayerlessness in our ignorance of and disobedience to the divine Instructor whom the Father has commissioned to teach us to pray?

If we wish to understand this truth even more clearly, we can look at Romans 8:26–27: "In the same way, the Spirit helps us in our weakness. We do not know what we ought to pray for, but the Spirit himself intercedes for us with groans that words cannot express. And he who searches our hearts knows the mind of the Spirit, because the Spirit intercedes for the saints in accordance with God's will." Is it not clear? The Christian left to himself does not know how to pray or what he ought to pray for. But God has stooped to meet us in this helplessness of ours by giving us the Holy Spirit to pray for us. That operation of His Spirit is deeper than our thoughts or feelings, but is acknowledged and answered by God.

Our first work, therefore, ought to be to come into God's presence not with our ignorant prayers, not with many words and thoughts, but in the confidence that the divine work of the Holy Spirit is being carried out within us. This confidence will encourage reverence and quietness and will also enable us, in dependence on the help that the Spirit gives, to lay our desires and deepest needs before God. The supreme lesson for every prayer is first of all to commit to the leading of the Holy Spirit and in total dependence on Him to give Him first place. Through Him your prayer will have value you cannot imagine. Through Him also you will learn to express your desires in the name of Christ.

Such faith would be protection against listlessness and despair in our place of prayer! Think of it! In every prayer the triune God takes a part—the Father who hears, the Son in whose name we pray, and the Spirit who prays for us and in us. How important it is that we are in right relationship to the Holy Spirit and that we understand His work!

The following points demand serious consideration.

1. *Let us firmly believe that the Spirit of God's Son, the Holy Spirit, is in us.* Do not assume that you know this and have no need to reconsider it. It is a thought so important and so divine that it can gain entrance to our hearts and be retained there only by the Holy Spirit. "The Spirit bears witness with our spirit." Our position ought to be that of reckoning with full assurance of faith that our heart is His temple and that He dwells within us and rules the soul and the body. Let us thank God heartily whenever we pray that we have His Spirit in us to teach us to pray. Thanksgiving will draw our hearts toward God and keep us in fellowship with Him;

it will take our attention from ourselves and give the Spirit room in our hearts.

No wonder we have been lacking in prayer and have felt this work too hard for us: we have tried to have fellowship with the eternal God apart from His Spirit, who reveals the Father and the Son to us.

2. *As we put this faith into practice with the certainty that the Spirit dwells and works in us, there must also be an understanding of all that He desires to accomplish in us.* His work in prayer is closely connected with His other work. In an earlier chapter we saw that His first and greatest work is to reveal Christ in His omnipresent love and power. So in prayer the Holy Spirit will constantly remind us of Christ, of His blood and His name, as the sure basis of our being heard.

Then, as the Spirit of holiness, He will teach us to recognize, hate, and be done with sin. He is the Spirit of light and wisdom, who leads us into the heavenly secret of God's overflowing grace. He is the Spirit of love and power, who teaches us to witness for Christ and to labor for souls with tender pity. The more closely I associate all these blessings with the Spirit, the more I will be convinced of His deity and the more ready I will be to commit myself to His guidance as I give myself to prayer. What a different life mine would be if I knew the Spirit as the Spirit of prayer! Another thing I need constantly to learn is:

3. *The Spirit desires full possession of my life.* We pray for more of the Spirit, and we pray well if alongside this prayer we hold the truth that the Spirit wants more of us. The Spirit would possess us entirely. Just as my soul has my whole body for its dwelling place and service, so the Holy Spirit would have my body and soul as His dwelling place, entirely under

His control. No one can continue long and earnestly in prayer without perceiving that the Spirit is gently leading him to an entirely new consecration of which he previously knew nothing. "I seek you with my whole heart." The Spirit will make such words more and more the motto of our lives. He will cause us to recognize that what remains in us of double-mindedness is truly sinful. He will reveal Christ as the almighty deliverer from all sin, who is always near to defend us. He will lead us in this way in prayer. He will help us to forget ourselves. He will make us willing to offer ourselves for training as intercessors to whom God can entrust the fulfillment of His plans and who day and night cry to Him to avenge His church of her adversary.

God, help us to know the Spirit and to revere Him as the Spirit of prayer!

Chapter 10

A Proper Knowledge of What Sin Is

To understand grace and to understand Christ aright, we must understand what sin is. How can we come to this understanding? Through the light of God and His Word.

Come with me to the beginning of the Bible. We see man created by God after His image and pronounced by his Creator to be very good. Then sin entered. It was rebellion against God. Adam and Eve were driven out of the Garden and brought, along with untold millions, under the curse and utter ruin. *That was the work of sin.*

Let us look further into Scripture at the story of Noah and his ark on Mount Ararat. Godlessness had become so rampant among men that God saw no remedy but to destroy humankind from the face of the earth. *That was the work of sin.*

What about Sinai? God wanted to establish His covenant with a new nation: the people of Israel. But because of man's sinfulness, He could do this only by appearing in darkness and lightning so frightening that even Moses was afraid and trembled. And before the end of the giving of the law, the message came that anyone who did not continue in all things written in the book of the law was cursed. *It was sin that made that decree necessary.*

When we visit Mount Calvary, we get a taste of what sin is: we see the hatred and enmity with which the world cast out and crucified the Son of God. Here sin reached its climax. Christ was made sin and became a curse as the only way to destroy the power of sin. In the agony of Gethsemane, when He prayed that He might be spared the terrible cup, and in excruciating pain on the cross with its deep darkness and desertion by the Father, He cried out, "My God, my God, why have you forsaken me?" we get a faint glimpse of the curse and the indescribable suffering sin brings. If anything can cause us to hate and detest sin, it is seeing Christ on that bitter cross.

Finally, let us look at the judgment seat of God on the Last Day and the bottomless pit of darkness, where countless souls will plunge under the sentence of Matthew 25:41: "Depart from me, you who are cursed, into the eternal fire prepared for the devil and his angels." When these words truly penetrate our hearts, they will fill us with a not-to-be-forgotten horror of sin.

Remember that you are a child of God. Sometimes you commit sin: you allow it to fulfill its desires. Are you forced to cry out with shame: "Woe unto me because of my sin"? The great power of sin is that it blinds us so that we do not recognize its true character. Even the Christian finds an excuse, thinking that he can never be perfect, and that daily sin is a necessity. He is so accustomed to the idea of sinning that he has lost the ability to grieve over it. But there can be no real progress in grace apart from an increased consciousness of the sin and guilt of every transgression against God.

And there cannot be a more important question than this: "How can I regain the lost tenderness of conscience and become prepared to offer to God the sacrifice of a broken heart?"

Scripture teaches us the way. Remember what God thinks about sin: His holiness burns against it; He sacrificed His Son to conquer sin and to deliver us from it. Wait in God's presence until His holiness shines upon you, and you cry out with Isaiah: "Woe unto me, for I am undone!"

Remember the cross and what the love of Christ endured there; what unspeakable pain sin caused Him. Take time, so that the suffering of Christ on the cross may have its full effect and influence. Think of sin as nothing less than giving your hand over to Satan and his power. This is one of the awful results of our prayerlessness and of our quick, careless "waiting" before God: a true knowledge of sin is all but lost.

Think not only of what redemption cost Christ but also of the fact that Christ is offered by the Holy Spirit as a gift of grace through whom divine forgiveness and renewal come to us. Ask how such love should be repaid. If only time were taken to linger in God's presence and ask such questions, the Spirit of God would accomplish His work of conviction of sin. He would teach us to take an entirely new viewpoint of sin. The thought would begin to arise in our hearts that we have truly been redeemed, so that in Christ's power we may live every day as partners in the great victory He obtained over sin on the cross and begin to manifest it in our walk.

Are you beginning to see that the sin of prayerlessness has had a greater effect than you first thought? Because of hasty and superficial communion with God, the sense of sin becomes weak and there is no motive strong enough to help you to hate sin and flee from it. Nothing except secret, humble, constant fellowship with God can teach you as His child to hate sin as God hates it. Nothing but the close fellowship and unceasing power of the living Christ can make it possible for you to understand what sin is and to detest it. Without this deeper understanding of sin, we cannot truly appropriate the victory that Christ made possible for us.

Chapter 11

The Holiness of God

It has often been said that the church has lost the concept of sin and the holiness of God. In the secret place of prayer we may learn anew how to give God's holiness the place it should have in our faith and our life. If you do not know how to spend half an hour in prayer, take up the subject of God's holiness. Bow before Him and give God time so that you may know His presence, and He may speak to you. It is an effort at first, but one that results in great blessing.

To strengthen yourself in the practice of His holy presence, take up the Word. Read the book of Leviticus and notice how God five times gives the command: "Consecrate yourselves and be holy, because I am holy" (11:44–45; 19:2; 20:7, 26). Still more frequent is the expression: "I am the Lord that sanctifies you." This great thought is carried over into the New Testament. Peter says (1 Peter 1:15–16): "But just as he who called you is holy, so be holy in all you do; for it is written: 'Be holy, because I am holy.' " Paul writes in his first epistle (1 Thessalonians 3:13; 4:7; 5:24): "May he strengthen your hearts so that you will be blameless and holy in the presence of our God and Father when our Lord Jesus comes with all his holy ones. For God did not call us to be impure, but to live a holy life. The one who calls you is faithful and he will do it."

Nothing but the knowledge of God as the Holy One will make us holy. How are we to obtain that knowledge of God unless we go alone to Him in the place of prayer? It is utterly impossible unless we take time and allow the holiness of God to reveal itself to us. How can anyone on earth obtain intimate knowledge of another if he does not associate with that person and remain under that one's influence? And how can God himself sanctify us if we do not take time to be brought under the power of the glory of His holiness? Nowhere can we get to know the holiness of God and come under its influence and power except in private prayer. It has been well said: "No man can expect to make progress in holiness who is not often and long alone with God."

And what is the holiness of God? It is the highest, most glorious, most all-embracing of all the attributes of God. *Holiness* is the most profound word in the Bible. It is a word that is at home in heaven. Both the Old and New Testaments tell us this. Isaiah heard the seraphs with veiled faces cry out: "Holy, holy, holy is the Lord Almighty; the whole earth is full of his glory" (6:3). John heard the four living creatures say, "Holy, holy, holy is the Lord God Almighty, who was, and is, and is to come" (Revelation 4:8). This is the highest expression of God's glory in heaven by beings who live in His immediate presence and bow low before Him. Do we dare imagine that we—by thinking, reading, and hearing—can understand or become partakers of the holiness of God? We need to begin to thank God that we have our private place of prayer, a place where we can be alone with Him.

If we remain prayerless, let our hearts be deeply ashamed. By so doing we make it impossible for God to impart His holiness to us. Let us ask God to forgive us this sin and to draw us to himself by His heavenly grace and to strengthen us to have fellowship with Him, the One who is holy.

The meaning of the words *the holiness of God* is not easily expressed. But we may begin by saying that they imply the unspeakable aversion and hatred with which God regards sin. If you want to understand what that means, remember that He preferred to see His Son die than that sin should reign in us. Think of the Son of God, who gave up His life rather than act in the smallest matter against the will of the Father. He had such a hatred of sin that He preferred to die rather than let men be held in its power. That is something of the holiness of God; it is a pledge that He will do everything for us in order to deliver us from sin. Holiness is the fire of God that will consume sin in us and make us holy sacrifices, pure and acceptable before Him. For this reason the Spirit came down as fire. He is the Spirit of God's holiness, the Spirit of sanctification in us.

Think about the holiness of God and bow in lowliness before Him until your heart is filled with the assurance of what He will do for you. Take a week, if necessary, to read and reread the words of God on this great truth until your heart is brought under the conviction: "This is the glory of the secret place of prayer, to be able to converse with God, the Holy One, and to bow in deep humility and shame before Him, because we have so offended Him and His love through our prayerlessness." There we shall receive the assurance that He will again take us into fellowship with himself. No one can expect to understand and receive the holiness of God who is not often and long alone with Him.

Someone has said that the holiness of God is the expression of the unspeakable distance by which He in His righteousness are separated from us, and yet also of the unspeakable nearness in which He in His love longs to hold fellowship with us and dwell in us. Bow in humble reverence as you think of the immeasurable distance between you and God. Bow in childlike confidence in the strong desire of His heart to be united with you in the deepest intimacy, and reckon most confidently on Him to reveal something of His holiness to the soul that thirsts after Him and waits upon Him and is quiet before Him.

Notice how the two sides of the holiness of God are united in the cross. So terrible was the aversion and anger of God against our sin that Christ was left in darkness; God had to hide His face from Christ when sin was laid upon Him. Still, so deep was the love of God toward us, and He so desired to be united to us, that He spared not His Son but gave Him over to unutterable sufferings so that He might receive us in union with Christ into His holiness and embrace us as His beloved children. It was of this suffering that our Lord Jesus said, "For them I sanctify myself, that they too may be truly sanctified" (John 17:19). He is our sanctification, and we are holy in Him.

I ask that you not think lightly of that grace: you have a holy God who longs to make you holy. Obey the voice of God that calls you to give time to Him in the stillness of your prayer room so that He may cause His holiness to rest on you. Let it be your habit every day, in the secrecy of your place of prayer, to meet the holy God. You will be repaid for the inconvenience it may cost you. The reward will be sure and rich. You will learn to hate sin and to regard it as cursed but conquered. The new nature will give you an abhorrence of sin. The living Jesus, the holy God, will as Conqueror be your strength, and you will begin to believe the great promise contained in 1 Thessalonians 5:23–24: "May God himself, the God of peace, sanctify you through and through. May your whole spirit, soul and body be kept blameless at the coming of our Lord Jesus Christ. The one who calls you is faithful and he will do it."

Chapter 12

The Importance of Obedience

In opposition to sin stands obedience. "For just as through the disobedience of the one man the many were made sinners, so also through the obedience of the one man the many will be made righteous. You have been set free from sin and have become slaves to righteousness" (Romans 5:19; 6:18). In connection with all that has been said about sin and the new life and the reception of the Holy Spirit, we must always give to obedience the place assigned to it by God.

It was because Christ humbled himself and became obedient unto death, even death on the cross, that God so highly exalted Him. In this connection Paul exhorts us: "Your attitude should be the same as that of Christ Jesus" (Philippians 2:5). We see, above everything else, that the obedience of Christ, so pleasing to God, must become the basic characteristic of our disposition and of our entire walk. Just as a servant knows that he must first obey his master in all things, so the surrender to an implicit and unquestioning obedience to God must become the essential characteristic of our lives.

How little this is understood by Christians! How many

allow themselves to be misled and rest satisfied with the belief that sin is a necessity and that one must sin every day! It would be difficult to say how much harm is done by this mistake. It is one of the main reasons why the sin of diso-bedience is so seldom recognized. I have heard Christians laughingly speak about the cause of darkness and weakness in their lives as "just disobedience again." Don't we as quickly as possible try to get rid of an employee who is habit-ually insubordinate? But when a child of God is disobedient every day, we do not regard it as anything extraordinary. Dis-obedience may be daily acknowledged, but there is no turn-ing away from it.

Perhaps this is why so much prayer is made for the power of the Holy Spirit and yet so few answers come. We read, "God has given His Holy Spirit to them that obey Him." Every child of God has received the Holy Spirit when he was born again. If he uses the measure of the Holy Spirit that he has with the definite purpose of being obedient to the utmost, then God can and will favor him with further man-ifestations of the Spirit's power. But if he permits disobedi-ence to get the upper hand day after day, he need not be surprised if his prayer for more of the Spirit remains unan-swered.

We have already said that the Spirit desires to possess more of us. How can we fully surrender ourselves to Him other than by being obedient? The Scripture says that we are to be led by the Spirit and that we must walk by the Spirit. My right relationship to the Holy Spirit is that I allow myself to be guided and ruled by Him. Obedience is the most important factor in our whole relationship to God.

Notice how the Lord Jesus, giving His great promise about the Holy Spirit on His last night, emphasized this point: "If you love me, you will obey what I command. And I will ask the Father, and he will give you another Counselor to be with you forever" (John 14:15–16). Obedience was essential as preparation for the reception of the Spirit. He often repeated this thought: "Whoever has my commands and obeys them, he is the one who loves me. He who loves me will be loved by my Father, and I too will love him and show myself to him" (John 14:21). So also in verse 23: "If anyone loves me, he will obey my teaching. My Father will love him, and we will come to him and make our home with him." And in chapter 15 of John, verse 7: "If you remain in me and my words remain in you, ask whatever you wish, and it will be given you." And verses 10 and 14: "If you obey my commands, you will remain in my love, just as I have obeyed my Father's commands and remain in his love. You are my friends if you do what I command."

Can words more plainly declare that our life in this new dispensation since the resurrection of Christ depends on obedience? That was the attitude of Christ's life. He lived to do not His own will but the will of the Father. And He cannot with His Spirit make an abiding home in the heart of one who does not surrender completely to a life of obedience.

It is truly sad how few are concerned about this disobedience! How little we believe that Christ asks for, expects this, from us—because He has undertaken to make it possible for us. How much is it manifested in our prayer, our walk, or in the depths of our spiritual life that we seek to please the Lord in all things? Too seldom we mention our disobedience or say, "I will be sorry for my sin."

But is obedience really possible? It certainly is for the

man who believes that Christ Jesus is his sanctification and relies on Him.

It is impossible for a man whose eyes have not yet been opened to see that Christ can at once forgive his sin. Such a man also finds it impossible to see that there is in Christ a sure promise of power to accomplish all that God desires of His child. Just as we found the fullness of forgiveness through faith, so through a new act of faith deliverance from the dominion of sin that so easily ensnares us is obtained. And by faith the abiding blessing of this continuous experience of Christ's keeping power becomes ours. This faith obtains new insight into promises whose meaning was not previously understood: "May the God of peace, who through the blood of the eternal covenant brought back from the dead our Lord Jesus, that great Shepherd of the sheep, equip you with everything good for doing his will, and may he work in us what is pleasing to him, through Jesus Christ" (Hebrews 13:20–21). "To him who is able to keep you from falling and to present you before his glorious presence without fault and with great joy—to the only God our Savior be glory, majesty, power and authority, through Jesus Christ our Lord" (Jude 24–25). "Therefore, my brothers, be all the more eager to make your calling and election sure. For if you do these things, you will never fall" (2 Peter 1:10). "May he strengthen your hearts so that you will be blameless and holy in the presence of our God and Father when our Lord Jesus comes with all his holy ones" (1 Thessalonians 3:13). "But the Lord is faithful, and he will strengthen and protect you from the evil one" (2 Thessalonians 3:3).

The fulfillment of these and other promises is secured for us in Christ. Just as certainly as the forgiveness of sin is assured to us in Him, so also is power against new or fresh attacks of sin assured to us. Then for the first time we understand that faith can confidently rely fully upon Christ and His abiding protection.

This faith sheds a totally new light on the life of obedience. *Christ holds himself responsible to work this out in me every moment, if I only trust Him for it.* I begin to understand the important phrase with which Paul begins and closes the book of Romans: "obedience that comes from faith" (Romans 1:5; 16:26). Faith brings me to the Lord Jesus not only for forgiveness of sin but also every moment to enjoy the power that enables me as a child of God to abide in Him and to be numbered among His obedient children. It is written of these children that as He who has called them is holy, so they also may be holy in all their behavior. Everything depends on whether or not I believe on the whole Christ with the fullness of His grace, and that He will be—not now and then but every moment—the strength of my life. Such faith will lead to an obedience that will enable me to "walk worthy of the Lord unto all pleasing, being fruitful in every good work, strengthened with all might, according to his glorious power."

The soul that feeds on such promises will experience instead of the disobedience of self-effort all that the obedience of faith means. All such promises have their measure, their certainty, and their strength in the living Christ.

Chapter 13

The Victorious Life

We viewed chapter 7, "The More Abundant Life," mainly from the side of our Lord Jesus. We saw that there is to be found in him—the Crucified One, the Risen One, and the Glorified One, who baptizes with the Holy Spirit—all that is needed for a life of abundant grace. Now, in speaking of "The Victorious Life," we will look from another standpoint. We want to see how a Christian can live as a true victor. We have often said that the prayer life is not something that can be improved upon in and of itself. So intimately is it bound up with the entire spiritual life that only when that whole life (previously marked by a lack of prayer) becomes renewed and sanctified can prayer have its rightful place of power. We must not be satisfied with less than the victorious life to which God calls His children.

Our Lord in the seven letters to the churches in Revelation concludes with a promise to each for those who overcome. The phrase "he that overcomes" is repeated seven times; and with it some glorious promises are given. They were given even to churches like Ephesus that had "forsaken its first love," to Sardis, that "[had] a reputation of being alive, but was dead," and Laodicea with her lukewarmness and self-satisfaction—as proof that if they would only repent, they might win the crown of victory. The call comes to every Christian to strive for the crown. If everything is not sacrificed to gain the victory, how is it possible to be a healthy Christian or to preach in the power of the Spirit? It is not; it is impossible.

How do we attain victory, then? The answer is simple. All is in Christ. "Thanks be to God, who always leads us in triumphal procession in Christ" (2 Corinthians 2:14). "In all these things we are more than conquerors through him who loved us" (Romans 8:37). It all depends on our right relationship to Christ, our complete surrender, perfect faith, and unbroken fellowship with Him. But how do you attain to all of this? These simple guidelines show the way by which the full enjoyment of what is prepared for you in Christ may be yours: (1) a new discovery of sin; (2) a new surrender to Christ; (3) a new faith in the power that will make it possible for you to persevere.

1. *A new discovery of sin.* In Romans 3 we find described the knowledge of sin that is necessary for repentance and forgiveness: "Now we know that whatever the law says, it says to those who are under the law, so that every mouth may be silenced and the whole world held accountable to God" (v. 19). And so you recognized your sin more or less consciously, confessed it, and obtained mercy. But if you would lead a victorious life, something more is needed. This begins with the recognition that in you, that is, in your flesh, there dwells no good thing (Romans 7:18). In the inner man you delight in the law of God, but you see another law in your members bringing you into captivity to the law of sin, and compelling you to cry out: "What a wretched man I am! Who will rescue me from this body of death?" (vv. 23–24). This is not like your experience at conversion, when you

386

thought over your few or many sins. This work goes much deeper. You find that as a Christian you have no power to do the good that you want to do. You must be brought to a new and deeper insight into the sin of your nature, and even though you are a Christian, you must see your utter weakness to live as you ought. You will learn to cry out: "What a wretched man I am! Who will rescue me from this body of death?"

The answer to this question is "Thanks be to God—through Jesus Christ our Lord!" (v. 25). Then follows the revelation of what there is in Christ. It is not limited to what is given in Romans 3. It is more. I am in Christ Jesus, and the law of the Spirit of life in Christ has made me free from the law of sin and death under which I was bound. I have been made free by the law (or power) of the life of the Spirit in Christ, and now am called in a new sense and by a new surrender to acknowledge Christ as the giver of the victory.

2. *A new surrender to Christ.* You may have used these words *surrender* and *consecration* many times but without a right understanding of what they mean. As you have been brought by the teaching of Romans 7 to a complete sense of the hopelessness of leading a true Christian life or a true prayer life by your own efforts, you begin to realize that the Lord Jesus must take you up by His own power in an entirely new way, and must take possession of you by His Spirit to an entirely new degree. This alone can preserve you from constantly sinning. Only this can make you truly victorious. This leads you to look away from yourself, to get free from yourself, and to expect everything to come from the Lord Jesus.

If we begin to understand this, we are prepared to admit that in our nature there is nothing good; it is under a curse and is nailed with Christ to His cross. We come to see what Paul means when he says that we are dead to sin by the death of Christ. Thus we obtain a share of the glorious resurrection life that is in Him. With this insight we are encouraged to believe that Christ through His life in us, through His continual indwelling, can keep us. Just as we had no rest until we knew He had received us at our conversion, so now we feel the need of coming to Him to receive from Him the assurance that He has undertaken to keep us by the power of His resurrection life. And so we feel that there must be an act as definite as His reception of us at conversion by which He gives us the assurance of victory. And although it appears to us to be too great and too much, still the man who casts himself without plea into the arms of Christ will experience that He does indeed receive us into such a fellowship as will make us, right from the beginning, "more than conquerors."

3. *A new faith in the power that will make it possible for you to persevere.* You have no doubt heard of the Keswick Convention, born out of the Moody-Sankey revival of 1875. The aim of this annual convention is to promote "practical holiness." The primary focus of the convention is that Christ is prepared to take upon himself the care and preservation of our lives every day and all day if we trust Him to do it. This truth is borne out in the testimonies given by many at the convention. Many have said that they felt called to a new surrender, to a complete consecration of their life to Christ, but they were hindered by a fear of failure. The thirst after holiness, after unbroken fellowship with Jesus, and after a life of persevering childlike obedience drew them in one direction. But the question always came up: "Will I continue to be faithful?" And to this question there came no answer until they believed that the surrender must be made not in their

own strength but in a power given them by the glorified Christ. He would not only keep them for the future, but He would also make possible the surrender of faith that expects future grace. It was in the power of Christ himself that they were able to present their lives to Him.

Oh, reader, believe it; a victorious life is possible. Christ, the Victor, is your Lord, who will undertake for you in everything and will enable you to do all that the Father expects of you. Be of good courage. Trust Him to do this great work for you, who has so freely given His life for you and forgiven you your sins. Only be bold to surrender yourself to a life kept from sin by the power of God. Along with the deepest conviction that in you dwells no good thing, confess that you see in the Lord Jesus all the goodness you will ever need for the life of a child of God. Begin literally to live "by the faith of the Son of God, who loved you, and gave himself for you."

For your encouragement, I will share the testimony of Bishop Moule, a man of deep humility. When he first heard of the Keswick Convention, he was afraid of "perfectionism" and would have nothing to do with it. Unexpectedly, during a vacation in Scotland, he came in contact with some friends at a small convention. There he heard an address that convinced him how entirely the teaching was according to Scripture. There was no word about sinlessness in the flesh or in man. Rather, it was a word about how Jesus can keep a man with a sinful nature from practicing sin. The light dawned in his heart. He who had always been counted a sensitive, obedient Christian came in touch with a new experience of what Christ will do for the one who gives himself completely to Him.

Here is what Bishop Moule says about the text "I can do all things through Christ who strengthens me":

I dare to say that it is possible for those who really are willing to reckon on the power of the Lord, for keeping and victory, to lead a life in which His promises are taken as they stand, and are found to be true. It is possible to cast all our care on Him daily, and to enjoy deep peace in doing it. It is possible to have the thoughts and imaginations of our hearts purified in the deepest meaning of the word, through faith. It is possible to see the will of God in everything, and to receive it, not with sighing, but with singing. It is possible, in the inner life of desire and feeling, to lay aside all bitterness, and wrath, and anger, and evil speaking, every day and every hour. It is possible, by taking complete refuge in divine power, to become strong through and through; and where previously our greatest weakness lay, to find that the things which formerly upset all our resolves to be patient, or pure, or humble, furnish today an opportunity to make sin powerless—through Him who loved us, and works in us an agreement with His will, and a blessed sense of His presence and His power. These things are divine possibilities, and because they are His work, the true experience of them will always cause us to bow lower at His feet, and to learn to thirst and long for more. We cannot possibly be satisfied with anything less than to walk with God—each day, each hour, each moment, in Christ, through the power of the Holy Spirit.

Thank God, a life of victory is sure for those who have a knowledge of their inward ruin and are hopeless in themselves but who, in "the confidence of despair," have looked to Jesus. They, in faith in His power to make the act of surrender possible for them, have done it in His might and now rely on Him alone every day and every hour.

Part Two

The Inner Room

—— Chapter 14 ——

Suggestions for Private Prayer

A brother who had earnestly confessed his neglect of prayer but who was later able to declare that his eyes had been opened to see that the Lord supplies grace for all that He requires of us, asked if some suggestions could be given for spending the most profitable time in private prayer. Since the question came after a conference, and there was no opportunity then to give him a sufficient answer, I will share the following now in the hope that it will be of help to some:

1. As you enter a time of private prayer, let your first focus be to give thanks to God for the unspeakable love that invites you to come to Him and to converse freely with Him. If your heart is cold and dead, remember that your faith is not a matter of feeling but first involves the will. Raise your heart to God and thank Him for the assurance you have that He looks down on you and will bless you. Through such an act of faith you honor God and draw your soul away from being occupied with itself. Think also of the glorious grace of the Lord Jesus, who is willing to teach you to pray and to give you the disposition to do so. Think too of the Holy

Spirit, who was given to enable you to cry, "Abba, Father" in your heart and to help your faltering prayer. Five minutes spent in this way will strengthen your faith. Once more I say: Begin with an act of thanksgiving, and praise God for your place of prayer and the promise of blessing there.

2. You must prepare yourself for prayer by Bible study. The first reason why the quiet time is not attractive to most is that people do not know how to pray. Their storehouse of words is soon exhausted, and they do not know what else to say, because they forget that prayer is not a soliloquy, where everything comes from one side; it is a dialogue, where God's child listens to what the Father says, replies to it, and then makes his requests known.

Read a few verses from the Bible. Do not concern yourself with the difficulties contained in them. You can consider these later; but take what you do understand, apply it to yourself, and ask the Father to make His Word light and power in your heart. In this way you will have material enough for prayer from the Word; you will also have the liberty to ask for things you need. Keep on in this way, and the prayer room will become at length not a place where you sigh and struggle, but one of living fellowship with the Father in heaven. Prayerful study of the Bible is indispensable for powerful prayer.

3. When you have thus received the Word into your heart, turn to serious prayer. But do not attempt it hastily or thoughtlessly, as though you knew well enough how to pray on your own. Prayer in our own strength brings no blessing. Take time to present yourself reverently and in quietness before God. Remember His greatness and holiness and love. Think over what you want to ask of Him. Do not be satisfied with going over the same things every day. No child goes on

saying the same thing day after day to his earthly father.

What you talk about with the Father is influenced by the needs of the day. Let your prayer be something definite, arising either out of the Word that you have read or out of the real spiritual needs that you long to have satisfied. Let your prayer be so definite that you can say as you go out, "I know what I have asked of my Father, and I expect an answer." It is a good idea to sometimes take a piece of paper and write down what you will pray for.

4. What has been said is in reference to your own needs. But you know that we are encouraged to pray for the needs of others and how we may help them. One of the main reasons why daily prayer does not bring more joy and blessing is that it is basically selfish. Selfishness is the death of prayer.

Remember your family; your church with its many interests and endeavors; your own neighborhood; your friends. Let your heart be enlarged and take up the interests of missions and of the church throughout the world. Become an intercessor, and you will experience for the first time the blessedness of being used of God to bless others through prayer. You will begin to feel that there is something worth living for as you see that you have something to say to God. You will find that He will do things in answer to your prayers that otherwise would not have been done.

A child can ask his father for his basic needs. A full-grown son converses with him about his business and family responsibilities. A weak child of God prays only for himself; a full-grown man in Christ understands how to consult with God over what must take place in the kingdom. Let your prayer list bear the names of those for whom you pray—your minister, other ministers in the community, and missionary affairs with which you are familiar. Thus the inner room will become a wonder of God's goodness and a fountain of great joy. It can become the most blessed place on earth. It may be hard to believe, but it is the simple truth that God will make it a Bethel, where His angels ascend and descend, and where you will cry out, "The Lord shall be my God!" He will make it a Peniel, where you will see the face of God, as a prince of God, as one who wrestled with the angel and overcame him.

5. Do not forget the close bond between the inner room and the outside world. The attitude of the inner prayer room must remain with us all day. The object of secret prayer is to unite us to God that we may know His abiding presence with us. Sin, thoughtlessness, yielding to the flesh or the world, makes us unfit for prayer and casts a cloud over our soul. If you have stumbled or fallen, return to your secret place; let your first task be to invoke the blood of Jesus and to claim its cleansing power. Do not rest until you have fully confessed, repented of, and put away your sin. Let the precious blood of Jesus give you a fresh freedom of approach to God. Remember that the roots of your life in the inner room reach far out through body and soul so as to manifest themselves in all of life. Let "the obedience of faith," in which you pray in secret, rule you constantly. The inner room is intended to bind man to God, to supply him with power from God, and to enable him to live for God alone. Thank God for that place and for the blessed life that He will enable you there to experience and nourish.

Chapter 15

The Use of Time and the Example of Paul

Before the creation of the world, time did not exist. God lived in eternity in a way that we little understand. With creation, time began, and everything was placed under its power. God has placed all living creatures under a law of slow growth. Think of the length of time it takes for a child to become a man in body and mind. In learning, in wisdom, in business, in leisure work, and in politics, everything somehow depends on patience and perseverance. Everything needs time.

It is the same in religion. There can be no dialogue with a holy God, no fellowship between heaven and earth, no power for the salvation of the souls of others, unless time is set apart for it. Just as it is necessary for a child to eat in order to grow and to learn every day for many years to develop his mind, so the life of grace entirely depends on the time we are willing to give to it day by day.

A minister of the gospel is appointed by God to teach and help those who are engaged in ordinary occupations of life to find sufficient time and use it correctly for the preservation of his spiritual life. Of course, the minister cannot do this unless he has a living experience of a life of prayer. His highest calling is not preaching, or speaking, or church visitation, but it is to *cultivate the life of God in himself daily,* and to be a *witness of what the Lord teaches him* and accomplishes in him.

It was true even of the Lord Jesus. Why was it necessary that He who had no sin to confess sometimes spent all night in prayer to God? It is because his spiritual life had to be strengthened through an intimate relationship with His Father. His experience of a life in which He took time for fellowship with God enabled Him to share that life with us.

I pray that each minister of the gospel might understand that he has received this precious space of time from God in order to wait on Him! God must have for fellowship with himself the first and the best of our time. Without this, our preaching and our service will have little power. Here on earth I may expend my time in exchange for money or learning. The minister exchanges his time for divine power and the spiritual blessings to be obtained from heaven. That, and nothing else, makes him a man of God and ensures that his preaching will be in the demonstration of the Spirit and power.

"Follow my example, as I follow the example of Christ" (1 Corinthians 11:1).

Paul was a minister who prayed much for his congregation. Read his words prayerfully so that you may hear the voice of the Spirit.

"Night and day we pray most earnestly that we may see you again and supply what is lacking in your faith. Now may our God and Father himself and our Lord Jesus clear the way for us to come to you. May the Lord make your love increase and overflow for each other and for everyone else, just as ours does for you. May he strengthen your hearts so that you will be blameless and holy in the presence of our God and Father when our Lord Jesus comes with all his holy ones" (1 Thessalonians 3:10–13).

"May God himself, the God of peace, sanctify you through and through. May your whole spirit, soul and body be kept blameless at the coming of our Lord Jesus Christ" (1 Thessalonians 5:23).

What food for meditation!

"May our Lord Jesus Christ himself and God our Father, who loved us and by his grace gave us eternal encouragement and good hope, encourage your hearts and strengthen you in every good deed and word" (2 Thessalonians 2:16–17).

"God, whom I serve with my whole heart in preaching the gospel of his Son, is my witness how constantly I remember you in my prayers at all times; and I pray that now at last by God's will the way may be opened for me to come to you. I long to see you so that I may impart to you some spiritual gift to make you strong" (Romans 1:9–11).

"Brothers, my heart's desire and prayer to God for the Israelites is that they may be saved" (Romans 10:1).

"For this reason, ever since I heard about your faith in the Lord Jesus and your love for all the saints, I have not stopped giving thanks for you, remembering you in my prayers. I keep asking that the God of our Lord Jesus Christ, the glorious Father, may give you the Spirit of wisdom and revelation, so that you may know him better. I pray also that the eyes of your heart may be enlightened in order that you may know the hope to which he has called you, the riches of his glorious inheritance in the saints, and his incomparably great power for us who believe. That power is like the working of his mighty strength" (Ephesians 1:15–19).

"For this reason I kneel before the Father, from whom his whole family in heaven and on earth derives its name. I pray that out of his glorious riches he may strengthen you with power through his Spirit in your inner being, so that Christ may dwell in your hearts through faith. And I pray that you, being rooted and established in love, may have power, together with all the saints, to grasp how wide and long and high and deep is the love of Christ, and to know this love that surpasses knowledge—that you may be filled to the measure of all the fullness of God" (Ephesians 3:14–19).

"In all my prayers for all of you, I always pray with joy because of your partnership in the gospel from the first day until now, being confident of this, that he who began a good work in you will carry it on to completion until the day of Christ Jesus. It is right for me to feel this way about all of you, since I have you in my heart; for whether I am in chains or defending and confirming the gospel, all of you share in God's grace with me. God can testify how I long for all of you with the affection of Christ Jesus. And this is my prayer: that your love may abound more and more in knowledge and depth of insight, so that you may be able to discern what is best and may be pure and blameless until the day of Christ, filled with the fruit of righteousness that comes through Jesus Christ—to the glory and praise of God" (Philippians 1:4–11).

"And my God will meet all your needs according to his glorious riches in Christ Jesus" (Philippians 4:19).

"For this reason, since the day we heard about you, we have not stopped praying for you and asking God to fill you with the knowledge of his will through all spiritual wisdom and understanding. And we pray this in order that you may live a life worthy of the Lord and may please him in every way: bearing fruit in every good work, growing in the knowledge of God, being strengthened with all power according to his glorious might so that you may have great endurance and patience" (Colossians 1:9–11).

"I want you to know how much I am struggling for you and for those at Laodicea, and for all who have not met me personally. My purpose is that they may be encouraged in heart and united in love, so that they may have the full riches of complete understanding, in order that they may know the mystery of God, namely, Christ" (Colossians 2:1–2).

This incredible study for our private prayer time teaches us that unceasing prayer formed a large part of Paul's service in the gospel. We see the high spiritual aim that he set before himself in his work on behalf of believers, and the tender and self-sacrificing love with which he always thought of the church body and its needs. Let us ask God to bring each one of us and all ministers of His Word to a life of which such prayer is the healthy and natural outflow. We will need to turn again and again to these pages if we would be brought by the Spirit to the apostolic life given to us here by God as an example.

Not only did Paul pray much for his congregation but he also asked his congregation to pray. Read again with prayerful attention:

"I urge you, brothers, by our Lord Jesus Christ and by the love of the Spirit, to join me in my struggle by praying to God for me. Pray that I may be rescued from the unbelievers in Judea and that my service in Jerusalem may be acceptable to the saints there" (Romans 15:30–31).

"Indeed, in our hearts we felt the sentence of death. But this happened that we might not rely on ourselves but on God, who raises the dead. He has delivered us from such a deadly peril, and he will deliver us. On him we have set our hope that he will continue to deliver us, as you help us by your prayers. Then many will give thanks on our behalf for the gracious favor granted us in answer to the prayers of many" (2 Corinthians 1:9–11).

"And pray in the Spirit on all occasions with all kinds of prayers and requests. With this in mind, be alert and always keep on praying for all the saints. Pray also for me, that whenever I open my mouth, words may be given me so that I will fearlessly make known the mystery of the gospel, for which I am an ambassador in chains. Pray that I may declare it fearlessly, as I should" (Ephesians 6:18–20).

"For I know that through your prayers and the help given by the Spirit of Jesus Christ, what has happened to me will turn out for my deliverance. I eagerly expect and hope that I will in no way be ashamed, but will have sufficient courage so that now as always Christ will be exalted in my body, whether by life or by death" (Philippians 1:19).

"Devote yourselves to prayer, being watchful and thankful. And pray for us, too, that God may open a door for our message, so that we may proclaim the mystery of Christ, for which I am in chains. Pray that I may proclaim it clearly, as I should" (Colossians 4:2–4).

"Finally, brothers, pray for us that the message of the Lord may spread rapidly and be honored, just as it was with you" (2 Thessalonians 3:1).

What a deep insight Paul had as to the unity of the body of Christ and the relationship of its members one to another! As we permit the Holy Spirit to work in us, He will reveal this truth to us as well. What a glimpse Paul gives us of the power of the spiritual life among these Christians by the way in which he knew that at Rome, Corinth, Ephesus, Colosse, and Philippi, there were men and women on whom he could rely for prayer because they had power with God! What a lesson for all ministers of the gospel, to lead them to inquire if they truly appreciate the unity of the body at its true value; ask if they are endeavoring to train up Christians as intercessors. Ask if they understand that the reason Paul had that confidence was because he himself was so strong in prayer for the congregation. Let us together learn the lesson, and seek God that we all may grow in the grace of prayer, so that all our service and Christian life may witness that the Spirit of prayer rules us. May we have confidence that God will avenge His own elect that cry out to Him day and night.

Chapter 16

Ministers of the Spirit

What is the meaning of the expression "The minister of the gospel is a minister of the Spirit"? (See 2 Corinthians 3:6–8.) It means:

1. The preacher is entirely under the power and control of the Holy Spirit, so that he may be led and used by the Spirit as He wills.

2. Many pray for the Spirit that they may make use of Him and His power for their work. This is an entirely wrong concept. It is He who must use you. Your relationship toward Him must be one of deep dependence and utter submission. The Spirit must have you completely and always and in all things under His power.

3. There are many who think they must only preach the Word, and that the Spirit will make the Word fruitful. They do not understand that it is the Spirit, in and through the preacher, who will bring the Word to the heart of the listeners. I must not be satisfied with praying to God to bless through the operation of His Spirit the Word that I preach. The Lord wants me to be filled with the Spirit; then I will speak as I should and my preaching will be in the manifestation of the Spirit and power.

4. We see this occurring on the day of Pentecost. They

were filled with the Spirit and began to speak, and spoke with power through the Spirit who was in them.

5. Thus we learn what the relationship of the minister toward the Spirit should be. He must have a strong belief that the Spirit is in him, that the Spirit will teach him in his daily life, and that He will strengthen him to bear witness to the Lord Jesus in his preaching and visiting. He must live in ceaseless prayer that he may be kept and strengthened by the power of the Spirit.

6. When the Lord promised the apostles that they would receive power when the Holy Spirit came upon them, and commanded them to wait for Him, it was as though He said: "Do not dare to preach without this power. It is the indispensable preparation for your work. Everything depends on it."

7. What is the lesson to be learned from the phrase "ministers of the Spirit"? How little we have understood this! How little we have lived in it! How little we have experienced the power of the Holy Spirit! What must we do? There must be deep confession that we have indeed grieved the Spirit, because we have not lived daily in dependence upon Him. There must be simple, childlike surrender to His leading, in the confidence that the Lord will work a change in us. Then there must be daily fellowship with the Lord Jesus in ceaseless prayer. He will bestow on us the Holy Spirit like rivers of living water.

Little time in the Word together with little prayer is death to the spiritual life. Much of the Word but little prayer yields a less than healthy spiritual life. Time spent in prayer with little time in the Word yields life, but without steadfastness. A full measure of the Word and much prayer each day produces a healthy and powerful life. Think of the Lord Jesus. In His youth and through to adulthood He treasured the Word in His heart. He showed that the Word of God filled His heart when he was tempted in the wilderness, as well as at every opportunity that presented itself—until He cried out on the cross in death: "My God, my God, why have you forsaken me?"

In His prayer life He manifested two things. First, He showed that the Word supplies us with material for prayer and encourages us to expect everything from God. The second is that it is only by prayer that we may live such a life that every word of God might be fulfilled in us. How can we come to the point where the Word and prayer each have their undivided right over us? There is only one answer. Our lives must be wholly transformed. We must get a new, healthy, heavenly life, in which hunger after God's Word and thirst after God himself are expressed in prayer as naturally as the needs of our earthly life. Every manifestation of the power of the flesh in us and the weakness of our spiritual life must drive us to the conviction that God, through the powerful operation of His Holy Spirit, will work out a new and strong life in us.

We must understand that the Holy Spirit is essentially the Spirit of the Word and the Spirit of prayer. He will cause the Word to become joy and light in our souls. He will also help us in prayer to know the mind and will of God and to find in it our delight. If we wish to explain these things to God's people that they may know the inheritance that is prepared for them, we must commit ourselves from this moment forward to the leading of the Holy Spirit. We must through faith in what He will do in us appropriate the heavenly life of Christ as He lived it on earth, with certain expectation that the Spirit who filled Him with the Word and prayer will also accomplish that work in us.

Let us believe that the Spirit who is in us is the Spirit of the Lord Jesus and that He is in us to make us truly partakers of His life. If we firmly believe this and set our hearts upon it, there will come a change in our involvement with the Word and prayer such as we could not have thought possible. Believe it firmly and expect it.

Chapter 17

Preaching and Prayer

We are familiar with the vision of the valley of dry bones. We know that the Lord said to the prophet Ezekiel: "Prophesy to these bones and say to them, 'Dry bones, hear the word of the Lord!' This is what the Sovereign Lord says to these bones: I will make breath enter you, and you will come to life" (Ezekiel 37:4–5). When he had done this, there was a noise, and bone came together to its bone, and flesh came up, and skin covered them—but there was no breath in them. The prophesying to the bones—the preaching of the Word of God—had a powerful influence. It was the beginning of the great miracle that was about to happen, and there lay an entire army of men newly made. It was the beginning of the work of life in them, but there was no spirit there.

Then he said to me, "Prophesy to the breath; prophesy, son of man, and say to it, 'This is what the Sovereign Lord says: Come from the four winds, O breath, and breathe into these slain, that they may live'" (v. 9). When the prophet had done this, the Spirit came upon them, and they lived and stood on their feet, a very great army. Prophesying to the bones, that is, preaching, has accomplished a great work. There lay the beautiful new bodies. But prophesying to the Spirit: "Come, O Spirit," that is prayer, and that has accomplished a far more wonderful thing. The power of the Spirit was revealed through prayer.

Is not the work of our preachers and ministers mostly prophesying to dry bones, making known the promises of God? This is sometimes followed by great results. Everything that belongs to the form of godliness has been done to perfection; a careless congregation becomes regular and devout, but it remains true for the most part that "there is no life in them." Preaching must always be followed up by prayer. The preacher must come to see that his preaching is comparatively powerless to bring new life until he begins to take time for prayer, and according to the teaching of God's Word, he strives and labors and continues in prayer; and he takes no rest and gives God no rest until He bestows the Spirit in overflowing power.

Do you agree that a change must be seen in our work? We must learn from Peter to continue in prayer for the ministry of the Word. Just as we are zealous preachers, we must be zealous in prayer. We must with all our strength, and as consistently as Paul did, pray unceasingly. For the prayer: "Come, breathe on these slain," the answer is certain.

Chapter 18

Wholeheartedness

Experience teaches us that anyone who engages in a work less than wholeheartedly will seldom succeed. Imagine a student, or his teacher, a man of business, or a warrior, who does not give himself to the task at hand. That one cannot expect success.

Wholeheartedness is even more essential in spiritual work, and above all, of the high and holy task of prayer and of being always well pleasing to a holy God. We are reminded of this in Jeremiah: "You will seek me and find me when you seek me with all your heart" (29:13).

Many of God's servants have said at one time or another, "I seek God with my whole heart"—but have you ever thought how many Christians there are of whom it is all too plain that they do *not* seek God with their whole heart? When in despair over their sins, they seem to seek God wholeheartedly. But once they know His forgiveness, even though they may display some Christian virtue, it would be difficult to say of them, "This man has surrendered his whole heart to follow God and to serve Him as the supreme effort of his life."

How is it with you? What does your heart tell you? Even though you have given yourself to fulfill your obligations

411

faithfully and zealously (even as a minister), perhaps you need to acknowledge: "I am convinced that the reason for my unsatisfactory prayer life is that I have not lived with a wholehearted surrender of all that would hinder my fellowship with God." What a deeply important question to consider in our prayer time and then to give the answer to God! How vital to arrive at a clear answer, and to confess it all before God alone!

Prayerlessness is not something that can be overcome as an isolated thing. It is related to the state of the heart. And it is a way of life. True prayer depends on an undivided heart. And I cannot give myself an undivided heart—one that enables me to say, "I seek God with my whole heart." It is impossible for us in our own strength; but God will do it. He said He would give us a heart to fear Him. He also said He would write His law on our heart. Such promises serve to awaken a desire to pray. However weak our desire may be, if there is a sincere determination to strive after what God has for us, He will work in our heart both to will and to do of His good pleasure. It is the great work of the Holy Spirit in us to make us willing. He enables us to seek God with our whole heart. May we acknowledge that we have been doubleminded, because while we have given ourselves to many earthly things with all our heart and strength, we cannot always say that we have given ourselves to fellowship with God with our whole heart.

"Follow Me"

The Lord did not say these words to all who believed on Him, or who hoped to be blessed by Him, but only to those whom He would make fishers of men. He said this not only when He first called the apostles but also later on to Peter: "Don't be afraid; from now on you will catch men" (Luke 5:10). The holy art of winning souls, of loving and saving them, can be learned only in a close and consistent relationship with Christ. What a lesson for ministers, Christian workers, and others! This intimate relationship was the great and particular privilege of His disciples. The Lord chose them that they might always be with Him and remain near Him. We read of the choice of the twelve apostles in Mark 3:14: "He appointed twelve . . . that they might be with him and that he might send them out to preach." And on the last night our Lord said, "And you also must testify, for you have been with me from the beginning" (John 15:27).

This fact was observed by outsiders. For instance, the girl who spoke to Peter after Jesus was taken away, said, "You also were with Jesus of Galilee" (Matthew 26:69). And the Sanhedrin, when they saw the courage of Peter and John: "They were astonished and they took note that these men had been with Jesus" (Acts 4:13).

The chief characteristic and indispensable qualification for the one who would bear witness to Christ is that he spend time in His presence.

Continuous fellowship with Christ is the only school for the training of students of the Holy Spirit. What a lesson for us all! Only he who, like Caleb, follows the Lord fully will have power to teach other souls the art of following Jesus. But what an amazing grace, that the Lord Jesus himself wants to train us to be like Him so that others may learn from us. Then we will be able to say with Paul: "Follow my example, as I follow the example of Christ" (1 Corinthians 11:1).

Never has a teacher taken such trouble with his scholars as Jesus Christ will with those who preach His Word. He will spare no pain; no time will be too limited or too long for Him. In the love that took Him to the cross, He wants to fellowship and converse with us, fashion us, sanctify us, and make us fit for His holy service. Dare we still complain that it is too much for us to spend so much time in prayer? Will we not commit ourselves entirely to the love that gave up all for us and look upon it as our greatest joy to have daily fellowship with Him? All you who long for blessing in your ministry, He calls you to abide in Him. Let it be the greatest delight of your life to spend time with God; it will be the surest preparation for fruitful service.

Lord, draw me, help me, hold me fast. Day by day teach me how to live by faith in your sweet fellowship.

Chapter 20

The Holy Trinity

God is an ever-flowing fountain of pure love and blessedness. Christ is the reservoir wherein the fullness of God was made visible as grace, and has been opened for us. The Holy Spirit is the stream of living water that flows from under the throne of God and of the Lamb.

The Redeemed, God's believing children, are the channels through which the love of the Father, the grace of Christ, and the powerful operation of the Spirit are brought to earth to be imparted to others.

What a clear picture we get here of the wonderful partnership in which God includes us as dispensers of the grace of God! The time we spend in prayer covering our own needs is only the beginning of the life of prayer. The glory of prayer is that we have power as intercessors to bring the grace of Christ and the energizing power of the Spirit upon those souls that are still in darkness.

The more closely the channel is connected with the reservoir, the more certainly will the water flow unhindered through it. The more we are occupied in prayer with the fullness of Christ and the Spirit who proceeds from Him, the more firmly will we abide in fellowship with Him, and the more surely will our lives be full of joy and strength. This,

415

however, is still only a preparation for the real work of prayer. The more we yield ourselves to fellowship with the triune God, the sooner we will gain the courage and ability to intercede for others in our families, in our neighborhoods, and in our churches.

Are we truly channels that remain open, so that water may flow through to the thirsty, lost souls in a dry, barren land? Have you offered yourself without reservation to God, to become a bearer of the energizing operation of the Holy Spirit?

Perhaps the reason we do not experience the full power of prayer is because we think so much of our own needs and of ourselves. We must understand that the new prayer life to which we have been called by the Lord Jesus can be sustained and strengthened only through the intercession through which we labor for the souls around us in order to bring them to know the Lord.

Meditate on this: God is an ever-flowing fountain of love and blessing, and I, as His child, am a living channel through which the Spirit and His life can be brought to earth every day!

Life and Prayer

Our daily life has a tremendous influence on our prayers, just as our prayers influence our daily life. In fact, our life is a continuous prayer. We are continually praising or thanking God by our actions and by the manner in which we treat others. This natural prayer and desire for God can be so strong in a man (who also prays to God) that the words of prayer that he actually utters cannot be heard. At times God cannot hear the prayer of your lips, because the worldly desires of your heart cry out to Him much more strongly and loudly.

As we have said, life exercises a mighty influence over prayer. A worldly life or a self-seeking life, for example, makes prayer by that person powerless and an answer impossible. With many Christians there is conflict between their everyday life and their prayer life, and the everyday life holds the upper hand. But as we have said, prayer can also exercise a strong influence over our everyday life. If I yield myself completely to God in prayer, prayer can overcome a life in the flesh and the practice of sin. The entire life may be brought under the control of prayer. Prayer can change and renew the life, because prayer calls upon and receives the Lord Jesus, and the Holy Spirit purifies and sanctifies us.

Because of their defective spiritual life, many people think they must make a supreme effort in order to pray more. They do not understand, of course, that only in proportion as the spiritual life is strengthened can the prayer life increase. Prayer and life are inseparably connected and the quality of each deeply related.

What do you think? Which has the stronger influence over you: five- or ten-minute prayers, or the whole day spent thinking on worldly desires? Do not be surprised if your prayers are not answered. The reason may easily be that your life and your prayers work against each other; your heart concentrates more on living than on praying. Learn this great lesson: My prayer must rule my whole life. What I request from God in prayer is not decided in five or ten minutes. I must learn to say: "I have prayed with my whole heart." What I desire from God must truly fill my heart the whole day; then the way is opened for a definite answer.

How sacred and powerful prayer is when it takes possession of the heart and life! It keeps one constantly in fellowship with God. Then we can literally say, *I wait on you, Lord, all day long.* Let us be careful to consider not only the length of time we spend with God in prayer but also the power prayer has to take possession of our whole life.

The Twelve said, "It would not be right for us to neglect the ministry of the word of God in order to wait on tables" (Acts 6:2). For that work deacons were chosen. And this word of the disciples serves for all time and for all who are set apart as ministers. "We will turn this responsibility over to them and will give our attention to prayer and the ministry of the word" (v. 3). Dr. Alexander Whyte once said, "I think sometimes, when my salary is paid to me so faithfully and punctually: the deacons have performed faithfully their part of the agreement; have I been just as faithful in my part, in persevering in prayer and the ministry of the Word?" Another minister said, "How surprised people would be if I proposed to divide my time between these two equally—one half given to prayer and the other to the ministry of the Word."

In the case of Peter, notice what perseverance in prayer meant. He went up on the roof to pray. There, in prayer, he received heavenly instruction as to his work among the heathen. There, the message from Cornelius came to him. There, the Holy Spirit told him to rise and go with the three men who sought him. From there he went to Caesarea, where the Spirit was unexpectedly poured out on the heathen. All this is to teach us that it is through prayer that God will give the instruction of His Spirit to enable us to understand His will, to let us know with whom we are to speak, and to give us the assurance that His Spirit will make His Word effective through us.

As a minister of the gospel, have you ever considered why you have a salary and a place to live, and so are freed from the need of holding a regular job? The reason is so that you can continue in prayer and the ministry of the Word. These will give you the necessary wisdom and anointing for your work. And that is the secret of a fruitful ministry.

No wonder there are often complaints about the ineffective spiritual life of a minister and his congregation. That which is of prime importance—perseverance in prayer—does not occupy its rightful place.

Peter was able to speak and act as he did because he was filled with the Spirit. Let us not be satisfied with anything less than full surrender to and undivided appropriation of the Spirit, as leader and Lord of our lives. Nothing less will empower us. Then, for the first time, we will be able to say, "God has made us able ministers of His Spirit."

Chapter 22

Are We Carnal or Spiritual?

There is a great difference between being carnal [living after the flesh] and being spiritual. This fact is little understood or pondered. The Christian who walks in the Spirit, and has crucified the flesh, is spiritual (Galatians 5:24). The Christian who walks after the flesh, and wishes to please the flesh, is carnal (Romans 13:14). The Galatians, who had begun in the Spirit, reverted to a life in the flesh. Yet there were among them some spiritual members, who were able to restore the wandering with true meekness.

What a difference between the carnal and the spiritual Christian (1 Corinthians 3:1–3)! With the carnal Christian, there may be the appearance of virtue and zeal for God and His service, but it is for the most part a manifestation of human power. With the spiritual Christian, on the other hand, there is a complete submission to the leading of the Spirit, a sense of personal weakness and total dependence on the work of Christ—it is a life of abiding fellowship with Christ brought into being by the Spirit.

How important it is for us to discover and to clearly

421

acknowledge before God whether we are spiritual or carnal. A minister may be very faithful in his teaching of doctrine and be enthusiastic in his service, and yet be so, for the most part, in the power of human wisdom and zeal. One of the signs of this is little pleasure or perseverance in fellowship with Christ through prayer. A love of prayer is one of the marks of the Spirit.

A tremendous change is in store for the carnal Christian who would become truly spiritual. At first he cannot understand what needs to change or how it will take place. But the more the truth dawns upon him, the more he is convinced that it is impossible unless God does the work. Yet to believe that God will do it requires diligent prayer. Meditation and a quiet, solitary place are indispensable, along with the end of all confidence in self. But along this road there comes the faith that God is willing, and He will do it.

How can you say to others: "Brothers, I could not address you as spiritual but as worldly—mere infants in Christ" (1 Corinthians 3:1) unless you yourself have the experience of having passed from the one state to the other? But God will teach you. Persevere in prayer and in faith.

Chapter 23

Examples in Godly Men

George Müller

Just as God gave the apostle Paul as an example in his prayer life for Christians of all time, so in more recent times He has given George Müller as proof to His church how literally and wonderfully He still hears and answers prayer. Not only did God give this man of God over a million pounds sterling in his lifetime to support his orphanages, but Müller also stated that he believed the Lord had given him more than thirty thousand souls in answer to prayer. These were not only from among the orphans but also many others for whom he had prayed faithfully every day (in some cases for fifty years), in the firm faith that they would be saved. When he was asked on what ground he so firmly believed this, his answer was: "There are five conditions that I always endeavor to fulfill. In observing these, I have the assurance of an answer to my prayer:

1. "I have not the least doubt because I am assured that it is the Lord's will to save them, for He wills that all men should be saved, and come to the knowledge of the truth

(1 Timothy 2:4). Also, we have the assurance 'that if we ask any thing according to his will, he hears us' (1 John 5:14).

2. "I have never pleaded for their salvation in my own name, but in the blessed name of my precious Lord Jesus, and on His merits alone (John 14:14).

3. "I always firmly believed in the willingness of God to hear my prayers (Mark 11:24).

4. "I am not conscious of having yielded to any sin, for 'if I regard iniquity in my heart, the Lord will not hear me' when I call (Psalm 66:18).

5. "I have persevered in believing prayer for more than fifty-two years for some, and shall continue till the answer comes: 'Shall not God avenge his own elect, which cry day and night unto him?'"

Take these thoughts to heart and pray according to these rules. Let prayer be not only the utterance of your desires but also fellowship with God, until you know by faith that your prayer is heard. The way George Müller walked is the new and living way to the throne of grace, *which is open to all of us.*

Hudson Taylor

When as a young man Hudson Taylor surrendered unreservedly to the Lord, he received a strong conviction that God would send him to China. He had read of George Müller, and how God had answered his prayers for his own support and that of his orphans. Taylor began to ask the Lord to teach him also to trust God in the same way. But he felt that if he wanted to go to China with such faith, he must first begin in England to live by faith. He asked the Lord to enable him to do this. He worked as a doctor's assistant, and asked God to help him not to ask for his salary, but to leave it to God to move the heart of the doctor to pay him at the right time. The doctor was a goodhearted man, but very irregular in payment. This cost Taylor much trouble and struggle in prayer because he believed, like George Müller, that the word "Owe no man anything" was to be taken literally, and that debt should not be incurred.

So he learned to move men through God—a profound lesson, which later became an unspeakably great blessing to him in his work in China. He believed that we should—in the conversion of the Chinese, in the awakening of Christians to give money for the support of the work, and in the finding of suitable missionaries who would keep this as faith's rule of conduct—make our desires known to God in prayer, and then rely on God to move men to do what He would have done.

After some years in China, he prayed that God would provide twenty-four missionaries, two for each of the eleven provinces, and two for Mongolia, each with millions of souls and no missionary. God did it. But there was no society to send them out. He had indeed learned to trust God for his own support, but he dared not take upon himself the responsibility of the twenty-four. He feared they might not have sufficient faith. This caused him severe conflict, and he became very ill under it, until at last he saw that God could just as easily care for the twenty-four as for himself. Then he assumed this responsibility in glad faith. And so God led him, through many severe trials of faith, to trust Him fully. These twenty-four increased in course of time to one thousand missionaries who relied wholly on God for support. Other missionary societies have acknowledged how much they learned from Hudson Taylor as a man who stated and obeyed this law: "Faith may rely on God to move men to do what His children have asked of Him in prayer."

Chapter 24

Light from the Inner Room

"But when you pray, go into your room, close the door and pray to your Father, who is unseen. Then your Father, who sees what is done in secret, will reward you" (Matthew 6:6).

Our Lord spoke of the prayer of the hypocrites who desire to be seen of men, and also of the prayer of the heathen who trust in their many words. They do not understand that prayer has no value except when addressed to a personal God who sees and hears. In the text, our Lord teaches a wonderful lesson concerning the inestimable blessing a Christian can have in his secret place of prayer. To understand the lesson fully, let us look at the light the prayer room sheds on:

1. *The wonderful love of God.* Think of God, His greatness, His holiness, His unspeakable glory, and then imagine the inestimable privilege to which He invites His children, that each one of them, no matter how sinful or frail, may have access to God anytime and may talk with Him as long as he wishes. God is ready to meet His child anytime he enters his prayer room; He is ready to have fellowship with him, to give him the joy and strength that he needs along with the assurance that God is with him and will undertake for him in everything. In addition, God promises that He will enrich His child in his outward life and work with those things he has asked for in secret. We ought to cry out with

joy. What an honor! What a salvation!

Do you see what a generous supply He offers for every need? One may be in great distress or have fallen into deep sin. Or he may in the ordinary course of life desire temporal or spiritual blessings. Perhaps he wants to pray for himself or for his family, or for his congregation or denomination. He may even want to become an intercessor for the whole world—the promise for private prayer covers all: "Pray to your Father, who is unseen . . . your Father . . . will reward you openly."

We might well imagine that no place on earth would be so attractive to the child of God as the prayer room, where the presence of God is promised and unhindered fellowship with the Father awaits. Think about the happiness of a child on earth who enjoys the love of his father, the gratefulness of a friend who meets a beloved benefactor, or the thrill of a subject who has free access to his king and may stay with him as long as he wishes. All these joyful privileges are nothing compared with this heavenly promise. In your prayer room you can converse with God as long as you desire. You can rely on His presence and fellowship there.

Do you see the wonderful love of God in the gift of a prayer room sanctified by such a promise? Let us thank God every day of our lives for the gift of His wonderful love. In this sinful world, He could devise nothing more suitable for our needs than this fountain of unspeakable blessing.

2. *The deep sinfulness of man.* Perhaps we also imagine that every child of God takes advantage of such an invitation with joy. But what is the response? From everywhere the conclusion is reached that private, personal prayer is as a general rule neglected by those who call themselves believers. Many make *no* use of the privilege; they go to church, they

confess Christ, but they know little of personal fellowship with God. Many do pray, but in a spirit of haste, and more as a matter of custom or for the easing of conscience. They cannot really testify to any joy or blessing from it. What is worse, the many who know something of prayer's blessedness, confess that they know little about faithful, regular fellowship with the Father throughout the day as something that is as necessary as their daily bread.

What makes the prayer room so powerless? Is it not the sinfulness of man and his fallen nature's aversion to God, which make the world more attractive than being alone with the heavenly Father?

Do Christians truly believe the Word of God that declares that "the flesh is enmity against God"? Do they walk so much after the flesh that the Spirit cannot strengthen them for prayer? Do Christians allow Satan to deprive them of the use of the weapon of prayer so that they are powerless to overcome him? Our response only shows the deep sinfulness of man, because no greater proof exists than this: We neglect private prayer and so turn our backs on the love that gave us the privilege.

More disturbing is the fact that even ministers of the gospel acknowledge that they pray too little. The Word tells them that their only power lies in prayer: through it they can be clothed with power from on high for their work. But it seems that the power of the world and the flesh has distracted them. While they devote time to their work and manifest zeal in it, the most necessary thing of all is neglected, and there is no desire or strength for prayer to obtain the indispensable gift of the Holy Spirit to make their work fruitful. *God, give us grace to understand the deep sinfulness of our neglect of prayer.*

3. *The glorious grace of Christ Jesus.* Is there no hope of change? Must it be always so? Or is there a means of recovery? There is, thank God!

The man through whom God has made known the message of the inner room is none other than our Lord Jesus Christ, who saves us from our sins. He is able and willing to deliver us from this sin, and He will deliver us. He has not undertaken to redeem us from all our other sins and then leave us to deal with the sin of prayerlessness in our own strength. In this also we may come to Him and cry out, "Lord, if you will, you can make me clean. Lord, I believe; help my unbelief."

How can you experience this deliverance? By the well-known way by which every sinner must come to Christ: Begin by acknowledging and then confessing before Him, in a childlike manner, the sin of neglect of the place of prayer. Bow before Him in true repentance and sorrow. Tell Him that your heart has deceived you by the thought that you, in your own strength, could pray as you ought. Tell Him that through the weakness of the flesh, the power of the world, and self-confidence, you have been led astray, and that you have no strength to do better. Do this with your whole heart. By your own resolution and effort you cannot put things right.

In your sin and weakness come into your prayer room, and begin to thank God, as you have never thanked Him before, that the grace of the Lord Jesus will make it possible for you to converse with your Father as a child ought to. Once again, hand over to the Lord Jesus all your sin and misery, as well as your whole life and will, for Him to cleanse and take possession of as His own.

Even though your heart may be cold and dead, persevere

in the exercise of faith that Christ is an almighty and faithful Savior. You may be sure that deliverance will come. Expect it. You will begin to understand that the prayer room is the revelation of the glorious grace of the Lord Jesus, which makes it possible for one to do what he could not do by himself—maintain fellowship with God and receive the desire and power that equip a person for walking with God.

Part Three

The Deepest Secret
of Pentecost

The Spirit of the Cross
in Our Lord

Sometimes we seek for the operation of the Spirit with the purpose of obtaining more power for work, more love in our life, more holiness in the heart, more light on Scripture or on our path. But all these gifts are subordinate to the great purpose of God. The Father bestowed the Spirit on the Son, and the Son gave Him to us for the purpose of revealing and glorifying Christ Jesus in us.

The heavenly Christ must become for us a real and living personality who is always with us and in us. Our life on earth can be lived every day in unbroken fellowship with our Lord Jesus. This is the first and greatest work of the Holy Spirit in the believer, that we should know and experience Christ as our life. God desires that we be strengthened with might by His Spirit in the inner man, so that Christ may dwell in our hearts through faith, so that we may be filled with all the fullness of God's love.

This was the secret of the joy of the first disciples. They had received the Lord Jesus—whom they feared they had lost—as the heavenly Christ into their hearts. And this was

their preparation for Pentecost: their attention was completely taken up with Him. He was literally everything to
them. Their hearts were empty of everything, so that the
Spirit could fill them with Christ. In the fullness of the Spirit
they had power for a life and service such as the Lord desired
for them. Is this the goal of our desires and our experience?
The Lord wants us to know that the blessing for which we
have so diligently prayed can be increased in no other way
than by the faithful cultivation of intimate fellowship with
Christ in prayer every day.

It seems to me that there is a still deeper secret of Pentecost to be discovered. The thought has come to me that
perhaps our concept of the Lord Jesus in heaven is too limited. We think of Him in the splendor and glory of God's
throne. We also think of the incredible love that moved Him
to give himself for us. But we forget that, above all, He was
known here on earth as the Crucified One. In this capacity
He has a place on the throne of God. "Then I saw a Lamb,
looking as if it had been slain" (Revelation 5:6).

As the Crucified One, He is the object of the Father's
eternal good pleasure and of the worship of the entire creation. It is, therefore, of prime importance that we on earth
should know and experience Him as the Crucified One, so
that we may manifest His disposition to others and share the
power that can make them partakers of salvation.

I feel deeply that the cross is Christ's highest glory. The
Holy Spirit neither has done nor can do anything greater or
more glorious than He did when He "through the eternal
Spirit offered himself unblemished to God" (Hebrews 9:14).
Because of this, it is evident that the Holy Spirit can do nothing greater or more glorious for us than to bring us into the
fellowship of that cross and work out in us the same spirit

that was seen in our Lord Jesus. The question has come: "Is this the reason why our prayers for the powerful operation of the Holy Spirit cannot be answered? Have we sought too little to receive the Spirit who might help us to know and become like the glorified Christ in the fellowship of His cross?"

Is this the deepest secret of Pentecost? The Spirit comes to us from the cross, where He strengthened Christ to offer himself to God. He comes from the Father, who looked down with unspeakable good pleasure on the humiliation, obedience, and self-sacrifice of Christ as the highest proof of His surrender to Him. He comes from Christ, who through the cross was prepared to receive from the Father the fullness of the Spirit that He might share it with the world. He comes to reveal Christ to our hearts as the Lamb slain in the midst of the throne so that we on earth might worship Him as they do in heaven. He comes especially to impart to us the life of the crucified Christ so that we may be able to say, "I have been crucified with Christ and I no longer live, but Christ lives in me. The life I live in the body, I live by faith in the Son of God, who loved me and gave himself for me" (Galatians 2:20). To understand this secret, we must first meditate on the meaning and the value of the cross.

The cross is to be viewed from two standpoints.

First, from the standpoint of the work it accomplished: the pardon and conquest of sin. This is the first message communicated to the sinner from Mount Calvary. It proclaims free and full deliverance from the power of sin.

Second, from the standpoint of the disposition that was manifested on that rugged piece of wood. We find this amply expressed in Philippians 2:8: "And being found in appearance as a man, he humbled himself and became obedient to death—even death on a cross!" Here we see *self-abasement* to the lowest place that could be found under the burden of our sin and curse; *obedience* to the uttermost to all the will of God; and *self-sacrifice* to the death of the cross. These three words reveal to us the holy perfection of His person and work.

Therefore, God has greatly exalted Him. It was the spirit of the cross that made Him the object of His Father's good pleasure, of the worship of the angels, of the love and confidence of all the redeemed. The self-abasement of Christ, His obedience to the will of God even to death, and His self-sacrifice even to death on the cross—these identify Him as the Lamb John saw in the vision of Revelation: "looking as if it had been slain, standing in the center of the throne."

May the Holy Spirit reveal to us the disposition that was in Christ to submit himself to such agony and loss for our sake.

Chapter 26

The Spirit of the Cross in Us

All that Christ was and did was for us. And He desires to manifest in us that same spirit. The spirit of the cross was His blessedness and His glory. May it be for us also. He desires to duplicate His likeness in us and to give us a full share of all that is His.

Paul wrote, "Your attitude should be the same as that of Christ Jesus" (Philippians 2:5). Elsewhere he writes, "We have the mind of Christ" (1 Corinthians 2:16). We are exhorted in Romans 12:1: "Do not conform any longer to the pattern of this world, but be transformed by the renewing of your mind."

The fellowship of the cross is not only a holy duty for us, but an unspeakably blessed privilege, which the Holy Spirit himself makes ours according to the promises: "Everything that I learned from my Father I have made known to you" (John 15:15) and "When the Counselor comes, whom I will send to you from the Father, the Spirit of truth who goes out from the Father, he will testify about me. And you also must testify, for you have been with me from the beginning" (John 15:26–27).

The Holy Spirit formed this disposition in Christ, and He will also form it in us if we allow Him to.

When the Lord told His disciples that they must take up the cross and follow Him, from their frame of reference, they could hardly have understood His meaning. But He wanted to stir up their thinking, and so prepare them for the time when they would see Him carrying His cross. From the Jordan forward, where He had presented himself to be baptized and counted among sinners, He carried the cross in His heart. That is to say, He was always conscious that the sentence of death, because of sin, rested on Him, and that He must bear it to completion. As the disciples thought about this, and wondered what He meant, only one thing helped them to grasp it: In their day, carrying a cross was the language of a man who had been sentenced to death and must carry his cross to the appointed place.

About the same time, Christ had said, "Whoever finds his life will lose it, and whoever loses his life for my sake will find it" (Matthew 10:39). He taught them that they must despise their present life when compared to their life in Christ. Their nature was so sinful that nothing less than death could deliver them. Gradually the conviction dawned on them that the taking up of the cross meant: "I am to feel that my life is under sentence of death, and that under the consciousness of this sentence, I must constantly surrender my flesh and my sinful nature, even unto death."

So in a small sense they were prepared to see that the cross that Christ carried represented the power to deliver them from sin, and that they must first receive from Him the true spirit of the cross. From Him they would learn what self-humiliation in their weakness and unworthiness was to mean; what the obedience was that crucified their own will in all things, in the greatest as well as in the least; what the self-denial was that did not seek to please the flesh or the world.

"If anyone would come after me, he must deny himself and take up his cross and follow me" (Mark 8:34).

Chapter 27

We Are Crucified with Christ

The lesson the Lord desired His disciples to learn from His statement concerning taking up their cross and losing their life finds its expression in the words Paul stated after Christ had died on the cross, was exalted on high, and the Spirit had been poured out: "I have been crucified with Christ and I no longer live, but Christ lives in me. May I never boast except in the cross of our Lord Jesus Christ, through which the world has been crucified to me, and I to the world" (Galatians 2:20; 6:14).

Paul wanted every believer to live a life that proved they were crucified with Christ. He wanted us to understand that the Christ who comes to dwell in our hearts is the Crucified One, who will impart to us the true mind of the cross. He tells us that "our old self was crucified with him" and that "anyone who has died has been freed from sin" (Romans 6:6–7). When believers receive by faith the crucified Christ, they in effect give their flesh over to the death sentence that was executed to the full on Calvary. Paul says, "If we have been united with him like this in his death, we will certainly also be united with him in his resurrection" (Romans 6:5), and, therefore, we must reckon that we are dead to sin in Christ Jesus.

These words of the Holy Spirit, through Paul, teach us that we must abide in the constant fellowship of the cross, in union with the crucified and now living Lord Jesus. It is the soul that lives under the cover and shelter and deliverance of the cross that alone can expect to experience the resurrection power of the Lord and His abiding presence.

There are many who place their hope of salvation in the redemption of the cross who understand little about the fellowship of the cross. These rely on what the cross purchased for them—the forgiveness of sins and peace with God—but seek to survive for long periods of time without fellowship with the Lord.

This is a tragedy.

Many do not know what it means to seek every day after heart communion with the crucified Lord as He is in heaven—"The Lamb in the midst of the throne." How wonderful if this vision of Christ could exercise its spiritual power upon us, that we might truly experience His presence with us every day here on earth!

You may ask, "Is it possible?" Without a doubt. Why was the Holy Spirit sent from heaven if it were not to make the presence of the glorified Jesus real to us on earth?

Chapter 28

The Holy Spirit and the Cross

The Holy Spirit always leads us to the cross. It was so with Christ. The Spirit taught Him and enabled Him to offer himself without spot to God.

It was so with the disciples. The Spirit, with whom they were filled, led them to preach Christ as the Crucified One. Later on He led them to glory in the fellowship of the cross, by which they were deemed worthy to suffer for Christ's sake.

The cross directed them again to the Spirit. When Christ had borne the cross, He received the Spirit from the Father that He might be poured out. When the three thousand newly converted, mentioned in the book of Acts, bowed before the Crucified One, they received the promise of the Holy Spirit. When the disciples rejoiced in their experience of the fellowship of the cross, they received the Holy Spirit afresh. The union between the Spirit and the cross is indissoluble; they belong inseparably to one another. We see this especially in the epistles of Paul: "Before your very eyes Jesus Christ was clearly portrayed as crucified. I would like to learn just one thing from you: Did you receive the Spirit by observing the law, or by believing what you heard?" (Galatians 3:1–2).

"Christ redeemed us from the curse of the law by becoming a curse for us, for it is written: 'Cursed is everyone who is hung on a tree.' He redeemed us in order that the blessing given to Abraham might come to the Gentiles" (Galatians 3:13–14).

"God sent his Son, born of a woman, born under law, to redeem those under law, that we might receive the full rights of sons. Because you are sons, God sent the Spirit of his Son into our hearts, the Spirit who calls out, '*Abba,* Father' " (Galatians 4:4–6).

"Those who belong to Christ Jesus have crucified the sinful nature with its passions and desires. Since we live by the Spirit, let us keep in step with the Spirit" (Galatians 5:24–25).

"You also died to the law through the body of Christ . . . that we [may] serve in the new way of the Spirit, and not in the old way of the written code" (Romans 7:4–6).

"Because through Christ Jesus the law of the Spirit of life set me free from the law of sin and death. For what the law was powerless to do in that it was weakened by the sinful nature, God did by sending his own Son in the likeness of sinful man to be a sin offering. And so he condemned sin in sinful man, in order that the righteous requirements of the law might be fully met in us, who do not live according to the sinful nature but according to the Spirit" (Romans 8:2–4).

Always, in everything, the Spirit and the cross are inseparable—even in heaven: "Then I saw a Lamb, looking as if it had been slain, standing in the center of the throne, encircled by the four living creatures and the elders. He had seven horns and seven eyes, which are the seven spirits of God sent out into all the earth" (Revelation 5:6).

"Then the angel showed me the river of the water of life, [is this the Holy Spirit?] as clear as crystal, flowing from the throne of God and of the Lamb" (Revelation 22:1; author's bracketed note). When Moses smote the rock, the water streamed out, and Israel drank of it. When the Rock Christ was smitten, and He had taken His place as the slain Lamb on the throne of God, there flowed out from under the throne the fullness of the Holy Spirit for the whole world.

How foolish it is to pray for the fullness of the Spirit if we have not first placed ourselves under the full power of the cross! Just think of the one hundred and twenty disciples. The crucifixion of Christ had touched, broken, and taken possession of their hearts. They could speak or think of nothing else, and when the Crucified One had shown them His hands and His feet, He said to them, "Receive the Holy Spirit." And so also, with their hearts full of the crucified Christ, now received up into heaven, they were prepared to be filled with the Spirit. They dared to proclaim to the people: "Repent and believe in the Crucified One"; and they also received the Holy Spirit.

Christ yielded himself unreservedly to the cross. It was the will of His Father. It was the only way to redeem the lost. Integral to the act of self-sacrifice and death was a disposition borne in Him by the Spirit—a disposition that would be imparted to His disciples and to all who put their trust in Him. The cross demands our entire life. To comply with this demand requires nothing less than an act of the will, and for this we are unfit in the natural sense. But if we submit our will to Him who stands waiting to receive us, we will be enabled to do what we could not otherwise do.

Chapter 29

The Cross in Contrast to the Flesh and the World

The cross and the flesh are deadly enemies. The cross would condemn and put to death the flesh. The flesh desires to cast aside and conquer the cross. Many, as they hear of the cross as the indispensable preparation for the fullness of the Holy Spirit, will find out what there is in them that must yet be crucified. We are to understand that our entire nature is sentenced to death, and we must die, by the cross, so that the new life in Christ may rule in us. Let us gain such an insight into the fallen condition of our nature and its enmity against God that we become not only willing but anxious to be wholly freed from it.

We must learn to say with Paul: "In me, that is in my flesh, there dwells no good thing. The mind of the flesh is enmity against God: it is not subject to the law of God, neither indeed can be." The very essence of the flesh is to hate God and His holy law. The wonder of redemption is that Christ has borne on the cross the judgment and curse of God on the flesh and has forever nailed it to the cursed tree. If a man only believes God's Word about this mind of the flesh, and then longs to be delivered from it, he learns to love the cross as his deliverer from the power of the Enemy.

Our old man—our former nature—is crucified with Christ, and our one hope is to receive this by faith and to hold it fast. "They that are Christ's have crucified the flesh." They have willingly declared that they will daily regard the flesh that is in them as the enemy of God, the enemy of Christ, and the enemy of their soul's salvation. They will treat it as having received its deserved reward in being nailed to the cross.

This is a part of the eternal redemption Christ has brought to us. It is not something we can grasp with our understanding or accomplish through our own strength. It is something the Lord Jesus himself will give us if we are willing to abide in His fellowship day by day and to receive everything from Him. It is something the Holy Spirit will teach us, and He will impart it to us as an experience. He will show how He can give victory in the power of the cross over all that is of the flesh.

What the flesh is in the small circle of my own person, so the world is in the larger circle of humankind. The flesh and the world are two manifestations of the same "god of this world," who is served by both. When the cross deals with the flesh as cursed, we at once discover what the nature and the power of the world are: "They hated both me and my Father." The proof of this was that they crucified Christ. But Christ obtained the victory on the cross and freed us from the power of the world. Now we can say with Paul: "May I never boast except in the cross of our Lord Jesus Christ, through which the world has been crucified to me, and I to the world" (Galatians 6:14).

Every day the cross was to Paul a holy reality, both in

Andrew Murray

what he had to suffer from the world and in the victory the cross continually gave Him. John wrote: "We know that we are children of God, and that the whole world is under the control of the evil one" (1 John 5:19). "Who is it that over-comes the world? Only he who believes that Jesus is the Son of God. This is the one who came by water and blood—Jesus Christ. He did not come by water only, but by water and blood. And it is the Spirit who testifies, because the Spirit is the truth" (1 John 5:5–6). Against the two great powers of the god of this world, God has given us two great powers from heaven: the cross and the Holy Spirit.

The Spirit and the Cross

Do you ever wonder why there are not more men and women who can witness, with joyful hearts, that the Spirit of God has taken possession of them and given them new power to witness? Another heart-searching question is more urgent: What is it that hinders us? The Father in heaven is more willing than an earthly father to give bread to his child, and yet the cry arises: "Is the Spirit restricted or hampered? Is this His work?"

Some will acknowledge that the hindrance undoubtedly lies in the fact that the church is under the sway of the flesh and the world. They understand too little of the heart-changing power of the cross of Christ. Because of this, the Spirit does not have vessels into which He can pour His fullness.

Many complain that the subject is too high or too deep. It proves how little we have appropriated and put into practice the teaching of Paul and of Christ about the cross. I bring you a message of joy. The Spirit who is in you, in however limited a measure, is prepared to bring you under His teaching, to lead you to the cross, and by His heavenly instruction to make you aware of what the crucified Christ wants to do for you and in you.

Take time, so that He may reveal the heavenly mystery to

you. He will show you how the neglect of private prayer has hindered your fellowship with Christ; He will reveal the cross to you and the powerful operation of the Spirit. He will teach you what is meant by self-denial, taking up your cross daily, and losing your life in order to follow Him.

In spite of your having acknowledged your ignorance, your lack of spiritual insight and fellowship with the cross, He is willing to teach you and to make known to you the secret of a spiritual life beyond all your expectations.

Begin at the beginning. Be faithful in private prayer. Thank Him that you can count on Him to meet you there. Even though everything may appear cold and dark, bow in silence before the loving Lord Jesus, who so longs for you. Thank the Father that He has given you the Spirit. Be assured that all you do not know and still need to learn about the flesh, the world, and the cross—the Spirit of Christ will make known to you. Only believe that this blessing is for you. Christ belongs to you, and He longs to obtain full possession of you through the Holy Spirit. But for this to happen, time and faith is necessary. Give Him time in prayer every day. You can be sure that He will fulfill His promise in you.

Our identity is in the way we love and serve one another: "Anyone who claims to be in the light but hates his brother is still in the darkness. Whoever loves his brother lives in the light, and there is nothing in him to make him stumble. But whoever hates his brother is in the darkness and walks around in the darkness; he does not know where he is going, because the darkness has blinded him. I write to you, dear children, because your sins have been forgiven on account of his name. I write to you, fathers, because you have known him who is from the beginning. I write to you, young men, because you have overcome the evil one. I write to you, dear children, because you have known the Father. I write to you, fathers, because you have known him who is from the beginning. I write to you, young men, because you are strong, and the word of God lives in you, and you have overcome the evil one. Do not love the world or anything in the world. If anyone loves the world, the love of the Father is not in him" (1 John 2:9–15).

Persevere—in addition to all that you ask for yourself—in prayer for your congregation, your church, your minister; for all believers; for the whole church of God, that God may strengthen them by the power of His Spirit, so that Christ may dwell in their hearts by faith. What a blessed time it will be when the answer comes! Continue in prayer. The Spirit will reveal and glorify Christ and His cross, the Lamb who was slain, standing in the center of the throne (Revelation 5:6).

Chapter 31

Christ, Our Example

Our Head, Christ, took the lowest place on the cross, and so He has marked out for us, His members, the lowest place. The radiance of God's glory (Hebrews 1:3) became the afflicted One of men (Isaiah 53:4). Since that time the only right we have is to be the last and the lowest. When we claim anything more, we have not yet fully understood the cross.

We seek for a higher life, and we will find it if we go deeper into the fellowship of the cross with our Lord. God has given the Crucified One the highest place (Revelation 5). Shall we not give Him the same place? We do this when from moment to moment we conduct ourselves as those who are crucified with Him (Galatians 2:19–20). In this way we honor the Lord who suffered for us.

We long for full victory. And we find it as we more fully enter into the fellowship of His cross. The Lamb obtained His greatest victory with His hands and feet nailed to the cross. We abide in the shadow of the Almighty only so long as we abide under the shadow of the cross. The cross must be our home. There alone are we sheltered and protected. We first understand our own cross when we have understood His. May we desire to get so close to it that we not only see it but we also embrace it, take it up, and make it our own.

Then the cross asserts itself in us, and we experience His power—to the point that we do not faint under it but carry it with joy.

What would Jesus be without His cross? His pierced feet have bruised the head of the Enemy, and His pierced hands have spoiled the devil's tactics completely (Matthew 12:29). What are we without the cross? Do not let the cross go, but hold it securely. Do we think we can go by any other road than that which the Master trod? Many of us will make no progress until we take up the cross of humility and self-denial.

Epilogue

Allow me a final word to the reader regarding the disposition of mind to which this book appeals.

It is not enough that one should understand and appropriate the thought of the writer and then rejoice because of the new insight he has obtained and the pleasure the knowledge has brought. There is something else that is of great importance. I must surrender myself to the truth, so that I will be ready with an undivided will to immediately perform all that I learn to be God's will.

In a book such as this, dealing with the life of prayer and intimate fellowship with God, it is indispensable that we should be prepared to receive and obey all that we see to be according to the Word and will of God. Where this disposition to receive and obey is lacking, knowledge only serves to make the heart less capable of receiving a fuller life. Satan endeavors to become the master of the Christian's prayer time. This is because he knows that the testimony of the one who has been unfaithful in prayer will cause little damage to his kingdom. Spiritual power to lead the lost to the Lord, or to build up the children of God, simply will not flow from a prayerless life. This power comes only through persevering prayer.

The great question is: Shall we earnestly set ourselves to win back again the weapon of believing prayer that Satan has, at least in a measure, taken away from us? Let us set before ourselves the serious importance of this conflict. As far as each minister is concerned, everything depends on whether or not he is a man of prayer—one who in the inner room is clothed each day with power from on high. We, in common with the church throughout the whole world, must acknowledge that prayer does not have the place in our service of God that it ought to have.

The public consecration that many believers have made at conferences, crusades, and other meetings, is not an easy thing. And even when the step is taken, old habits and the power of the flesh will tend to nullify it. The power of faith is not yet alive and well. It will cost us great effort and great sacrifice to conquer the devil in this area in the name of Christ. Our churches are the battlefields in which Satan will muster all his power to prevent us from becoming people of prayer. So much depends on this for our congregations, God's kingdom, and for us as individuals.

With fear and trembling and much prayer, I have written what I trust will help to encourage Christians in this conflict. With a feeling of deep unworthiness, I venture to offer myself as a guide to the place of prayer—which is the way to holiness and to true fellowship with God.

I have asked the Lord to give this book a place in the prayer rooms of many, and that He would assist the reader, when he sees God's will, to immediately yield himself to do it. In war, everything depends on each soldier's being obedient to the word of command, even though it might cost him his life. In our struggle with the wiles of Satan, we will not conquer unless each one of us stands ready to say from the heart: "What God says, I will do; if I see that anything is according to His will, I will immediately receive it and act upon it."

May there be in each one of us a spirit of surrender to immediate obedience to all we read here that is in accord with the Word of God.

God grant that by His great grace this book may prove a bond of fellowship by which we may think of one another, help each other, and strengthen everyone we know for the conflict in prayer by which the Enemy of our souls may be overcome and the life of God be gloriously realized!

ANDREW MURRAY was born in South Africa in 1828. After receiving his education in Scotland and Holland, he returned to Africa and spent many years as a missionary pastor. He and his wife, Emma, raised eight children. He is best known for his many devotional books, including some of the most enduring classics of Christian literature.

You May Also Like . . .

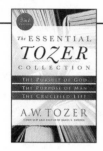

This 3-in-1 collection of A.W. Tozer's writings will strengthen your walk with Jesus.

The Pursuit of God is sure to resonate if you long for a life spent in God's presence.

The Purpose of Man is a call to worship as God reprioritizes your life and fills your soul.

The Crucified Life will lead you to the cross so you can be raised to new life in Christ.

The Essential Tozer Collection